Studying Child Psychology

Studying Child Psychology

Malcolm Hardy
Steve Heyes
Jennie Crews
Paul Rookes
Kevin Wren

Weidenfeld and Nicolson
London

George Weidenfeld and Nicolson Ltd
91 Clapham High Street, London SW4 7TA

ISBN 0 297 82004 4 cased
ISBN 0 297 82005 2 paperback

Printed in Great Britain by Butler and Tanner Ltd
Frome and London

Contents

Preface

The two five-year-olds are fighting in the kitchen. Dad is calmly explaining that they really have got the same amount of orange juice, but Matthew is not having any of it: 'It's not fair, Tim has got more than me!' This discussion goes on for some time. Dad knows that he poured the same amounts of juice because he always makes a point of being fair. A little later Dad, not quite so calm by now, is shouting that there is no more orange juice anyway and that if they don't shut up there will be no more for the rest of the week.

Why do we get into these situations with our children? There are many reasons. Perhaps Dad has had a rough day (some days he would just ignore the argument and let them get on with it), perhaps the argument about the orange juice is simply an extension of a fight that has been simmering all day partly as a result of the late bedtimes that the children have kept over the last few days.

If we were in a real-life situation we might be aware of these factors and take the appropriate action. This book doesn't try to solve family difficulties like this one but it does try to discuss some of the background to these events. For example, it is interesting that the children (or at least one of them) are arguing that they have different amounts of orange juice even though Dad knows that they have the same and may even have gone out of his way to pour equal quantities. It has been known for a long time that children do not judge quantity in the same way as adults do; if Matthew had a short, wide glass and Tim had a tall narrow glass we would not be surprised that Matthew believes that he has less juice that Tim, because children of this age usually base their decisions about quantity on just one dimension – Matthew notices that Tim's juice comes higher up the glass but ignores the fact that it is a thinner container. Children don't seem to see the world in the same way as 'grown-ups' – they are not simply miniature adults.

This book looks at some of the findings of Developmental Psychology and is based around the syllabus of the Southern Examining Group's Psychology (Child Development) GCSE syllabus.

Our thanks are due to the following grown-ups who helped type the manuscript: Pam Hardy, Eileen Heyes and Tracy Rookes.

Cheshire, May 1990

Mal Hardy
Steve Heyes
Jennie Crews
Paul Rookes
Kevin Wren

Chapter 1

Intellectual and Moral Development

Jean Piaget's Theories

If a two-month-old child finds something in her cot she will probably put it in her mouth; her brain is not yet ready to do much more than decide whether an object is good to suck or not. When she finds the same object a few months later, she may spend a lot of time moving parts of it with her hands: these parts move round and round – the thing wasn't much fun before but now it is very interesting. A couple of years later the toddler comes across the same thing again; now she pushes it back and forth across the room singing 'brmmm, brmm, and 'honk, honk'. As the child has grown older the toy has stayed the same but in her mind it has changed from some sort of dummy to a toy car.

Babies, toddlers, infants and adults all live in the same *physical* world but because their minds work differently their *psychological* worlds are very different. Psychologists use the term *Cognitive development* when talking about the changes which occur in thinking, perceiving and memory as we grow up.

Despite great differences in the way that children are treated, general patterns of development can be observed, showing that behaviour is not simply at the mercy of the particular environment in which the individual is placed.

Piaget was interested in how children understand the world. He observed behaviour and produced a theory that stressed that children think in a different way from adults. He argued that children go through a series of stages in their cognitive development (the development of thinking, memory, perception, etc.). The order of these stages does not vary, and each one brings with it a different way of thinking. The theory is not simply maturational, because although children move from one stage to the next as they get older, development depends upon interaction with the environment. In a stimulating environment an active child will progress from stage to stage more quickly than in a deprived environment.

The child's intellectual development takes place through the development of what Piaget calls *schemata* (singular: *schema*). He says nothing about the form that they take in the brain, but that they are the internal representation of a series of physical or mental actions; they can be likened to a set of rules about how to interact with the environment.

Once a child has a particular schema he is motivated to use it. Piaget stresses that this motivation causes the activity which allows the child to discover more about the world and this activity results in cognitive development. What the child actually does in his environment depends upon his existing schemata. The motivation to repeat the actions related to a schema can be seen particularly in children a few months old who can spend long periods of time just kicking their legs; while doing this, objects may move in the pram, they may make a noise, they may move in and out of sight. In continually doing this the child has many experiences that he could otherwise have missed. At about ten months the child may drop a toy out of the cot as often as an adult will retrieve it. As parents we may find this game tiring but if the child does not have the opportunity to play like this, cognitive development may suffer.

The child understands his world through his schemata. This is why the child we discussed above saw her toy as a dummy at one age but as a car at another. This process of understanding the world through an existing schema is known as *assimilation*. The assimilation of things into existing schemata allows the child to remember more and more information about the world, even though in some cases fitting things into the existing mental frameworks makes the child act in a way that adults consider odd. Four-year-old children, for example, have a series of schemata about numbers which are not the same as those of adults; these schemata are such that when asked which of the rows below has more dots in it, they answer 'The top one'.

The child gains feedback from the environment as to how accurate his perceptions are; when he experiences a mismatch between his schema and this feedback he is said to be in a state of *disequilibrium*. For example, as a baby in his first few months exercises the grasping and sucking schema, some objects will make a noise when grasped. The existing mental organization cannot deal with this, and disequilibrium exists, causing alteration of the schema so that it can deal with the new stimulation. A new schema, which will allow the child to use rattles, has now been formed and equilibrium exists once more. The child can now assimilate objects into his new schema and starts to decide which are good rattles and which are not. The equilibrium is, of course, only temporary, since continued action will bring new forms of stimulation to the child and the process of changing schemata, known as *accommodation*, will occur again. If a child is only exposed to information and experiences that can be easily assimilated, no accommodaton will occur and development will be retarded. On the other hand, accommodation cannot occur if experiences are too far removed from those with which the child is familiar.

The assimilation of information into schemata, and the accommodation of schemata to cater for the demands of new experiences, occurs throughout the stages of development. At each stage the organization of schemata becomes more complex.

The Sensorimotor Stage

The sensorimotor stage runs from birth until well into the second year. Newborns have a few, very limited, in-built schemata which allow them to grasp, suck and look at objects. The child is only concerned with what is going on at the present time; as soon as an object disappears from sight, the baby seems to forget it altogether. It is not until about eight months that children seem to become aware that objects still exist even when they cannot be seen; before this age they will not reach for an object that has been hidden behind something even if the object was moved while the baby was watching. Piaget called this the development of *object permanence*. Object permanence is not fully developed until about the age of one year. When a toy is hidden behind a pillow, a child of eight to twelve months has no difficulty in retrieving it. Children will play this game over and over again but the 8–12-month-old seems to pay more attention to his own habitual actions than to the actual position of the object. If the toy is first hidden in the usual place and then moved to another hiding place while the child watches, he will search behind the original pillow and may show surprise that he cannot find the toy.

By the end of the sensorimotor stage, infants have developed some understanding of the relationships between their muscle movements and effects on the environment. They have developed schemata which allow them to symbolize the world and think about objects that are out of sight. Children begin to produce words in the latter part of this stage, and use these as well as physical actions to represent and act upon their environment.

The Pre-Operational Stage

This stage generally runs from 2 to 7 years of age. With the development of language and memory the child can remember more about the environment and is able to predict it better. These predictions are still simple ones, and the child tends to over-generalize – calling all men 'daddy' for example. The child's intellect is limited by *egocentricity*; he is unaware that other people may have a different view of the world. This was shown by Piaget and Inhelder (1956), who placed a model landscape on a table, and seated a teddy on one side

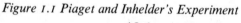

Figure 1.1 Piaget and Inhelder's Experiment

and a child on the other. The child was then asked to draw what the teddy could 'see'. Children in the pre-operational stage drew a picture of what they could themselves see, showing egocentricity.

The intellect is also limited by the way in which only one aspect of a problem can be considered at a time. This causes the child to show lack of *conservation*. Lack of conservation of volume can be demonstrated by pouring water into two wide glasses until the child agrees that there is the same amount in each. If the water from one of the glasses is then poured into a tall, thin glass, pre-operational children will report that there is more water in the tall glass than in the short one. The child appears to concentrate only on the height of the liquid; he cannot focus on its width at the same time. When judging a quantity of sweets the same children may say that there are more when they are spread out than when they are bunched together, thereby showing lack of conservation of number. So it is not surprising that children of four or five squabble about shares of orange juice or sweets even when an adult has been scrupulously fair in making sure that everyone has the same amount.

As the pre-operational stage comes to an end, the child starts to conserve number and then volume.

The Concrete Operational Stage
In the *concrete operational* period, from seven to eleven years, the child is still dependent on the appearance of objects but is becoming able to learn the rules of conservation and can use simple logic to solve problems, provided that they involve real (concrete) objects. Children during this stage can, for example, put a number of different-sized dolls into order of size, but cannot solve the same type of problem when it is presented verbally; for example Doll A is taller than Doll B; Doll A is smaller than Doll C; which doll is the tallest?

The Formal Operational Stage
The *formal operational* phase covers the period from eleven years to adulthood. The child learns the more sophisticated rules in this time and can now develop general laws and use scientific reasoning. Thoughts are no longer always tied to the concrete; children can form hypotheses and make rules about abstract things. The learning of new rules does not end with the ending of childhood, but continues throughout life.

Some Reservations about Piaget's Theories
A number of researchers have argued that Piaget underestimated the ability of young children. Marvin *et al.* (1976) asked children to choose an object from a table while their mother had her eyes closed; when asked if Mum knew what object had been chosen, two-year-

olds said yes – the egocentric response – but four-year-olds realized that their mothers could not know. It appears that the extent to which pre-operational children show egocentricity depends on the type of task, rather than being an overall characteristic of the stage.

N. Freeman, S. Lloyd and C. Sinha (1980) investigated the situation where a toy is hidden first behind object A for a series of trials and then moved, while the child is watching, from behind A to behind B. Children between about eight and twelve months of age generally continue to search for the toy behind object A. Freeman and his colleagues discovered that twelve-month-old children had little difficulty with this task when the toy was hidden in an upright cup, but were much less successful if the cups were inverted. Children seem to know how a cup is normally used and are distracted from the task when the cup is inverted. When the cup is used in its normal fashion the child can concentrate on finding the toy. It seems that the child may be concerned with more aspects of the task than the Piagetian psychologist is!

Some people have argued that children's problems with conservation tasks simply reflect the way in which they understand the words used; the words 'more than' or 'less than' do not have the same links with number and volume that they do for adults. Piaget believed that failure in the conservation tasks reflected something much more central to the whole of the child's understanding of the world.

J. McGarrigle and M. Donaldson suggested that children use a *social logic* when they fail to conserve on a Piagetian task. They argue that under normal circumstances if an adult asks a child about something such as a set of counters, then rearranges the counters and asks the same questions again, it is a safe bet that the child's answer should now be different. They backed this up by devising a task where the social logic did not force the child into an incorrect answer. Instead of having an adult both asking the questions and changing the length of a row of counters, they introduced a 'naughty teddy' to rearrange the counters. The researcher asked whether there were more in one row than the other, or whether there were the same number in each. The 'naughty teddy' puppet then joined in and disturbed the rows. After 'fighting off' the puppet, the researcher asked the question again. Out of 80 children tested, 54 conserved in the test compared with only 33 of them when tested in the traditional way. The children in this situation seem to regard the second question as a reasonable request for information and concentrated on the rows of counters, rather than applying the social logic that something must have changed or the grown-up wouldn't have bothered asking again.

Piaget pointed out that the order of the stages is invariable, but that some children pass through them more quickly than others. The stages themselves are not so rigidly separated as might appear from summaries such as the one that we have made in this chapter. It is often quite difficult to decide whether a child is in one stage or another since in reality the stage boundaries are blurred.

Piaget's early studies were based on a very small sample of subjects, often his own children, but follow-up studies have shown that his results have much wider applicability. His work has stimulated a great deal of research designed to support, expand or contradict his theories, and as a result it has been one of the most valuable contributions made to psychology.

Piaget's and Kohlberg's Theories of Social and Moral Development

As in his theory of cognitive development, Piaget argues that maturation, experience and social interaction are all vital factors in social and moral development. Processes such as assimilation and accommodation of schemata are as relevant to ideas about right and wrong as they are to decisions about the physical world. The stages of moral development are not as clearly defined as the stages of cognitive development but obviously the child's moral reasoning will be different in the concrete operational stage compared with the pre-operational stage, where the child is unable to take into account the views of others (egocentricity).

Much of the theory comes from the observation of a relatively small number of children during normal behaviour or in question-and-answer sessions. Despite the few subjects observed in the initial work, many other researchers have found similar patterns in the development of children's social and moral behaviour.

Piaget was interested in three areas of social development:

(a) The child's ideas about rules.
(b) How a child decides what is right and what is wrong.
(c) The child's ideas about punishment and justice.

The Child's Ideas about Rules

Piaget studied how children learnt and internalized rules, by studying their understanding of the game of marbles. (The rules of which, incidentally, show wide variations from culture to culture.) To do this, he used a questioning technique: 'When I was little, I used to play a lot, but now I've quite forgotten how. I'd like to play again. Let's play together. You teach me the rules, and I'll play with you.' Other questions were: Have the rules always been the same? Where do the rules come from? Could new rules be made up, and would they be fair?

Piaget noticed that there seemed to be a sequence of development in children in the understanding of these rules; that is, the children's answers changed as they got older. Piaget believed that the main causes of this development were maturation of the child's schemata, and assimilation and accommodation of information from the child's environment.

Very young (below three years) children had no rules – each child devised and played its own version of the game.

Three-to-six-year-olds (still at the pre-operational stage) notice new rules but still play egocentrically – even when two children are playing together, they do not interlink their behaviour or co-operate. Although both know the rules, they often ignore them and, in effect, play as individuals.

Such children (even though they ignore the rules) regard them as being absolutes. They cannot be changed, and have the same force as physical laws – they have always existed, but were probably invented by God. Piaget called this the stage of heteronomous morality, or the stage of *moral realism*.

There is a gradual development from age 6 up to about 11 or 12 (late concrete operational), at which point the rules have become fully internalized and understood. Whereas the younger child believes that the rules were given semi-mystically by older children, parents, God, or have always existed, the concrete operational child realizes that the rules are developed by children themselves, and can be changed by the agreement of all the players. Piaget called this the stage of autonomous morality, or the stage of *moral reciprocity*.

How the Child Decides What Is Right and What Is Wrong

In this research, Piaget was interested in how the child comes to assess the seriousness of a crime. The research technique used here was to put hypothetical situations before the child and ask him to assess how wrong the action was, and why it was wrong. For example, children would be told a story about a boy called John, and one about a boy called Henry.

> 'A little boy who is called John is in his room. He is called to dinner. He goes into the dining room. But behind the door there was a chair, and on the chair there was a tray with fifteen cups on it. John couldn't have known that there was all this behind the door. He goes in, the door knocks against the tray, bang go the fifteen cups and they all get broken!'

> 'Once there was a little boy whose name was Henry. One day when his mother was out he tried to get some jam out of the cupboard even though he knew he was not allowed to do this. He climbed on a chair and stretched out his arm. But the jam was too high up and he couldn't reach it and have any. While he was trying to get the jam he knocked over a cup. The cup fell down and broke.'

The child would then be asked 'who was the naughtiest, John or Henry?' Young children in the stage of moral realism usually say that John was naughtiest because he broke so many cups; for them, a crime's seriousness depends upon its visible effects rather than the intention behind the act. This reflects pre-operational and concrete operational thinking.

The adult type of morality (the stage of moral reciprocity) which involves judging by intention, begins to develop about age 7, and is usually well developed by about 10 years of age. For the under-seven (pre-operational) child, however, an adult's punishments for misdeeds must seem very odd – a large punishment for Henry but a small or negligible one for John, because the adult's judgement is based on intention, not damage, and the child cannot yet understand this.

In adult moral standards, intention and seriousness are often separated. For example, a driver whose car kills somebody who walked right into its path is not held to blame – in fact, is often given comfort (but still feels remorse and guilt) – whereas a near-identically serious act (killing someone with a car) when committed by a drunken

driver, or committed intentionally, is severely penalized and criti-
cised.

The ways in which children judge lies follows a similar pattern
too, but with a intermediate third stage:

Stage 1   *(moral realism)* A lie to a 6-year-old can be an actual untruth,
or an oath – both are punished by parents, and the child cannot tell the
difference between them. Some 6 year-olds believe that any behaviour
which leads to a punishment is a lie.

Stage 2   *(intermediate stage)* 8–9-year-olds' lies are statements which
are not factual – the bigger the unreality of the statement, the bigger the
lie to them. For example, 'Today, I saw a dog as big as a cow' would be
judged as a much bigger lie than a child saying he did well at school when
he really did poorly. Because the former is a bigger department from fact,
and is less believable, it is a bigger lie.

Stage 3   *(moral reciprocity)* 10–11-year-olds would call the former
statement a joke – it is so obviously untrue that it is not a lie. The second
statement, however, was made with intent to deceive and is therefore
considered the bigger lie. At this stage, therefore, intention again becomes
the criterion for judgement.

The Child's Ideas about Punishment and Justice

Children in the stage of moral realism believe that the size of the
punishment should fit the crime (although their ideas of what is a
crime are different from ours, as shown above), but below 7 years
Piaget found no evidence that the child wanted to match the type of
punishment to the type of crime. By the age of 11 or 12, Piaget found
that 80 per cent of children favoured 'letting the punishment fit the
crime'; so that they favoured being made to sleep in a cold room as
a punishment for breaking a window or being smacked for hitting a
smaller child. Unlike the younger child the twelve-year-old felt that
restitution (making good for the damage caused) was also important
(the stage of moral reciprocity).

Piaget argues that the child moves from a stage of moral realism
when he is largely swayed by physical, observable effects of action
and thinks of rules as 'tablets of stone' which cannot be changed, to
a stage of moral reciprocity (some researchers call this stage *moral
insight*) when he takes intention into account, is able to fit the
punishment to the crime, and sees rules as things which allow groups
to function and can be changed by agreement.

The movement between moral realism and moral insight is gradual, and people of any age may show characteristics of both types of moral thinking. Although maturation is important, social interaction is vital to the change from one stage to the other. For example, the pre-school child may only have experienced one set of rules about how to play a game (so his schema for the game at this stage consists only of this one set of rules). In order to assimilate the behaviour of another child who plays by different rules, he regards the other child as cheating. However, when he comes across many children with many different rules it becomes more difficult to simply assimilate these differences into his schema by saying that they are all cheating, and the child has to change his schema (i.e. he has to accommodate these different rules). The child's schema for rules now includes a recognition that there are other rules than his own. Further social experience enables the child to accommodate the idea that the rules of a game may be changed if all the players agree.

Kohlberg's Theory of Moral Development

Kohlberg's technique and his belief that social and moral development occur in stages is a direct follow-on from Piaget. However, Kohlberg believed that these stages were much more clearly defined than did Piaget. Like Piaget, Kohlberg posed questions to people about what was right and what was wrong. For example:

> 'In Europe, a woman was dying from cancer. One drug might save her, a form of radium that the druggist in the same town had recently discovered. The druggist was charging 2,000 dollars, ten times what the drug cost him to make. The sick woman's husband, Heinz, went to everyone he knew to borrow the money, but he could only get together about half of what it cost. He told the druggist that his wife was dying and asked him to sell it cheaper or let him pay later. But the druggist said "No". The husband got desperate and broke into the man's store to steal the drug for his wife.' 'Should the husband have done that? Why?'

By using stories like this, and by asking people to explain the reason for their answers, Kohlberg, like Piaget, produced a 'stage' theory of moral development – but as you will see, the stages are more clearly defined than Piaget's; he also asked a wider range of age-groups than did Piaget.

Kohlberg believed that there were three levels of morality, each level being divided into two stages, giving six stages in all.

We set out below the levels and stages of Kohlberg's theory, together with some of the sorts of decisions which people at each stage might make about Heinz's dilemma. (Note, though, that whilst most of these decisions say that Heinz was right, it is perfectly possible at each stage to get answers which say that Heinz was wrong.)

Level 1
Pre-conventional morality

Stage 1   *(Called 'Punishment and obedience orientation' by Kohlberg.)*   People in this stage believe that something is wrong if it is punished or punishable. If the behaviour is not punished, then it is right. Heinz would therefore be wrong to steal the drug, because stealing is punishable.

Stage 2   *(Instrumental hedonism)*   In this stage, people conform to rules and laws to gain rewards, or to have a favour they have done to somebody returned. Heinz would not gain by obeying the law, and he doesn't owe the druggist any favours, so probably he is right to steal.

Level 2
Conventional morality

Stage 3   *('Good child' morality)*   What is good is that which pleases others (particularly the family), and the intention behind an action begins to be taken into account. Heinz' behaviour would not have pleased the druggist, and perhaps also not pleased his friends and family. However, the intention behind the theft was to save a life, so he was probably right to steal the drug.

Stage 4   *('Law and order orientation')*   What is right and wrong is not so much determined by family and friends, but by society. Society's laws are designed to maintain social order, and should only be disobeyed in extreme circumstances. Heinz was wrong to break society's laws, but the possible death of his wife is an extreme circumstance, so stealing the drug is not entirely wrong.

Level 3
Post-conventional morality

Stage 5   *('Social contract orientation')*   Whilst laws should be upheld, they can be changed by agreement. Anyway, one should behave so as to bring the greatest good to the greatest number of people. Despite the law, some things are more important – a person's right to life and freedom. Therefore, Heinz was right to take the drug.

Stage 6 *('Universal ethical principles')* People in this stage have developed their own moral principles, based on the sacredness of life and respect for the individual. Most laws conform with these principles, but where they do not, it is better to uphold the principles. Heinz was right to steal the drug – the universal ethical principle of the sacredness of life is more important than any law.

Evidence For and Against Piaget's and Kohlberg's Theories

There are really two questions to answer in connection with Piaget and Kohlberg's theories. First, what evidence is there that people's moral development occurs in stages?. Second, Kohlberg's and Piaget's theories are about the development of moral thinking; what evidence is there that what a person actually does (i.e. his moral behaviour) develops in the same way as his moral thinking?

ARE THERE STAGES IN MORAL DEVELOPMENT?

Since Kohlberg's stages are more clearly defined than Piaget's, we will concentrate on the evidence for or against Kohlberg's stages. The best way to study this question is to perform a longitudinal study (see p.ooo), by testing the same people's moral development over a number of years. Kohlberg performed a six-year longitudinal study on Turkish city and village boys and American middle – and working-class boys aged between 10 and 16 years at the start of the study.He found, when he tested the boys at three-year intervals, that fifty per cent of them stayed at the same stage and the other fifty per cent had moved up or down a stage.

A twenty-year study by Rest supported the idea that moral development occurs in stages, but Rest also found that the amount of development through the stages was not as great as Kohlberg's theory predicted – in fact on average, Rest's subjects only increased by two stages. Kohlberg himself found very few subjects who showed stage 6 morality, and fewer than predicted at stage 5. (Kohlberg is now in doubt as to whether there is in fact a separate stage 6 at all.)

Although there seems to be some evidence for the existence of stages in the development of moral thinking, it is not exactly strong evidence. (Some of Kohlberg's subjects dropped a stage, and Rest's subjects did not seem to make much moral progress in twenty years!) Kohlberg believes (like Piaget) that the stages in moral thinking are due to maturation, but an alternative explanation may be that parents reward or punish different kinds of moral thinking in their children at different ages. For example, children in Kohlberg's stage 1 obey to avoid punishment. This may be due (as Kohlberg believes) to their level of maturation, or it may be because with young children, reasoning with the child by the parents doesn't work as well as punishment does.

ARE MORAL THINKING AND MORAL DEVELOPMENT THE SAME THING?

Piaget and Kohlberg both believed that a person with a higher level of moral thinking would also behave more morally than a person at a lower stage. Kohlberg set up situations where children were able to cheat, and looked at whether the child's stage of moral thinking (as measured by Heinz-type questions) predicted their moral behaviour (i.e. whether or not they actually cheated). He found that 70 per cent of stage 1 and 2 children cheated, 55 per cent of stages 3 and 4 children cheated, and only 15 per cent of stage 5 children cheated. This result, however, is very much an exception. Other studies show a much weaker relationship between moral thinking and behaviour. In particular, a massive study by Hartshorne and May conflicts with Kohlberg's findings.

In a 1928 study of 11,000 children, Hartshorne and May first gave them a series of moral thinking tests. Some children took all the tests in the same environment (e.g. in a school classroom), whilst other children took different tests in different places (e.g. some in a schoolroom, some at home.) Children who took all the tests in one place showed great consistency in their answers – for example if a child obtained a high score on one test, he was likely to obtain a high score on other tests. However, much less consistency was found in the test results of children who took different tests in different situations. Hartshorne and May concluded that these results '... indicate quite clearly that a child does not have a uniform generalised code of morals, but varies his opinions to suit the situation in which he finds himself.'

After these tests of their moral thinking, the children's moral behaviour was tested. They were given the opportunity to cheat, lie or in other ways be dishonest in many different situations. In one situation the children were given a multiple-choice test and asked to circle the right answers; later they were given the correct answers and asked to mark their own work. A copy of their original answers had been taken without the child's knowledge and so it was possible to tell if he or she had cheated. Another exercise involved a set of puzzles, one of which included a coin; when the puzzles were returned the researchers checked whether the coin had been stolen. Many other situations were set up which varied in type, in the likelihood of being caught and in the rewards for being dishonest. The results showed very little consistency of honesty for particular children across a range of situations. The children's honesty seemed to be governed by the situation rather than a consistent underlying characteristic of honesty or lack of it (as Piaget and Kohlberg would predict).

Another study by Damon also fails to support Piaget's and Kohlberg's theories. Damon found that some children who thought that there ought to be an equal division of sweets amongst a group of children who had worked together, behaved differently in a real situation – they demanded more sweets than other children. Similarly, children who thought that the hardest worker should get most sweets changed their view in the real situation if that child was not themselves!

The general trend of research evidence suggests that, whilst there might be some evidence for the existence of stages in the development of moral thinking, there is not much evidence for a strong link between moral thinking and moral behaviour – what people say they would do in a situation, and what they actually do in that situation are often different.

Piaget's and Kohlberg's theories have been very influential in directing other psychologists' research towards the development of moral thinking in children. Both theories, however, are weak at predicting how children actually behave when faced with moral decisions.

Summary

1 Piaget believed that the development of the intellect proceeds through four main stages: sensorimotor, pre-operational, concrete operational and formal operational.
2 This development occurs through the growth of internal structures called schemata which interact with the environment through the mechanisms of assimilation (adding in new information to an existing

schema) and accommodation (changing schema or developing a new one, in order to store new information).

3 Recent research has begun to throw some doubt on the validity of Piaget's stages of development. In particular, it has been found that using different tests (or even instructions) can change the child's apparent stage of intellectual development.

4 Piaget also studied children's moral development – their ideas of right and wrong, punishment and justice, and their understanding of rules. He found links between moral development and the child's stage of cognitive development.

5 Kohlberg developed a more detailed sequence of stages of moral development. Both Piaget's and Kohlberg's theories concentrate more on what the child says than on what it actually does.

Further Reading

Donaldson, M., *Children's Minds* (1978, Fontana).
Osofsky, J.D. (ed.) *Handbook of Infant Development* (2nd edn, 1987, Wiley).

Chapter 2

Developmental Scales and IQ Tests

Intelligence, like other complex examples of human behaviour such as love and hate, is very difficult to define. We often know what love, hate, intelligent behaviour is when we see it but when asked to say just exactly what it is, we find it difficult. Alice Heim produced a reasonably common sense definition of intelligence: 'Intelligent activity consists of grasping the essentials of a situation and responding appropriately to them.' (Though it should be noted that this definition does not have widespread acceptance among psychologists.)

If we have such difficulty in describing intelligence then how can we measure it? This problem is not new in science. For centuries scientists have been measuring phenomena or their effect on a situation (i.e. experiment) in order to understand them, yet without having a precise knowledge of the nature of the phenomena. In the physical sciences, for example, scientists have been measuring light and its effects on our environment for many years, without having a detailed knowledge about such aspects of light as its colour, wave length or speed.

The psychologist uses intelligence tests in a similar manner. He measures aspects of human behaviour he feels intelligence influences in some way, e.g. memory, general knowledge or the ability to see relationships between shapes. Basically, these aspects can be divided into two broad areas, verbal intelligence and non-verbal intelligence, the latter being sometimes called 'performance'. By verbal intelligence we mean those aspects of behaviour influenced by language and speech such as general knowledge and vocabulary. Non-verbal intelligence is essentially those parts of our environment we have to try and understand by using our ability to perceive the world in terms of shape, time and number.

Pioneers of intelligence testing such as Binet and Simon concentrated too much on seeing intelligent behaviour as only being expressed through the verbal mode. Modern psychologists have moved on and often use tests such as the Wechsler Intelligence Scale for children (WISC-R), designed for children between the ages of 6 and 16 years, and the Wechsler Pre-school and Primary Scale of Intelligence (WPPSI), designed for children of 3–6 years old. Both tests try to measure fully aspects of both verbal and non-verbal (performance) intelligence. In addition, psychologists use the test situation as a clinical interview, in order to obtain information regarding the child's motivation, personality and attention span. Before the administration of an intelligence test, the psychologist would have to obtain background information regarding the child's behaviour at school and his physical development and well-being. Such information helps the psychologist to decide whether the result-ant IQ is a true reflection of the child's ability. Often other tests are completed, such as tests of visual and auditory perception, of reading and spelling and free drawing. This is done in order to gain a greater understanding of the child as an individual. Modern psychologists realize that the IQ score gained from an intelligence test has only limited value in terms of understanding the child as, say, a learner in school for example.

Let us look at a case history in order to understand this process better.

A Case Study

Simon, at the age of 8 years, had barely made any headway in reading and writing. In school he was still on very basic reading books aimed at children a good 18 months younger than him. He could write his first name but sometimes he would reverse the S.

His free writing was illegible since he could not spell, neither could he keep his writing to the line or space it accurately. In arithmetic he was a little bit better although he still had to count with counters or on his fingers. His teacher assessed him as below average in all subjects and certainly as bottom of her class in reading and spelling. On being referred to a psychologist for assessment he was found to be well above average intellectually as the profile in Figure 2.1 shows.

Clearly Simon is under-functioning in school although he is a bright child and therefore should be very able in the 3 Rs. On further investigation, the psychologist found that he was breech birth, was

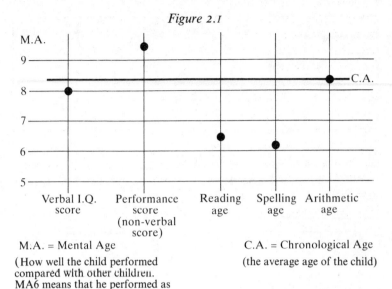

Figure 2.1

M.A. = Mental Age
(How well the child performed compared with other children. MA6 means that he performed as well as an average 6-year-old.)

C.A. = Chronological Age
(the average age of the child)

ambidextrous and had recently been taken to his family doctor by his parents as they felt he was slightly deaf.

The resultant diagnosis was that Simon was a bright child with specific learning difficulties. Birth abnormalities, partial deafness, ambidexterity, minor eyesight problems and the late development of language are all reasons why some children experience difficulties learning in school. As you can see, without such biographical details and Simon's attainment scores in the 3 Rs, the psychologist would have found great difficulty in trying to decide why Simon was doing badly in school on the basis of his IQ only. Simon's profile shows that of the two aspects of intelligence tested for, he did best on the performance scale. This could explain to some extent why he was better in arithmetic than reading and writing since, for example, the WISC performance scale measures aspects of intelligence one often associates with ability in arithmetic and mathematics. The WISC performance scale includes items very similar to those listed below.

Types of Question Found in the WISC Performance Scale
(1) *Picture arrangement*. The child is shown a series of pictures which reflect a sequence of events except that the sequence is out of order. The child is asked to arrange them correctly. For example:

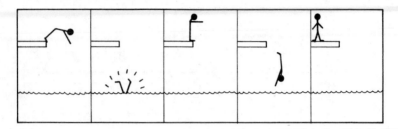

(2) *Picture completion*. The child is shown a picture with something missing, for example a kettle without a spout, and the child is asked to say what is wrong. For example:

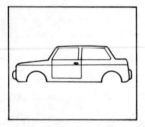   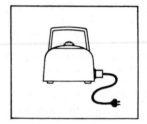

(3) *Block design*. The child is shown a design which he has to complete by using blocks. The blocks have some sides plain, some coloured, and some half plain and coloured. For example:

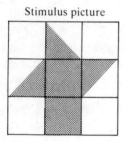   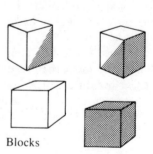

(4) *Object assembly*. The child has to put together a jigsaw of parts into a picture of a dog, a human foot, etc. For example:

(5) *Codes.* The child has to match symbols with numbers according to a code. For example:

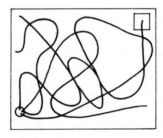

(6) *Mazes.* The child has to trace a route on a series of mazes which gets progressively more difficult. For example:

On the verbal scale items, the child has to deal with the following:

(1) *Information.* The child has to answer a number of general knowledge questions to do with history, geography and nature, for example 'Through which country does the River Mississippi flow?'

(2) *Comprehension.* The child has to explain a rule, saying or social convention, for example 'What do you do if you find a wallet in the street?'

(3) *Digit span.* The child is asked to repeat after the tester a series of numbers which increase in length, for example
(a) 8 – 9   (b) 6 – 4 – 1 etc.

(4) *Similarities*. The child is asked to say how two items are similar, for example 'How are a stool and a chair alike?'

(5) *Arithmetic*. The child is asked to answer a number of arithmetic problems presented verbally, for example 'If I take 6 away from 19, what is left?'

(6) *Vocabulary*. The child has to define words progressing in level of difficulty. He must answer orally rather than demonstrate his answer. For example 'What does the word cap mean?'

In theory a child should score about the same on both scales. Children with specific learning difficulties or who are mentally handicapped or come from a home where English is not the language of everyday interaction, often have dissimilar scores on the two scales. Simon's lower score on the verbal scale, for example, might well be a result of his deafness. Partial deafness can retard normal language development and this lag in development would impede the child's performance on, say, the vocabulary items. So, for example, in response to the psychologist's questions 'What does the word tap mean?' the child may mistakenly answer 'It's when cats drink' and therefore achieve a 0 score for that item. Indeed, this is one of the great problems in testing a child's intelligence level: How far can you be sure you are not testing something else, like hearing, as well?

Problems with IQ Tests

Pencil-and-paper-type tests for screening purposes such as the 11-plus selection test are also testing the ability to read. Performance items are also testing visual perception and discrimination. But there are other more subtle aspects of individual behaviour at work here. A test item, for example asking the child to put town, village, city and hamlet into order of size from largest to smallest, is making the assumption that all children are familiar with urban and rural life. To a city child or recent immigrant there may be no difference between a hamlet and village. Similarly, the non-verbal test at the top of the next page would confound a child with a minor sight problem such as a glide, or a child who was dyslexic. (Which one would complete the pattern – 1, 2, 3 or 4?)

Even with tests such as the Progressive Matrices (designed by M. Raven) where language has been eliminated in order to make it

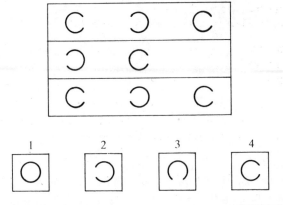

culture-free, some children would obtain a depressed score because of a visual or learning disability. The following problem is similar to the type of problem presented to young children. From the six alternatives to the left of the diagram the child must choose the one he or she thinks will complete the pattern.

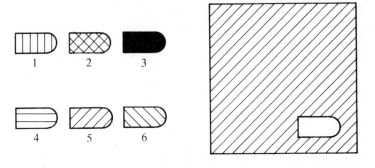

A learning-disordered child who constantly gets left and right mixed up, and like Simon often reverses letters, stands a good chance of choosing number 6 instead of 5 because as well as a test of general intelligence it requires the child to be able to visually discriminate. between / and \ and |.

If testing children's intellectual attainment is difficult, how easy is it to assess the intelligence of a baby or a toddler?

Developmental Scale

The further down the age scale you go, the more difficult it becomes to measure intelligence. Very young children, i.e. below the age of three years, have limited language both in terms of speech and comprehension, very short spans of attention and tire easily. Formal intelligence testing as in tests like WPPSI or the Raven Coloured Progressive Matrices (especially designed for school-age children) would not be advisable, since it is highly likely that the test would never be completed or that the psychologist could not be sure that responses towards the end of the test session were valid.

When dealing with very young children, psychologists and pae-diatricians use another form of assessment called a *developmental scale*. This form of assessment is subtly different from tests like the WISC or the Raven tests, as most developmental scales are *criterion-referenced* tests rather than *norm-referenced* tests. By this we mean that the developmental scale compares the child's present per-formance in such areas of development as co-ordination and lan-guage development, to a set of levels of ability, called criteria. So, for example, in physical co-ordination the test might ask the psy-chologist to rate the child's ability to manipulate objects in his hand in the following way:

	Can do	Cannot do
(1) Can point to an object.	*	
(2) Can grasp an object given to the child.	*	
(3) Can hold onto an object given to the child.	*	
(4) Can pick up an object with finger and thumb.		*

The psychologist in conjunction with the parent or nursery nurse would indicate with a mark on each line to the right of each criterion whether (a) the child can perform this act or (b) cannot; or if the mark was in the middle, that the child had nearly mastered the skill.

As we can see in the above example, this child can point at, grasp and hold onto objects, but as yet has not mastered the skill of picking things up with his index finger and thumb; a very necessary skill needed to help develop other behaviour such as that required for dressing and eating. In contrast, norm-referenced tests generally compare the child's scores on verbal and non-verbal scales with scores obtained by others in the child's age-group. Criterion-referenced tests are generally not tightly age-related in this way although infant developmental scales and checklists are often based on the pioneering work of paediatricians like Dr Mary Sheridan (1973), who produced the Stycar sequences, i.e. a list of development milestones reached by all normal children as they develop through childhood.

These milestones are divided into five main categories: motor development and its co-ordination; the development of speech and hearing; the development of visual competence; the development of social behaviour; and the development of play. In this sense, then, criterion-referenced tests are similar to norm-referenced tests because as many developmental milestones, e.g. moro reflex, grasping and crawling are very age-specific. But, and this is the important difference, they are not seen as pass or fail tests. If a newborn baby exhibits the moro reflex (startle response), this is considered to be normal in newborn infants. If the reflex was slow to come or sluggish in nature, this would be noted and the child's responses to other tests and procedures would be watched carefully because slow or sluggish reflexes could be a sign that something was wrong – for example, the child might be ill or handicapped. Similarly, a child who sits up with supporting pillows at about 6 months of age would be considered normal for his age. The child who was late to reach this milestone in his development, and who has been late to reach other developmental milestones in his history, might well be mentally handicapped. The child who consistently reaches developmental milestones early might well become a very intelligent school pupil.

One such screening test is the 'Schedule of Growing Skills' devised by Dr M. Bellman and Dr J. Cash (1987) and based on Mary Sheridan's Stycar sequences. The child's development is checked against a set of prescribed criteria across nine areas of activity including physical development, language acquisition and the development and co-ordination of the senses. Delays and deficiencies identified in the nine areas can help health visitors and paediatricians to identify children with problems.

Conclusions
Those presently involved in assessing children on a regular basis such as infant-school teachers, paediatricians and child psychologists are

moving away from norm-referenced tests towards attainment testing, criterion-referenced tests and the use of development scales and checklists. Understandably, many feel that IQ scores on their own cannot explain all aspects of a child's behaviour. As we saw with Simon, it is not until we begin to compare a child's mental age with his level of attainment in areas such as literacy and numeracy and relate these to his physical and mental health and development, that we can hope to obtain a thorough picture of the child as an individual.

One educational test which seems to go some way towards meeting some of these requirements is the 'British Abilities Scale' (Elliot *et al.* 1979). The BAS can be used with children as young as 2 years and as old as 17 years. Like the WISC, it measures various aspects of cognition such as memory, spatial ability and problem-solving. In addition, because it is more flexible than WISC it can be used to measure changes in particular abilities over time, as well as for calculating a full IQ score.

Summary

1 Intelligent activity consists in grasping the essentials of a situation and responding appropriately to them.

2 Intelligence testing often tries to sample two aspects of behaviour: verbal and non-verbal (performance).

3 The WISC contains the following non-verbal sub-tests: picture completion, picture arrangements, block design, object assembly, codes, mazes. The verbal half of the test contains: information, comprehension, digit span, similarities, arithmetic, vocabulary.

4 Test results may be influenced subtly by minor sensory difficulties, culture and upbringing.

5 When testing very young children (i.e. 3 years and below) testers use a developmental scale which is a criterion-referenced test rather than a norm-referenced test.

6 Children who are late to reach developmental milestones may be handicapped, and children who reach milestones very early may be very bright.

7 Developmental scales tend to sample behaviour in the areas of: co-ordination, language acquisition, sensory development, social behaviour and play.

8 Those involved in assessing young children are moving more towards criterion-referenced tests, attainment tests and developmental scales and checklists.

Further Reading

Bellman, M. and Cash, J., *The Schedule of Growing Skills in Practice* (1987, NFER-Nelson).

Sheridan, M.D., *Children's Developmental Progress from Birth to Five Years. The Stycar Sequences* (4th ed, 1976, NFER-Nelson).

Chapter 3

The Development of Language and Communication in Children

When we think about language development and children we must get away from the idea that communication between people is only about face-to-face contact, where one person speaks and the other listens. If we look around our environment we will see communication taking place in many guises, for example letters, telephones, megaphones, morse code. People often smile at each other to signal approval or friendship without using speech. In the animal kingdom a whole variety of methods are used to convey simple ideas such as anger, the approach of danger or the location of food. Dogs, for example, will whine and bark to signal annoyance or threat. Beavers, on the other hand, smack their tails on the ground to signal danger.

Another general point which needs to be made at the beginning of this chapter is that communication, whether in the form of speech or non-verbal communication (body language), is a social act. As such, therefore, you need a talker and a listener, a signaller and an observer, a sender and a receiver. In other words, the smallest group within which effective language development and the development of communication behaviour can take place is a group of two (linguists call it a dyad). As a result of technological advances, the video recorder in particular, research scientists are able to record and analyse in great detail naturalistic observations. Examination of video data has revealed communicative behaviour in babies as young as one week old. A famous psychologist called Daniel Stern, who has investigated this area of human behaviour extensively, noticed that babies will focus attention and then withdraw attention when in the presence of the mother; and that this cycle of attention and withdrawal is different to the attention the child gives to other objects in the environment.

Stern also noted that one of the child's earliest social acts was to enter the mutual turn-taking exchanges which resemble adult speech. Catherine Snow (1977) studied the conversation between mothers and babies. She noticed how the baby's behaviour including yawns, smiles, blinks and gurgles were treated by the mother as communication; they acted as a stimulus to the mother to respond in speech. She also noticed the turn-taking sequence of events between mother and child. This is sometimes referred to as mutual reciprocity.

It would seem from recent studies like Snow's that the obvious aspects of adult caring behaviour such as talking to, singing to, rocking and handling are closely linked with the child's own (rather limited) communicative behaviour, including crying, cooing, babbling and smiling. Researchers are coming round to the idea that a child's speech development does not exist in isolation from its social and intellectual development and therefore should not be studied in isolation. Accordingly, modern psychologists are shifting to the notion that language development, the development of social behaviour and the growth of intelligence and thinking, are all inter-related and that this interrelatedness has its beginnings in the child's earliest behaviour. This stage in child development has come to be known as the *pre-linguistic stage* and researchers have been particularly interested in five aspects of this, namely: crying, cooing, babbling, pointing and smiling. But before we embark on a detailed description of these let us first take a brief look at how language is constructed.

Phonemes, Morphemes, Words and Sentences

Language begins with breathing because, to make a speech sound, air must pass over the vocal cords to make them vibrate. By subtly changing the shape of the mouth, by using the cavities of the nose and skull and involving the use of the tongue, teeth and palate we are able to vary the sound. In fact by this means we are able to make many more than the 56 or so individual sounds which go to make up spoken English. In addition, we are able to perform other verbal variations such as whisper, sing, shout and scream.

The smallest individual sounds which go to make up any language are called *phonemes*. The 'keh' sound at the beginning of 'cat' is one such phoneme in spoken English. By changing only one phoneme in many English words it is possible to change its meaning, e.g. 'cat' can be changed to 'rat' by substituting 'reh' for 'keh'.

Phonemes are put together to form *morphemes*. The morpheme can be described as the smallest unit of sound which has meaning.

So, for example, the word 'walked' has two morphemes, 'walk' and 'ed', the former meaning a type of movement and the latter indicating actions which take place in the past. Morphemes help us to be clear about what we mean. 'Walks', 'walking' and 'walker' all have the morpheme 'walk' in them, but the first may be used as a plural, the second as indicating the future and the third might be used to describe a device for assisting a child to learn to walk as in 'baby-walker'.

Morphemes are put together to form words. With words come meanings and shades of meaning or what linguists call semantics. Many linguists are in disagreement as to just what it is that constitutes a word. Leaving this debate on one side the child psychologist is more interested in how children develop vocabulary and how they come to know and understand that, say, the word 'green' can mean a colour as well as a patch of lawn.

Finally, to convey precise meaning to a listener we must put words into sentences which will make sense. To do this we follow a set of rules called syntax. This is why competent users of our language say: 'I went for a walk in the park.' A recent immigrant to this country in the process of learning English might say instead 'I go for in the park walkings.' This is because as a learner of English as a foreign language he or she is not as yet a proficient speaker. Similarly, a very young child might say: 'I goed for a walk in the park.' The child, unlike the immigrant who may never become a fully proficient speaker, will become a very effective communicator in a relatively short period of time, and without formal teaching! It seems quite staggering to think that at such an immature stage in the child's development, when he or she is both physically and mentally immature and socially very limited, the child will progress from the primitive cry to generating sentences independently and that all this will take about four years; and in addition the child will learn to interpret and use facial expression and gesture. It is with this thought in mind that we will return to the pre-linguistic stage of development to examine the role of crying in speech production.

Stages in Language Development

The first two months or so of a baby's life are characterized by crying, sleeping and feeding. In normal children the pattern of events which leads up to speech development begins with crying. Crying is very important not only as a signal to the child's parents of the baby's needs but because it helps to exercise the child's lungs and in turn improve cardiovascular development. As a signal, crying is used by the baby to indicate hunger, sickness, pain, over-stimulation, tiredness and discomfort. In fact, there is some evidence provided by Friedman et at. (1982) that children with physical problems, e.g. small-for-dates babies, have a different cry to normal infants.

Another set of researchers, including Mary Ainsworth (1972), observed 26 mothers and their babies in their own homes. Ainsworth's general conclusion was that sensitive mothers, i.e. those more responsive to their baby's cries, had babies who cried less than mothers who took longer to respond. Ainsworth sees the mother's sensitivity to her baby's needs as laying the foundations for later social development.

At about four weeks of age babies begin to 'coo' to signal pleasure. These cooing noises crudely equal what we would call vowel sounds. It is here that the child begins to learn the basics of adult spoken language. In addition, the child is developing its ability to recognise spoken sounds. Research has shown that infants as young as four weeks old can discriminate between individual speech sounds. A classic experiment to demonstrate this was carried out by Eimas (1971) and his associates. By linking a child's dummy to a loudspeaker the baby was able to hear a 'pa' noise if he sucked vigorously enough. At first the babies sucked frequently and vigorously enough to keep the sound on continuously, but after a short period of time their interest waned. At this point in the experiment the researchers changed the sound to 'ba' and this was enough to reawaken their interest so that they began to suck more vigorously again. A similar group of infants underwent the same experiment except that they heard the stimuli in reverse order, i.e. 'ba' first and 'pa' second. In this second group a similar result was obtained. It would seem therefore that the infants could make the distinction between the phoneme 'p' and 'b'. These two sounds are so close in the way they are uttered (try saying them aloud) that the experiment seems to show that babies have very good auditory acuity, i.e. they can hear clearly and distinctly.

There is other evidence too which seems to demonstrate that auditory acuity is quite advanced in infants. Bower (1977) showed that infants under 20 weeks of age can locate audible objects in the dark provided the object is presented in front of them. Condon and Sanders (1974) noticed that babies of a few days old will move their limbs in time (synchrony) with the rhythm of human speech. Two other researchers, De Casper and Fifer (1980), observed that infants of only a few days old are able to distinguish between their mother's voice and the voice of a female stranger. This ability to distinguish between sounds is obviously very important to speech and language development, as we can clearly see from the retarded speech and language in deaf children. In addition, it also tells us that it is important to talk to babies from early in their infancy, although we can tell they understand little, if anything, of what we say.

Researchers like Daniel Stern and Catherine Snow have done much to improve our understanding of the communication between mother and infant. Both observed mutual turn-taking smiling games at about six weeks of age. The smile, it would appear, is a very powerful social signal for a child and adults. In a survey carried out by Macfarlane (1971) of mothers of two-month-old, first-born infants, 75 per cent included smiling as being one aspect of their baby's behaviour they much enjoyed. The 'strange case of the smile', as Dr Bower has called it, is definitely taken by adults as a social signal from the baby and therefore as a piece of purposeful non-verbal communication. Scientists like Bower and Stern are still unsure as to its precise purpose, from the child's point of view, although many have theorized about it.

Another important communicative gesture which appears shortly after the fourth month is that of pointing. Bower (1977) noticed that there was a difference between reaching out to and pointing at a desired toy. He also noted that pointing was accompanied by 'give me' or 'what is it?' type noises. These noises are not aspects of adult speech but unique to the child. He cites two pairs of twins he was working with. Each twin developed a noise to accompany pointing and each noise was different. It is striking that so early in the child's development, i.e. about 5–6 months of age, the child has linked sound and gesture and is able to use them communicatively.

At about six months of age the child begins to use a wider range of sounds. These sounds are often consonants and are combined with vowel sounds to form small syllables, e.g. 'ga', 'ki'. Linguists refer to this increase in speech production as babbling. At first babies make many different combinations of sound but by the time they have reached their first birthday much of their babble is specific to the language community in which they have been living. So, for example, English babies tend only to make the specific sounds of spoken English, and German babies only the specific phonemes which go to make up the German language. In addition, they frequently repeat the same syllables over and over and begin to imitate the intonational patterns of adult speech. This pattern of development is not limited to English children. Children in other cultures do the same. Babbling, along with crying and cooing, seem to be universal. But the likeness does not end there; Slobin (1973) and Brown (1973), both famous psycholinguists who have involved themselves in cross-cultural studies, tell us that children learning *any* spoken language progress through very similar stages of development.

These stages can be summarized as:

1 Crying, cooing and babbling.

2 First word (as approximation of adult speech). Some comprehension of simple words.

3 Use of meaningful expressions, e.g. 'up', 'more'. Comprehension of simple instructions.

4 Two-word utterances.

5 First grammatical sentences.

6 Appearance of questions, negatives, over-generalization (e.g. 'goed').

7 Complex sentences.

8 In literate societies the appearance of graphic representations of language, using signs, alphabets and writing.

Another important feature about this developmental pattern is that children all over the world, irrespective of the spoken language to be learned, or their culture, progress through these major stages in the same order and roughly at the same rate – even retarded children.

The Effects of Deprivation on Language Development

Perhaps the most surprising thing of all is the case of feral children, i.e. those children who as babies, toddlers and young children have suffered extreme forms of deprivation. They, too, show a similar linguistic development after being rescued from their plight and placed in a more caring environment. A very recent case was that of

Genie who was discovered in California at the age of 13 years. Most of her life had been spent tied to a potty chair in isolation. Although she had been fed, no one apparently had spoken to her. When she was discovered she weighed just 59 lbs, unable to walk or talk or toilet herself. Susan Curtis (1977), who worked with Genie, has provided us with a detailed record of her speech and language development. The most striking aspect of this development is that it resembles very closely the stages one observes in normal children. Genie could understand more than she could say and her first utterances were very similar to the vocabulary of 12–18-month-olds, e.g. 'no more', 'sorry'. Similar results to this were reported by Mason (1974) about a girl called Isabelle, Koluchova (1972) about a pair of Czechoslovakian twins, and Douglas and Sutton (1978) about two sisters called Alice and Beth. All these children were speech- and language-retarded when found and all progressed through similar stages of development to those of normal children.

First Words
At the beginning of the second year, children begin to speak in one-word utterances. The first word is often idiosyncratic, i.e. peculiar to the child. Although the word may not resemble any word in adult speech, the child uses the utterance as a word, often accompanying it with pointing. A little boy well known to the authors used the word 'gogoz' as a means of indicating solid food. These utterances are called holophrases by linguists, and such speech is called holophrastic speech.

Over the next four to six months the baby acquires new words, again not always recognizable as adult words. By eighteen months of age the child begins to acquire new words quite rapidly, of which many are recognizable. By twenty-four months the typical child has a vocabulary of around 300 words. But it must be said that physical defect, poor general health, mental handicap or being a member of a bilingual family can impede this progression.

Halliday (1975) and de Villiers (1979), who both documented the early speech development of a number of infants, have drawn our attention to other interesting aspects of children's early vocabulary development. Early words, for example, are often simplifications of the adult form of speech, e.g. 'da' for 'dog', or 'ada' for 'anything'. They will often simplify clusters of consonants which are difficult to pronounce, e.g. 'nack' for 'snack'. Halliday noticed in particular that many early words are situation-specific, i.e. the child will only use the word in a certain set of circumstances although the word could be used elsewhere. For example, the child may say 'more' but only when asking for a drink. Finally, many researchers like Halliday have noted that the child's vocabulary consists mainly of nouns very specific to his daily routine, e.g. 'bed', 'nan', 'dog'. The rest are verbs with a few personal pronouns, e.g. 'I do'. In order of appearance nouns come first, possibly because children understand the naming of objects better than the naming of actions, although Wells (1985) points out that many parents deliberately teach names of objects at about this stage.

First Sentences

At about eighteen months of age, and for reasons not yet fully understood, two utterances are said together. This is a massive step forward for the child because by combining words – 'more juice', 'daddy go' – the child can convey a whole new variety of things, such as:

Requests	–	'more drink'
Actions	–	'car go'
Possession	–	'Nana bag'
Location	–	'Mummy chair' (pointing)
Negation	–	'no dog'

For some months after this event the child still continues to use one-word utterances, but by the second birthday many one-word utterances have dropped out of his vocabulary and he is just beginning to string three and sometimes four words together. What is more significant than the fact that his vocabulary is extending is that the child is using grammar, albeit a very crude one. He is using rules to create sentences: sometimes sentences he could not possible have heard before. Most of the sentences generated by children would not normally be heard in adult speech. We do know that adults modify their speech when talking to children. Linguists refer to this as *motherese*. But as Wells (1985) and Maratsos (1983) have observed, adults (usually parents) do not speak to their offspring in this simplified form all the time, but only in certain circumstances, for example to hold the child's attention. Very often the adult model of speech presented to the child is complex, disjointed and sometimes ambiguous.

These early simple sentences have been described by Roger Brown (1973) as telegraphic speech, i.e. they are in speech what a telegraph message looks like in writing. When collected together and analysed they reveal some very interesting distinctive features:

(1) Sentences consist only of words which carry important meaning. The child leaves out all the functor words, e.g. articles (a, the), auxiliary verbs (am, is) and conjunctions (and, but).

(2) The word order is very similar to adult word order, seemingly showing that they have a rudimentary knowledge of grammar, e.g. subject-verb-object; in the case of two-word utterances, it is often subject plus verb or object.

(3) With this rudimentary grammar the child can generate new sentences, often unique. A child well known to the authors would say 'fofa come' when the bath taps were turned on and 'fofa bye-bye' when they were turned off.

(4) Braine (1963) noticed that some words like 'gone', 'come', 'all gone' were regularly linked with others, e.g. 'daddy gone', 'mummy gone', 'toy gone'. He called these pivot words. He also noticed that the pivot word would often be in the same place: in the above example 'gone' would more likely be the second rather than the first word.

(5) As at other stages of development, the child can understand more than he can say.

The next stage in development is to move on to more complex, grammatically correct sentences. The child begins to include auxiliary verbs like 'is' and 'am', plurals, past tenses and prepositions. In other words the child adds the many functor words he was not including in his previous two-word sentences. At what age children do this is debatable. Roger Brown, whom we mentioned earlier, found that the three children he studied made the transition at different ages. Eve was about 21 months old when she made the transition, whereas Adam and Sarah were 34 months and 35 months respectively before they began to make more complex sentences.

Like the previous stages, this progression also has distinctive aspects not observed elsewhere in the child's developmental process. These include:

(1) The child begins to include plurals, past tenses, auxiliary verbs, prepositions and some adverbs and adjectives, e.g. 'this is a big one', 'give me book mummy'.

(2) The use of regular and irregular past tenses begin to appear in the child's speech, these sometimes being used in unique ways, e.g. 'it goned now'. (See 6 below.)

(3) The 'wh-?' words appear too, although the child finds it difficult to cope with the changed word order of a question. Instead, the child will tag a wh-word onto a statement, thus: 'why the dog come in?'

(4) Similarly, the same type of thing happens with negation. At first the child finds difficulty in using 'wasn't', 'can't', 'isn't'. So instead he will say 'there no boats' or 'I not pull it', rather than 'there aren't' or 'I can't'.

(5) As with the previous stage in development the child is able to make sentences which are unique, such as the little girl who described two people arguing as 'fight with big talkings'. These cute sentences are of great interest to linguists particularly those interested in how children assimilate and come to use syntax, since many of these sentences never appear in adult speech. Children in other cultures do the same. (Russian, German and Polynesian mothers, for example, also relate to their relatives and friends the novel sayings of their offspring!)

(6) Another interesting phenomenon during this stage is the way in which children over-use grammatical rules they have acquired. The past tense often gets over-used in that children will often add an '-ed' ending to irregular past-tense verbs, e.g. 'I not sawed him'. In some languages there is no past tense as we understand it, but similar observations have been made of children over-using recently acquired grammatical forms in other cultures.

By the time the child enters the reception class of his local infant school he is a very competent language-user. Much of his speech is very similar to the adult form and his general vocabulary is growing rapidly although he may still delight his parents with amusing questions and statements. One such child asked his parents if ham grew on bushes or came from pigs. His parents, rather perplexed, asked him why he wanted to know, to which the child replied that he had heard his teacher say there had been an 'ambush' in his village. Although not all mistakes are as amusing as this one, the fact that the child can form questions and string sentences together means he now has access to more complex grammatical speech and, more importantly, a wider vocabulary. The child is now in a position to gain clarification on matters of language usage that he finds confusing.

Learning to Read and Write

Once at school, the child soon learns to represent language in the written form: both as reading and writing. Usually he learns to write his name first as a memorized pattern (picture), rather than as an understanding of phoneme (sound) – grapheme (written letter) representation. Early reading takes the form of learning off by heart a series of simple vocabulary which form the basis of a very simple reading book. The words are learned as visual patterns and shapes first and not as a phoneme-grapheme relationship such as 'keh-a-teh' makes 'cat'. The child is first shown a flash card cat and asked to repeat 'cat'. Sometimes to help the child's retention of the shape the word will be presented thus: cat. The reason for this is that reading, like speaking and listening, is a very complex skill requiring complicated neurological co-ordination. As a result young children, at first, often have problems relating a sound with a letter. Some children, often referred to as children with 'specific learning difficulties', have persistent problems learning to read, write and spell. Others, however, are very slow to acquire these skills despite adequate intellectual ability. In some of these cases, but not all, language development, or rather the lack of it, can account for their poor performance in reading. Clark (1976), Wells (1980) and Francis (1982) have all found a general relationship between spoken-language acquisition and the successful development of reading and writing.

Language – Innate or Learned?

Having reviewed the complicated developmental stages in language acquisition in children, is there any one theory which will adequately explain how language is acquired? Theorists from opposing sides have tried to explain language acquisition as either due to learning (empiricists) or as a result of innate biological processes (nativists).

Empiricists see the child learning language as a result of being a member of a language-using family. The family contains important people which the child imitates. His language becomes refined through parental reinforcement, i.e. parents tend to reinforce verbal behaviour which is desirable. Nativists, on the other hand, see language as innate and its development as being dependent on specific biological and environmental conditions. Linguists like Chomsky and Lenneberg feel that human language (any language), is so vast and complex that the child's mind is somehow triggered in a pre-determined way to cope with the sorts of structures which go to make up his native language. The inborn trigger for language development is referred to as a language acquisition device (LAD).

The current view of language acquisition is not one-sided and is a result of several fields of study converging. So, as well as linguists studying the development of speech in children, others, such as cognitive psychologists like Piaget and Bruner, have concerned themselves with how children grow to understand the world around them as both thought (concepts) and language. Consequently theorists seem to uphold the view that children:

(a) have some innate predisposition to make sense out of speech sounds;
(b) build together language, learning and social experiences;
(c) have some of their experiences moulded and shaped through environmental influences.

At one time the acceptance by psychologists of (a) above would have been sufficient proof to argue that humans and only humans were language-users. The fact that man was innately predisposed to be a language-user was the one single piece of evidence which separated him from the animal kingdom. The fact that we can talk and listen and represent our language communication in written forms sets us apart from the animal world. Not only that, theorists offered other evidence in that man had specialized structures for language in the left hemisphere of the brain.

In 1966 an experiment with a chimpanzee called Washoe radically changed our view of man's place in the universe and seemed to bring into question the whole idea that, as the only language-users, humans were unique. Allen and Beatrice Gardner acquired an infant female chimpanzee in June 1966. She was about one year old. They began to teach her to communicate with them by teaching her American Sign Language or Ameslan, as it is referred to by the deaf for whom it is intended. This shift from spoken language to sign language was a very clever move on the part of the Gardners since earlier experiments by people like the Hayes and Hayes (1952) and Kellogg and Kellogg (1933) had seemed to show that primates were physiologically unable to produce and co-ordinate vocal sounds to form speech. By teaching Washoe sign language they were able to bypass the problem of speech production but still teach her language.

The Gardeners started to teach Washoe Ameslan as soon as they got her. By experimenting with a number of behaviourist techniques they found that a combination of shaping and moulding were quicker. By 'shaping' is meant the rewarding of successive approximations to the desired behaviour. In the case of Washoe she was rewarded every time she came closer to making the correct sign. 'Moulding' involved taking Washoe's hands and forming them into the proper sign. So, for instance, to teach her the sign for hat the Gardeners would take her hand and pat the top of her head with it, having first shown her a picture of a hat. This would be repeated until she made the sign properly, and she would be reinforced.

The Gardners' original intention was to find out at what point in the acquisition process children overtake chimpanzees. They hypothesized that Washoe would show certain abilities loosely associated with language but that eventually the chimpanzee would reach a ceiling. They thought the chimp would never be able to ask questions, understand negatives or cope with word order (syntax). By completing their experiment they would be able to isolate the unique linguistic processes used by children but beyond the capability of chimpanzees. Their assumptions were completely contradicted by Washoe; and, one might add, by similar studies carried out since.

As a result of living in this very enriched environment, Washoe was able to use eight signs within months of starting her training and by April 1967 had signed her first spontaneous combination. She signed 'gimme sweet'. This was 10 months after the start of the project when she was between 18 months and 24 months of age, which is about the age at which children use two-word utterances. Not only that, but she was able to demonstrate that she knew the signs had a wider application than the context in which they were taught, e.g. she was able to sign 'dog' for a picture of a dog as well as a real one. She had some understanding of the semantic value of signs in that 'dog' indicates a number of things with characteristics one normally associates with 'dogness'. But most surprising of all was that she spontaneously, on occasions, invented her own signs (for example for 'bib'). To the Gardners this meant that they were not just training Washoe to use sign language in the way one might condition a performing seal for the circus, but were releasing abilities previously assumed not to be there. But more surprises were in store!

In 1971 Washoe, who by now was about five years of age, was transferred from the Gardners to work with Dr Robert Fouts at the University of Oklahoma. By this time she knew 160 signs which she used singly and in combinations in a variety of contents and used a fairly consistent word order, roughly subject-verb-object. Fouts had other chimps at the University who had been taught Ameslan. On entering her new environment Washoe began signing to both other chimpanzees and her new handlers within the first day. Later she learned new signs from the other chimps.

Despite these impressive results we must keep them in perspective. Ameslan is a gestural language, so one could argue that it is only an extension of the chimp's natural behaviour. In relation to children of the same age Washoe's attainment is much lower than that of quite retarded children. More recently, other researchers have tried to teach chimpanzees Ameslan. Terrace tried, but reported that his chimp (called Nim Chimpsky) did not start conversations himself – he would only talk if Terrace talked first. Most of Nim's talking was repetition of Terrace's words, and many of Nim's utterances were not grammatical, e.g. 'Go-sweet-gimme good'.

The general feeling among psychologists is that, whilst attempts to teach human language to animals have shown some interesting results, there's not yet enough evidence to support the idea that non-humans can learn human language.

Summary

1 Language, speech and social behaviour are interrelated and this can be observed in the earliest turn-taking exchanges between mother and baby.

2 Language consists of phonemes, morphemes, words and grammar. By subtly changing these we can express an almost infinite number of sentences.

3 Language has its earliest beginnings in the pre-linguistic stage of development and consists of crying, cooing, babbling, smiling and pointing.

4 The pre-linguistic stage is followed by: first words (approximations

of adult speech); use of meaningful expressions; two-word utterances; grammatical sentences; the appearance of negatives and questions; complex sentences and, in literate societies, the appearance of reading and writing.

5 This pattern of events seems to be universal, even in deprived children and children who are handicapped.

6 Theorists have tried to explain this development as learned behaviour (empiricists) or as due to innate processes (nativists).

7 The current view is that children learn language partly as a result of an innate predisposition to make sense out of speech sounds and partly through environmental experiences.

8 Over the last twenty years experiments in teaching chimpanzees language has brought into question the uniqueness of man as the only language-user. Information from these experiments seems to be conflicting, and there is as yet insufficient proof for the idea that non-humans can possess human language.

Further Reading

De Villiers, P.A. and de Villiers, J.G., *Early Language* (1979, Fontana).

Cook, V.J., *Young Children and Language* (1979, Arnold).

Garvey, C., *Children's Talk* (1984, Fontana).

Chapter 4

The Growth of Attachment

The close bond between the parents and offspring of many species has obvious survival value. There is a tendency for animals to be born in a vulnerable state the higher up the evolutionary scale you go. The offspring of insects and amphibians can usually fend for themselves the moment they are born, but human infants cannot survive alone until much later. This prolonged period of childhood in the higher animals allows the offspring to learn from parents and others, so that each generation can built on the accomplishments of the past. In order to be successful, a strong attachment between parent and infant is necessary especially during early infancy.

A group of scientists known as the *ethologists* have made a close study of this bonding process in animals. They have called the development of the bond *imprinting*. Konrad Lorenz believed that imprinting was an inborn ability in goslings and ducks to follow the first relatively large moving object which they saw after hatching. (In the wild, this would usually be the animal's mother.) After following her for a while, the infant would learn to recognize her and would avoid all other objects. It would have imprinted on the mother, thus forming an attachment with her.

Lorenz was an ethologist – ethologists attempted to study an animal's behaviour in its natural environment, and believed that much animal behaviour was innate, rather than learned.

Conditioning Explanations of Attachment

At one time psychologists who attempted to use the ideas of conditioning to explain most of behaviour (the *Behaviourists*) argued that the thing which caused the attachment between infant and parent was the fact that the parent fed the child and so became associated with food and pleasure; affectionate behaviour is reinforced by the food.

Harlow tested this idea by using two mother-surrogates or substitutes, one of which was made of wire and contained the food bottle while the other was covered with terry-towelling cloth – rather like the mother's fur – and did not provide food. Behaviourists would argue that the infant would spend most time with the wire-covered mother, because 'she' supplied food. In fact the infants preferred the cloth-covered mother; it was also noticeable that monkeys reared with the cloth-mother showed much more exploratory behaviour then those reared with the wire-covered mother. These latter showed strange behaviour, they would only rarely embrace the wire mother, and most of the time stayed a short distance away, seeming very timid and clutching and rocking themselves for long periods of time. When both cloth- and wire-reared infants were, at maturity, placed with other monkeys it was found that they were largely inefficient mothers, they ignored or mistreated their own offspring.

Harlow believed that the preference for the cloth-covered mother showed an innate preference – possibly for the feel of monkey-fur rather than for the mother herself. In young monkeys such behaviour would have survival value: their mothers move around a lot, and this preference would keep them with their mothers, and therefore in safety. Although conditioning may have some role to play in the growth of attachment to other people, Harlow's work shows that it cannot be regarded as the major factor.

Critical Period for Attachment

In 1970 R. A. Hinde found that even brief separations of the infant from its true mother can produce long-lasting harmful effects: the baby switches between periods of great maternal contact and periods when it rejects the mother. Such effects were found by Hinde to continue for as long as two years after a brief separation. Thus if an infant monkey is deprived of its mother in infancy it cannot form an affection bond with her later. Harlow believed that there is a Critical Period which lasts roughly from birth to eight months. A Critical Period is a genetically determined period of time during which a particular kind of behaviour (e.g. attachment) can occur. If the correct stimuli (e.g. the mother) are not present during this period, the behaviour cannot develop. Infants reared in isolation for more than eight months were unable to form strong bonds with a mother when they were introduced to her and showed no distress if she was parted from them.

Human infants take longer to develop than monkeys, but Harlow believed that the same principles still apply, except that the Critical Period for attachment behaviour in humans is up to about three years old. Maternal deprivation in infancy can therefore have severe effects on later development.

The Growth of Attachment in Humans

Babies show more interest in human beings than other objects from the moment that they are born. This may be due to the variety of movement, sound and touch that humans provide or it may simply be an innate preference. Fantz (1966) showed that babies as young as two weeks preferred to look at a picture of a human face with all the parts in the correct position rather than a jumbled face; this indicates that if recognition of the human face is not innate, it is learnt very quickly!

Babies display their real social natures when they first start to smile which is usually noticeable during the fifth of sixth week. The smile is most often given to people rather than objects but Ahren (1954) showed that at about the age of five or six weeks a pair of eyes drawn onto the outline of a face was enough to initiate smiling. Later more details needed to be added, and by five months all the major features of the face, plus shading to give a three-dimensional effect, were required to elicit a smile. The most noticeable effect of the child's smiling is the way that it reinforces adults and maintains interaction.

Schaffer and Emerson (1964) studied 60 babies at monthly intervals during the first 18 months of life, and identified a regular pattern in the development of attachments. The children were all studied in their own homes to cut down any effect of unfamiliar surroundings. The level of attachment to their mother and other significant adults were measured in two ways. The first was a measure of the amount of distress shown by the child when separated from the mother, combined with the relief shown when she returns; this combined factor is known as *separation anxiety*. The second was a judgement of the extent to which the child showed fear of strangers.

They demonstrated the following pattern of development:

Birth to six months. This is the *indiscriminate attachment phase*.

The child smiles at parents and strangers alike, and shows no particular preference about who picks him up.

Seven months to one year. This is the *specific attachment phase*. The child shows fear of strangers and great separation anxiety, usually in relation to the mother.

One year and older. The *multiple attachment phase*. The number of attachments to significant adults and children gradually increases. This phase usually starts at about three months after the beginning of the specific attachment phase.

The ages are only a rough guide; in fact Schaffer and Emerson found children who started the second phase as early as six months and others as late as one year. The same pattern seems to occur in all cultures, and Kagan (1967) has shown it in cultural groups as diverse as Americans, Israelis and Kalahari Bushmen.

There is a tendency for us to use the word 'mother' whenever we are discussing the closest relationship that the young infant has with an adult, and in the majority of cases it is in fact the mother that holds this special relationship. Schaffer and Emerson showed, however, that it is not unusual for the infant to show its closest attachment to a different adult. Although the majority of the babies showed their main or primary attachment to the mother, nearly one-third formed the primary attachment to the father, and one-sixth to another person such as a brother, sister, grandmother, aunt or friend of the family. A couple of children showed no attachment at all. It is the quality of interaction between adult and child rather than the amount of time spent together which is the most important factor in determining attachment. The primary attachment figures were usually the people who fed and changed the child, but this was not always the case; the most important factor in the development of the relationship was the way in which the adult interacted with the child. The primary attachment figure was more likely to be sensitive to the child's behaviour and modify their own appropriately; in other words they are the ones who play and communicate with the infant. Schaffer used the term *reciprocity* to describe the way that a parent responds to the behaviour of their child and the child in turn modifies its behaviour in the light of what the parent is doing.

Children of a very young age seem to be able to interact with adults; they are not the passive receivers of stimulation that we once thought they were. Meltzoff and Moore (1977) have demonstrated that babies of 12 days old and less were able to imitate their mother when she put her tongue out at them. In one film which they made, Meltzoff and Moore showed a 42-minute-old child who followed his mother's action of putting her tonque out with putting his own in and out, and when the mother then moved her mouth to an 'Ah' shape the baby frowned and changed to opening his mouth.

Stern (1974) showed that mothers and three-month-old babies show many of the non-verbal signals that adults make to each other during conversation; they look at each other and move their heads in time with each other. He found that mothers and children maintain a lot of eye-contact and that it is the child which breaks off the interaction by looking away. Trevarthen describes the interaction of two-month-old babies and their mothers as conversations; the pair take it in turns to babble or make facial or body movements and do not interrupt each other. Schaffer argues that mother (or another primary attachment figure) and child develop a particular pattern of non-verbal communication, and that it is this that cements their relationship. The pattern that develops is unique to a particular adult/child pair. Once it has developed the child finds difficulty communicating with others, and it may be this that causes the so-called 'fear of strangers' which occurs in the specific attachment period. This dialogue between the primary attachment figure and infant is known as *interlocution*.

Although strong fear of strangers is not shown until about seven or eight months, children show milder forms of the reaction much earlier. Sander (1969) showed that children as young as two weeks cried for longer than usual when their nurse was changed after ten days during which the nurse had looked after the child for 24 hours a day.

Ainsworth observed the reactions of children in the specific attachment phase when they entered a new room with their mothers. The typical child when first entering the room stayed close to their mother, at first physically touching her. Later the child moves away to explore, looking back from time to time. When a stranger entered the room the children tended to rush back to mother and would only play with the new person after some time-lapse. If the mother left the room at any time the child tended to cry and cease playing. Harlow found that young monkeys show very similar behaviour in strange environments. It is as though the primary attachment figure provides a base from which the infant can explore the world, returning from time to time for the assurance of the familiar, while he or she explores new places or meets new people.

Children vary greatly in the extent to which they show their attachments. Ainsworth, Bell and Slayton (1971) noted that the most common attachment relationship shown in situations like the strange room (above) was what they called *secure attachment*. These children tend to play positively with strangers, although they avoid getting too close early in the meeting. When their mothers return after an absence they go to her and then get on with playing. They contrast this with the *avoidant* child who tends to be unaffected by the position of the mother and ignores her when she returns after an absence, and the *resistant* child who seems to be torn between seeking and resisting contact with the mother.

Observers tend to rate the mothers of secure children as more responsive to the child's behaviour. They tend, for example, to be consistent in the way that they respond to the child's crying, rather than varying their behaviour with their own mood. Ainsworth (1973) isolated four dimensions of maternal behaviour that are related to the type of attachment the child has. The four dimensions are:

Sensitive – Insensitive. Sensitive parents are more able to see things from the child's point of view.

Accepting – Rejecting. Accepting parents see the baby as making a positive change to their lives and don't show a great deal of resentment about the restrictions that babies impose.

Co-operating – Interfering. Co-operating parents tend to work with the child rather than imposing their own wishes.

Accessible – Ignoring. Accessible parents take more notice of the child.

Ainsworth showed that the mothers of secure children tended to be more sensitive, accepting, co-operating and accessible. The children with resistant and avoidant attachments both tended to have mothers who were rejecting, but this was combined with insensitive for the avoidant children, and with interfering and ignoring for the resistant children.

Ainsworth believes that the behaviour of the mother plays the most important part in determining the type of attachment that will be formed, but we must not forget the two-way nature of the relationship: both the mother and the child respond to each other. Some children are more easy to relate to right from the word go because they cry less, sleep longer, smile more, etc.

The attachments of early life are reflected in later behaviour. Waters, Wippman and Sroufe (1979) showed that children who had been classified as either secure or insecure in their attachments at the age of 15 months showed different social behaviour at three and a half years. Their nursery-school teachers rated the secure children as more popular, more likely to get involved in games, more self-directed and more eager to learn than children who had been categorized as insecure. Other studies have shown similar differences, but it is not possible to be certain that these behavioural differences are caused by the type of relationship that the child has with its parents. A child who is easy to get on with may start life with the sort of characteristics that encourage parents to be accepting, sensitive, etc, and these same characteristics may make him popular in later life – more likely to get involved in games, more self-directed and more eager to learn than children who had been categorized as insecure. A study by Waters et al. shows this possibility in practice: infants who at the age of 12 months had been rated as being resistant to attachment, and who did not show a consistent desire for interacton, had also been rated as more irritable and less responsive to stimuli at the age of 7 years. Chess and Thomas found what they called 'temperament differences' between infants at the age of one week. Such differences included irritability and taste preferences as well as a wide variety of strengths of response to stress – ranging from mild interest to outright panic when a toe was dipped in ice-cold water!

If such differences in behaviour can be observed so early in life, it might be that some infants are more 'difficult' than others, so that the parents do not respond to it in the same way they would to a more pleasant child. This does not mean that all irritable babies develop insecure attachments, however. Some parents may overcome the child's irritability, or be less put off by it, so that the child develops secure attachments to them. (This may explain why a child can form a secure attachment to one parent, but an insecure attachment to the other.)

Maternal Deprivation

In 1951 a paper for the World Health Organization by John Bowlby suggested that maternal deprivation could be a major cause of many social, emotional and intellectual disorders: 'mother-love in infancy and childhood is as important for mental health as are vitamins and proteins for physical health' (*Maternal Care and Mental Health*, 1951).

Bowlby's ideas were influenced by two main sources – psychoanalysis (see p.91) and ethology (see p.43).

From psychoanalysis, Bowlby took the case-study method (see p.000) and most of the ideas which formed his basic theory. These were:

(a) That the first five years of life are the most important in a person's development.

(b) That a child's relationship with its parents (particularly its mother) has a massive effect on its development.

(c) That psychological trauma ('trauma' means 'wound') in childhood has long-lasting effects.

(d) That loss of a parent, particularly loss of the mother or separation from her, is a major cause of psychological traumas.

Bowlby was also influenced by the ethologists' studies of imprinting, and the concept of Critical Periods (now called Sensitive Periods) in development.

This section will look at Bowlby's theory and the evidence for and against it.

In line with the results of Harlow's experiments (described on p.43), Bowlby believed that if a child were not permitted to form an affection bond with its mother it would develop *affectionless psychopathy* – an inability to feel much emotion for anybody else and a lack of interest in anybody else's welfare. He also believed that children who had been deprived of a mother or mother-surrogate were far more likely to show delinquent behaviour later in life. Many people have assumed that, in order to prevent these tragic situations, full-time mothering is essential, but Bowlby never said this. He simply believed that there must be someone available with whom the child can form an affection bond; he did not say that this person had to be the mother.

Nevertheless, the findings of Bowlby and other researchers seemed at the time to point to the conclusion that lack of a mother or mother-substitute can lead to social, intellectual and general developmental impairment. We shall summarize some of the best-known findings.

Delinquency. In a study of 44 juvenile thieves, Bowlby found that 17 of them had suffered separation from their mothers for more than six months in their first five years of life. Only two people from his control group of disturbed adolescents who did not steal were found to have been maternally deprived.

Affectionless psychopathy. Two of Bowlby's maternally deprived delinquents showed this inability to form emotional relationships with other people.

Depression. In 1945 R. A. Spitz observed that maternally deprived children frequently showed apathy, slow development and general depression.

Dwarfism. In 1963 R. G. Patton showed that maternally deprived children often did not develop physically, and were undersized compared to normally-reared children.

Slowed development of intelligence and language. In 1943 W. Goldfarb found that children raised in institutions were often retarded in their intellectual and linguistic development.

Enuresis. In 1970 J. I. Douglas studied children who were separated from their parents in the first four years of life due to hospitalization; they were liable to fairly persistent enuresis (bedwetting) for several years.

All the above behaviour problems have thus at some time been lumped together under the heading 'caused by maternal deprivation'. But we shall now turn to an examination of each of these problems, to determine whether it is certain that maternal deprivation is the cause, and to investigate alternative explanations.

DELINQUENCY

Bowlby's original study of 44 juvenile thieves has been much criticized. He tended to ignore the fact that more of his delinquents were not maternally deprived. Another problem related to his method of study: it was a retrospective study – that is, it took people who were already thieves and looked back on what had happened to them in the past. He therefore relied on the memories of the boys to discover what had happened to them in the first few years of life. In addition he was not able to see whether all people who suffered maternal deprivation later became delinquents. In 1961 L. J. Yarrow confirmed that there is quite a high positive correlation between broken homes and delinquency. However, the fact that two things correlate highly does not mean that one need cause the other – a third factor may cause both (see page 213).

Broken homes often mean separation of a child from its mother; but not all broken homes lead to delinquency, which seems to depend more on the type of break-up. Death of a parent, which obviously disturbs home life, does not seem to lead to delinquency, while domestic upheaval as a result of a parental separation or divorce often does (Douglas, 1969). Thus it may be that divorce or separation causes delinquency; equally, however, divorce, or separation, and delinquency could all be caused by an unstable relationship between parents, or the child's delinquency might be a cause of the break-up of the home.

In 1965 M. M. Craig showed that families with a high level of internal conflict were those most likely to have delinquent children. Similarly, in 1971 M. L. Rutter found that deliquency and disturbance were found most commonly in children who had left unhappy homes.

Power and others (1974) studied children who had appeared in courts for juvenile crimes. Some children only appeared once but others ('recidivists') appeared in court several times. Power looked into the home situations of both 'once-only' offenders and recidivists. Why was it that some children committed crimes only once, while others kept on committing them? The answer seems to lie, as Craig and Rutter had suggested, in the amount of stress and conflict in the child's home – the higher the level of emotional stress, the more likely was the child to commit a crime. If the problems at home were solved, and the stress lowered, children would stop committing crimes (the 'once-only' delinquents). However if the levels of stress in the home stayed high, the child would continue to commit crimes (the recidivists).

In the studies that link maternal deprivation and delinquency, maternal deprivation is only one factor amongst others such as an unhappy home background and so it is not possible to say that maternal deprivation causes delinquency.

AFFECTIONLESS PSYCHOPATHY

On the basis of the two maternally deprived delinquents who had severe problems in relating to other people, Bowlby asserted that affectionless psychopathy was caused by maternal deprivation. Simple separation does not seem to be a good enough explanation of this problem, however, since children separated from their mothers to go into a tuberculosis sanatorium did not show the disorder.

Maybe Harlow's study of infant monkeys could give us a clue here. The monkeys seemed to show affectionless characteristics after having been separated from their biological mothers. Rutter points out that Harlow's monkeys were not truly deprived of their mothers, because 'deprivation' implies having something and then losing it. Never having something is known as *privation*. Harlow's monkeys therefore suffered from privation, not deprivation. The monkeys had never been allowed to form an affection bond with their mothers and were later unable to do so with anybody. If, however, a child is allowed to form an affection bond with his mother, who then disappears, at least he has had some experience with bond formation. Privation does not permit any such experience.

Thus maternal deprivation cannot be identified as the cause of affectionless behaviour, while privation can be thus identified. But need it be maternal privation? Anna Freud and S. Dann (1951) investigated a group of six children left parentless by Nazi persecution and raised together, first in a series of concentration camps and finally in an English nursery. The children developed strong bonds with each other, because no parents or parent-substitutes were available. The children were all pre-school age at the start of their group life; as time went on, it became clear that, although some of the children showed various emotional problems, there was no sign in any of them of the affectionless character investigated by Bowlby.

At the age of 37, four of the six orphans were contacted again and their development investigated. Three of the four had been adopted between the ages of 5 and 8, and two of them were described as being happily married, effective and successful at work, and as having warm personalities. The third child was reported as still feeling insecure and was suffering bouts of depression. The fourth child, who was not adopted, was reported to be still upset and concerned about the damage and insecurities of his childhood. None of them, however, showed any sign of the affectionless character which Bowlby's theory predicts should have developed.

A pair of Czech twins were reared almost in isolation in cellars or even cupboards from 18 months of age until they were seven (apparently their mother had died and their father had married a woman who turned out to be a psychopath). When they were at last released from the cellar, they were taken into care and were studied by Koluchova (1972). On their release, they could hardly walk, showed almost no speech and were severely intellectually retarded. It was noticed, however, that they were very attached to each other, and when they were adopted, both formed strong attachments to their foster mother. Koluchova tested them again when they were 14 years old, and it was found that their IQ scores were now average, and that they were happy, lively and popular at school. Although (not surprisingly) they were still afraid of going into cellars, they showed none of the affectionless psychopathy (nor any of the intellectual and language retardation) that Bowlby would have predicted.

If early experience does cause affectionless psychopathy it is as a result of never having the opportunity to develop an attachment to anybody. Schaffer showed that it is not unusual for children to make their closest attachments to their father rather than their mother. H. B. Biller (1971) even suggests that bond formation with the mother only may in itself be inadequate; he suggests that in order to be able to form stable relationships with both sexes in adulthood, the child needs the opportunity to form bonds with both parents. If a child develops a close relationship with its mother, or any other person, affectionless psychopathy is unlikely to result from later deprivation.

DEPRESSION

Spitz studied children who were long-stay hospital patients. He found that separation from both parents and from the home environment could cause general emotional upset. But these effects could be significantly lessened by counteracting the upsetting strangeness of the hospital atmosphere; this could be achieved either by providing interesting playthings (H. Jolly, 1969) – preventing boredom which could aggravate the problem – or by accustoming the child to the hospital before his actual admission, by allowing him to visit it with parents (J. and J. Robertson, 1955).

Death of a parent was found by Douglas to lead occasionally to long-term depression in the child, but this was only found in children who had been fostered after the parental death.

Maternal (or parental) deprivation can be related to long-term depression but cannot be regarded as the most important factor.

DWARFISM

Like the other problems we have examined, stunted growth is not caused simply by maternal deprivation. Two main factors seem to be at work here. First, the standard of care for the child, whether given by the mother or not, may be so low that the child is simply not given enough foot to eat. Secondly, even though enough food may be offered, the child may not eat it because it is emotionally upset. Again, this emotional upset may be caused by the lack of someone – not necessarily the mother – with whom to form an affection bond, or it may be caused by poor relationships between the child and parent or guardian – much scolding or spanking, for example.

RETARDATION OF LANGUAGE AND INTELLECTUAL DEVELOPMENT

Goldfarb asserted that the major cause of slow development was maternal deprivation. He compared the developmental rates of a group of 15 institutionalized children of the age-range 10–14 with a group – matched for heredity as far as possible – who were raised in foster homes, all children having been removed from their natural parents at a few months of age. The group kept in the institution were significantly retarded developmentally, compared with the other group. However, he had not considered other possible variables, in particular the amount of stimulation that the children received.

J. B. Garvin (1963) for example, found a gain in IQ of nine points in children going from unstimulating homes into institutions where they received more stimulation. H. M. Skeels (1966) found a similar effect occurring in children who were moved from a non-stimulating orphanage to an institution for the mentally subnormal where they received more stimulation. W. Dennis (1960) surveyed those institutions where children did not appear to gain much intellectually. He found that a 'poor' or non-stimulating institution was one where the children were rarely handled or talked with; where there were few toys or opportunities for play; and where there was a general lack of sensory, motor and linguistic experience for the children.

Perhaps in a way Bowlby was right: children whose mothers reject them are less likely to be receiving the right kinds and amounts of stimulation. But it is the lack of stimulation which seems to be the major cause of retardation, rather than the lack, or severance, of an emotional bond between mother and child.

ENURESIS OR BED-WETTING

Much of the evidence suggests that prolonged enuresis often occurs in children who have faced a great deal of stress during their first years, up to the age of six. In 1970 J. W. B. Douglas and R. K. Turner investigated the kinds of situation which may lead to stress in the child. Separation from the mother, father and home appears to be one factor; but there are many others. Like delinquency, enuresis was frequently found in children from homes where there was family discord, because discord produces stress. Stress is also obviously present in children who are in hospital for surgical operations, which often leads to discomfort. These children, too, show a high rate of enuresis. Burn and fracture cases, who usually suffer the most pain, also have the highest rate. Again, maternal deprivation may be one contributory factor, but it cannot be said to be a major one.

Conclusions

After reviewing the evidence, Rutter and Tizard suggest that Bowlby was wrong to take research carried out on poor-quality institutional care and to assume that its results applied just as strongly to day care or to any brief separation of the child from its mother. However, far more damning is that the evidence suggests that Bowlby's original theory (a mixture of psychoanalysis and ethological theories) was wrong. This section looks at the flaws in Bowlby's theory.

(1) Separation from the mother or mother surrogate does not seem to cause long-term damage to the child, as Bowlby predicted.

(2) The idea that the child's bond with its mother is always strongest (since babies have an innate tendency to imprint on their mothers) is not supported by the evidence. For example, in addition to Schaffer and Emerson's findings (see p.46), Grossman and Grossman found that it is quite possible for a child to

be securely attached to its father, but insecurely attached to its mother. Rutter found that children who had a good relationship with either parent were less severely affected by discord and conflict in the home. Similarly, Hetherington found that, if a child's parents divorced, children who stayed with the parent with whom they had a very good relationship were much less upset by the effects of the marriage break-up.

(3) Bowlby and Ainsworth believed that day care was harmful to the child, because it involved separation from the mother. (Institutional care was believed to be even more harmful, because it involved a longer separation.) However, Clarke-Stewart compared the results of 28 studies on the effects of day care and home care on the child's attachment to its mother. Only in one out of the 28 studies was it shown that day-care children were more likely to be anxiously or insecurely attached to their mothers. Tizard believes that whilst some British research into day-care centres supports Ainsworth's views, this may be because in Britain, families with severe difficulties are given priority for day-care places which are in very short supply. Clarke-Stewart looked at research carried out in Scandinavia and in the USA, where day care is more easily available. Day-care children, it was found, were more sociable and co-operated better with other children than did home-reared children.

(4) Bowlby and Ainsworth both stressed the tremendous importance of the mother's behaviour towards the child. However, research by Waters, for example, strongly suggests that the baby's behaviour affects the mother's, and that what is important is the two-way (or reciprocal) relationship between parent and child.

(5) According to Bowlby and Ainsworth, the first five years of the child's life were by far the most important; events which occurred during these years had a greater effect on the children than anything which happened in later years. Again, the research evidence does not support this point of view. Freud and Dann's study (p.53) and the study by Koluchova (p.54) show the limited effect of early experience. More evidence comes from a study by Tizard of children from residential nurseries who were adopted between the ages of two and seven years:

Before this time the children were looked after by a large number of constantly changing nurses – on average 50 by the time they were four and a half – who were encouraged to relate to them in a detached, 'professional', manner. In other respects the care of the children was good. The staff-child ratio was high, the children were well supplied with books and toys, and their intellectual development was average. At 24 months, however, they tended to be excessively clinging to whoever was looking after them. By the age of four and a half 70% of the children still in institutions were said by the staff 'not to care deeply about anyone'.

Nevertheless, after adoption most of the children quickly formed deep, reciprocated attachments to their new parents – evidence which seems to disconfirm Bowlby's belief that mothering is almost useless if delayed until after the age of two and a half. By the age of eight, their IQs and school work were well above average. On the other hand, about half of the children had difficulties at school and with their peers – that is, they were considered attention-seeking and restless by the teachers, and quarrelsome and unpopular with their peers. At age sixteen, their relations with their new parents in most cases continued to be good. But as a group they still had more problems with their peers than the control children, and they also tended to be more anxious. Whilst these differences could be due to some aspects of the children's current situation, on balance it seems more likely to be caused by the continuing effects of their unusual early social experiences. These effects, however, were much less drastic and of a different nature from those predicted by Bowlby – that is, those children who seemed to be affected had problems with their peers. They had experienced no difficulty in developing attachments to their parents.*

(6) Rutter has proposed that, instead of early experiences being the only factor affecting an individual's development, events throughout life can cause behaviour problems – or reduce them. Early experiences, Rutter believes, may have a drastic effect, but only if the individual's behaviour or situation keeps him exposed to harmful effects. On the other hand, if the person's situation is changed, his behaviour may change and there may be no permanent damage.

A study by Dowding, Quinton and Rutter shows how this idea might work. Women who had spent most of their early life in care were studied as adults, and compared with a control group of women who had lived at home in early childhood. 30 per cent

* Barbara Tizard, *The Care of Young Children – Implications of Recent Research* (1986, Thames Coram Research Foundation), p.17.

of the 'in-care' women were described as having marked psycho-social problems, and 40 per cent were rated as being poor parents (because they tended to ignore their children's need for attention and they were not good at controlling their children, though they smacked them more frequently than home-reared women smacked theirs). So far, the results resemble Harlow's results from his 'Love in infant monkeys' study. However the results also showed that 20 per cent of the 'in-care' women did not show any psycho-social problems, and 31 per cent were rated as good mothers. Why were some women apparently affected by their institutional upbringing, and some not? Rutter and Quinton researched the lives of the women and found that what determined whether they developed behaviour problems and became poor mothers could not have been their early life in institutions, because they had all been institutionally reared. A whole range of factors was found stretching from childhood to early adulthood, which had affected the women's behaviour. For example, their experiences at school, how supportive their husbands were, and the levels of income and job security were all related to their behaviour problems. The women who did not show behaviour problems were the ones who had tended to have more pleasant school experiences, more supportive husbands, and were less likely to be under economic stress.

If Bowlby was right, children with happy and secure early experiences should be in effect inoculated against unpleasant events in later life – that is, they should be less harmed by them. Brown and Harris studied women from a range of backgrounds – some secure, some insecure – who had suffered the death of a parent during adolescence, or death of a husband in adulthood. According to Bowlby's theory, women from secure backgrounds should experience less psychological damage than women with insecure early experiences. Brown and Harris found that there was no difference in the frequency of depression between the two groups of women. Secure early experiences may not, therefore, inoculate us against psychological problem in later life.

Although Bowlby's theories are now largely regarded as being incorrect, he focused researchers' attention on the sorts of factors which may affect the child's development. Later researchers, instead of concentrating on the effects of maternal deprivation, now look at the effects which other people can have on the child, particularly on the child's relationship with its father, brothers and sisters (siblings) and with other children of its own age (peers).

The Child's Relationship with Father, Siblings and Peers

Schaffer and Emerson (p.46 above) showed that up to 30 per cent of children had formed their most important attachment to their fathers. Lamb found that the type of interaction between father and child tend to be different from those between mother and child; for example, mothers tend to hold the child more and to show more smiling and displays of affection than do fathers, who tend to become more involved in physically exciting play. Lamb found that these differences in parents' behaviour continue even when the father is the child's main caretaker. Maccoby suggests that fathers interact more with sons than with daughters, and may therefore be important in developing boys' gender roles. Lamb found that one of the major (though indirect) effects of the father is that the strength of his support of the mother increases her sensitivity and responsiveness to the children.

It used to be thought that the main relationship between siblings was one of the emotional and physical rivalry. More recent research, however, suggest that siblings can be important attachment figures for the child, and may play a vital part in assisting the child's intellectual development.

In some cases, one-year-olds spend nearly as much time interacting with older siblings as they do with their mothers. Dunn believes that older siblings are important to younger children because they provide a wider range of stimulation – for example they can act as teachers, playmates, protectors, comforters and as models for imitation as well as being aggressors and competitors for the parents' attention. Abramovich has shown that friendly behaviour between siblings is far more common than hostile or aggressive behaviour. Older siblings can also become attachment figures – Stewart found that in the strange situation test, over half of the 10–20-month-old children studied could be comforted by an older sibling when the mother left the room.

The importance of peers to a child's development obviously

depends on the length of time the child plays with them, as well as on the intensity of the interaction. In the first year of life, although children will smile and touch other children of the same age, they do not usually form strong relationships with them. In their second year, however, children begin to be able to take turns with playthings (although there are sometimes squabbles over whose toy it is), and helping and comforting behaviour is shown between them. Ispa in the Soviet Union found that pairs of two-year-olds who had attended the same nursery group were able to comfort each other in the strange situation test, whereas solo children or children with another but unfamiliar peer, showed distress.

The Freud and Dann study (p.53 above) showed how important a child's peers could become, and that attachment to its peers could almost act as a substitute for attachment to its parents. For children with parents, however, relationships with peers and siblings give a wider range of people to interact with and therefore give them wider opportunities for learning social behaviour and physical and intellectual skills.

From the evidence above, it seems that the child's relationships with a range of other people are what is important – the child does not necessarily have one all-important bond with the mother. These other relationships, as well as providing emotional comfort, can also be important in stimulating the child and in helping it to learn.

Summary

1 Attachment (the bond between parent and offspring) has survival value.

2 Harlow believed that there was a Critical Period for attachment in monkeys from birth to eight months of age (birth to 2 or 3 years in humans).

3 Schaffer and Emerson found three stages in the attachment of human babies to their parents: the indiscriminate phase, the specific phase and the multiple phase.

4 Schaffer and Emerson also found that many children can have fathers or other relatives as their primary attachment figure.

5 Meltzoff & Moore and Stern all showed that babies can have non-verbal conversations with their mothers at a very early age.

6 Ainsworth discovered that some children form secure attachments with their mothers, some form insecure attachments and some children avoid or ignore their mothers.

7 Bowlby believed that maternal deprivation could have long-lasting and harmful effects on a child's development. In particular, he believed that maternal deprivation was a major cause of affectionless psychopathy, delinquency, dwarfism, enuresis, depression and intellectual and language retardation.

8 Much of the later research suggests that maternal deprivation is not a major cause of these behaviour problems.

9 In recent years, researchers have stopped concentrating exclusively on the child's relationship with its mother, and have begun to look at the importance of the child's relationship with other members of its family and with other people.

Further Reading

Rutter, M.L., *Maternal Deprivation Reassessed* (2nd edn, 1981, Penguin Books).

Tizard, B., *The Care of Young Children – Implications of Recent Research* (1986, Thomas Coram Research Foundation).

Chapter 5

Behaviourist and Social Learning Theories of Development

Behaviourism was the dominant school of British and American psychology from the late 1920s into the 1960s and still has an influence today.

It first developed as a reaction against the psychology of the early part of the century which was concerned with the mind and 'explained' most kinds of behaviour as being caused by instincts; women were supposed to make good mothers due to the maternal instinct, people tend to gather in groups due to the herd instinct, and so on. This type of explanation doesn't get you very far especially since every writer seemed to have a different list of basic instincts and there was no real attempt to check that the behaviours really were in-built as the concept of instinct implies. Since psychology in the early 1900s was seen by many as the study of the mind, something which is *non-physical*, it was difficult to use the methods of science which had grown up in the study of the *physical* world.

John Watson, the first of the Behaviourists, changed the emphasis of psychology to the study of behaviour, concentrating on the relationship between *stimuli* and *responses* both of which could be observed. Watson was not concerned with the mind or any other unobservable structure which thought or made decisions about what an individual should do. Even if they existed they were not open to scientific enquiry, since they could not be observed. Watson also discarded the concept of instinct and started with the assumption that learning was the major driving force in development. This emphasis on observable behaviour and on learning was the key to the success of behaviourist psychology because it generated masses of testable hypotheses, the food and drink of research.

Learning, said the behaviourists, is 'a relatively permanent change in behaviour as a result of experience; this does not include changes in behaviour brought about by physical damage, disease, drugs or

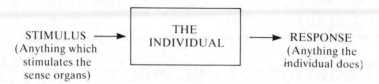

maturation processes'. This definition includes the formal learning of the schoolroom but also that which occurs in less formal settings such as learning to play cards, learning how to react to other people or learning what we enjoy and what we hate.

When Watson first started there had been very little formal study of the way in which learning occured but the work of Ivan Pavlov showed how animals could learn to produce reflex responses in new situations by a process known as *classical conditioning*. We will first look at Pavlov's work and then discuss its application to human development.

Classical Conditioning

Pavlov was a physiologist, working on the salivary reflex in dogs. As part of his experiments he devised an apparatus for measuring the amount of saliva secreted by a dog. Then he noticed that whenever the dog caught sight of the laboratory assistant carrying the bucket which contained its food the rate of its salivation increased, even when the dog could not actually see the food. Dogs normally salivate only at the sight, smell or taste of food, yet the dog was definitely salivating at the sight of the bucket. Pavlov wanted to know why this dog should show such a change from its normal behaviour. He wondered whether, if the dog could associate the bucket with its food, it could also associate some completely different object or event with the food and begin to salivate in response to that.

For the next few feedings, each time the dog received its food a bell was sounded for a few seconds, and the amount of saliva secreted was measured. After several such trials Pavlov sounded the bell without the accompaniment of food and the dog still salivated, nearly as much as it normally did when food was presented.

Pavlov gave scientific names to the parts of this procedure. The food is termed the *unconditional stimulus* or UCS: it is the stimulus which normally elicits the salivary reflex response. It is 'unconditional' because it works by itself; it needs no other help, or 'conditions', to allow it to work. The bell is a *conditional stimulus* or CS because it will only activate the reflex *on condition that* it is presented at the same time as the food. Salivation to the food is therefore the *unconditional response* or UCR; it is a response to an unconditional stimulus; and salivation to the bell is a *conditional response* or CR – a response to a conditional stimulus.

We can summarize Pavlov's procedure in this formula:

The Classical Conditioning Formula

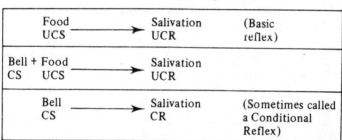

Dogs learn to salivate when they hear the sound of a bell alone, after hearing the bell rung at the same time as they have received food, which does make them salivate. Thus the salivation of a dog to the sound of a bell is conditional upon the bell having been associated with food. Please note that we have used the terms 'unconditional' and 'conditional' here. In some books, you may see the terms 'unconditioned' or 'conditioned' used instead. However, both sets of terms mean the same thing. The use of both endings – 'al' and 'ed' – arose from an error when Pavlov's work was first translated from the original Russian into English. Pavlov actually wrote 'conditional' but this was mistranslated as 'conditioned'.

Pavlov found that the conditioning technique was most effective when the conditional stimulus was presented very slightly before the unconditional stimulus.

EXTINCTION OF THE CR

The UCS *reinforces* the response to the CS; it strengthens it. Without the UCS the CR would not develop. If we now continue to sound the bell but never reinforce the response of the animal with food, the (UCS, the CR – salivation – will gradually die out, a process known as *extinction*. If the CS is again rung after a time lapse to give the animal time to rest, the CR may reappear, although it will be much weaker in form. This is known as *spontaneous recovery*.

GENERALIZATION

The basic conditioning process doesn't only affect the original connection between the conditioned stimulus and the conditioned response. Other stimuli, if they are fairly similar to the original CS, will also be found to elicit the response; a bell with a slightly higher or lower tone than the original, for example, or a tapping noise, will probably elicit the salivary response in the experiment just outlined. The response gets weaker as the new stimulus gets more and more different to the original CS. The way in which other stimuli can elicit the CR is known as *generalization*.

DISCRIMINATION

The animal can be taught to 'choose' between stimuli, to *discriminate*; for example, we can condition animals to respond only to specific shapes. If we pair a circular shape with the presentation of food, the animal becomes conditioned to salivate at the appearance of the circle. However, it may, and usually does, generalize the response so that, although a white circle may have been presented originally, the animal will also respond to circles of other colours. In this case we can get the animal to discriminate between these circles by reinforcing only presentation of the white-circle stimulus; because the appearance of differently coloured circles is not reinforced, salivation at their presentation soon stops.

Discrimination is often used for experiments assessing perception in animals. If we want to see whether an animal has colour vision we may condition it to salivate when it sees, say, a red square. If other coloured squares are presented the animal will probably generalize but if only the red square is paired with food an animal with colour vision should learn to discriminate; whereas one that has only black and white vision will not learn the discrimination (it would be necessary to make sure that all the squares were exactly the same except for colour so that discrimination could not be made simply on the grounds of brightness or other qualities). If we want to see whether an animal can perceive a triangle among several other shapes, we condition the animal to salivate at the presentation of a triangle and eliminate any tendency towards generalization so that the animal responds to triangles only. Then the triangle, together with other shapes, is presented to the animal. If it salivates only on the presentation of the triangle we can conclude that the animal can actually perceive that the shapes are different; some animals have great difficulty discriminating between triangles and squares which are obviously different to human observers.

Classical Conditioning and Human Development

John Watson felt that most of our emotions were developed by classical conditioning based on a few reflex emotions to painful or pleasant experiences. To demonstrate this idea Watson and Rayner (1920) conditioned an emotional response in a young child who is often known as 'little Albert'.

They first tested Albert's emotional reactions at the age of nine months. They found that Albert showed no fear to a range of stimuli which included a white rat; he did, however, start crying and showing other fear reactions when Watson made a sudden loud noise by banging a steel bar with a hammer.

When Albert was eleven months old Watson and Rayner paired the white rat with the loud noise of the hammer on the steel bar. After a number of pairings, which were spread out over a period of fifty days, Albert showed a fear response to the white rat on its own.

They demonstrated generalization of the fear response to other

UCS (noise)	→	UCR (fear)
CS + UCS (rat) (noise)	→	UCR (fear)
CS (rat)	→	CR (fear)

(similar) stimuli such as a rabbit, a dog and cotton wool. None of these stimuli had evoked fear before the study. These fear responses were still shown a month later, though they were not as strong. Most people would have qualms about doing research like this these days because it might have long-term effects on the child. Watson and Raynor did not see Albert again after this final test and so they were not able to extinguish the response.

Watson argued that the emotional development of children could be explained by the process of classical conditioning occuring in the normal day-to-day experience of the child, causing new situations to lead to emotional responses which the child may generalize to similar situations in the future.

The behaviourists went on to explain abnormal emotional development in the same way; for example the development of phobias. Phobias are strong irrational fears of things like dogs, cats, open spaces, crowds or many other stimuli that most of us take for granted. A terrifying experience obviously causes fear and anxiety; according to classical conditioning, anything which becomes associated with that terrifying experience may thus become a CS and may itself induce fear and anxiety. The table below shows how a person's cat phobia could develop.

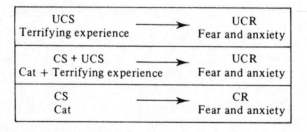

Such a phobia can last for years and yet in Pavlov's experiment when the CS was presented several times without the UCS, the CR was extinguished. Why does this not happen with a phobia? The answer seems to be that the phobic individual never allows himself to get anywhere near the CS – a cat in this case – and will even go to the extreme of refusing to be out of doors, watch television or read a newspaper, in case he sees or hears mention of a cat. In this case of course the CS is not being presented over and over again, either with or without the UCS, so the CR is not extinguished. In order to help a patient with a strong phobia a clinical psychologist might set up a situation in which extinction can occur. He would do this in two ways:

(1) *Flooding or implosion therapy*. Using this technique the patient is presented directly with the object of fear. In the unlikely event that anyone would use this technique for our cat phobia described above, it would mean locking the patient in a room with the cat until the CS–CR bond is extinguished. This can of course be a fairly dangerous procedure, especially when the phobia is very strong, so in general the second method (below) would be preferred for the cat phobic. The technique is more appropriate to an individual who has had a bad car accident or fallen from a horse; under these conditions it is a good idea to get back in a car or onto the horse as quickly as possible to extinguish possible phobic reactions. This may be easier to do immediately after the accident rather than later because there is some evidence that phobias may increase in intensity over the first few days or weeks following the incident.

(2) *Systematic desensitization*. Instead of being directly exposed to the feared object the patient is only gradually exposed to it. The first part of the procedure involves discussing the patient's fears and building up an *anxiety hierarchy*; that is, a list of the things that the person is afraid of, running from extreme fear to slight anxiety. The cat phobic might be terrified of a real cat in the same room, disturbed by a photograph of a cat but only slightly anxious about a cartoon figure of a cat (anxiety hierarchies are usually a lot longer than that). The patient is then introduced to objects low down on the anxiety hierarchy. As the anxiety response to each object is extinguished so the next item on the hierarchy is presented. In addition, as each object is shown, the patient is trained in various relaxation methods so that he can learn to associate relaxation with each of them in turn. By the time the object of the phobia is presented the level of anxiety will be much less than it was originally, due to the effect of extinguishing the anxiety responses all the way up the hierarchy (a sort of generalization of extinction).

Notice that with this system it is not really necessary to know what the original terrifying experience was; all the behaviour therapist must find out is the type of stimulus that triggers off the fear response, and then he can set about extinguishing the bond between them.

Freudian psychologists and psychiatrists, however, feel that it is important to find out the underlying cause of a phobia because they believe that phobias are a result of deep unconscious conflicts (see page 93). If they are right, curing the phobia won't help and the conflict will find another way of showing itself – it would be a bit like trying to cure measles by simply removing the spots. Eysenck argues that there is very little evidence of this *symptom substitution* (the production of a new problem once the phobic reponse has been removed).

Operant Conditioning

Classical conditioning cannot explain the whole process of learning. When early behaviourists tried to use it to explain all learning and behaviour they utterly confused themselves. In order to explain even fairly simple behaviour, such as getting up and opening the door when the door bell rings, they had to invent such strange terms as 'door-opening reflexes' in order to follow the classical conditioning formula. The process could explain the learning of emotions where an existing response was produced in a new situation but in order to explain the development of new pieces of voluntary behaviour another form of learning, *operant conditioning,* was required.

From his work with animals E.L. Thorndike put forward the following hypothesis: if a certain response has pleasant consequences, it is more likely than other responses to occur again in the same circumstances. This became known as the *Law of Effect.* B.F. Skinner, who is regarded as the father of operant conditioning, introduced a new term into the Law of Effect – *reinforcement.* Behaviour which is reinforced tends to be repeated; behaviour which is not reinforced tends to die out, or to be extinguished. To reinforce is to strengthen, so behaviour which is strengthened tends to be repeated – obvious enough perhaps, but Skinner's contribution was to show what sort of things or events could act as reinforcers. In the first type of experiment described below a reinforcer is used in very much the same way as a reward, but it should be remembered that rewards are not the only possible type of reinforcers (see positive and negative reinforcement on page 76).

Skinner developed machines for operant conditioning which have been named 'Skinner boxes', and in which rats and pigeons are the subjects most often used.

Figure 5.1. A Skinner Box

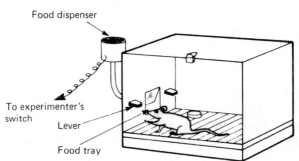

When placed in a Skinner box the animal has to press a lever to open a food tray and thus obtain reinforcement in the form of food. In any situation an animal has a certain repertoire of behaviour; a rat, for example, will show exploratory behaviour when first placed in the Skinner box, such as scratching at the walls, sniffing and looking round. By accident in the course of its exploration, it will press the lever and food will be presented. Every time the rat does so it is given food; thus its pressing of the lever is reinforced by the presentation of food and the animal comes to associate this particular action with receiving this reward. Any other responses such as those mentioned above are not reinforced, and so tend to die out. After several presentations of the reinforcement the rat will press the lever far more often than it did formerly. When the animal has been conditioned in this way the lever pressing, previously an accidental response, has become a conditional response.

Although the experimenter may wait for the rat to press the lever accidentally a much quicker way of ensuring the response is to use the process of *shaping* (sometimes called 'successive approximation'). When shaping is used, the animal is first reinforced for moving closer to the lever and then for being close to the lever. When this has been done the rat is far more likely to accidently press the lever which is then the only response that is reinforced.

In classical conditioning the unconditional stimulus itself provides

Figure 5.2. The 'Formula' for Operant Conditioning

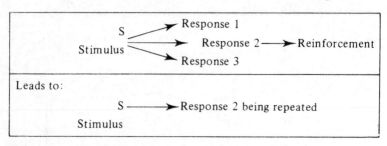

the reinforcement; this is presented before the conditional stimulus. In operant conditioning, however, the reinforcement is presented after the response. Operant conditioning, then, uses reinforcement to single out one specific action from the animal's normal behaviour and to ensure that it is repeated more often than the rest. The reinforcement in classical conditioning causes the response to be made in the first place.

Schedules of Reinforcement

So far we have described how an animal in the Skinner box receives a pellet of food each time it presses the lever. If we stopped giving this reinforcement the lever-pressing behaviour would gradually be extinguished, usually after only a few minutes. What makes operant conditioning important as an explanation of learning, however, is Skinner's development of schedules of reinforcement – different ways of providing reinforcement, which can have different effects on both the rate at which the animal presses the lever, the *response rate*, and the rate at which the lever-pressing behaviour is extinguished, the *extinction rate*. It is these schedules of reinforcement which make operant conditioning a very flexible form of learning. Any response, once it has been conditioned, can be made to last as long as it is required. The various schedules of reinforcement and their effects on response and extinction rate are described below.

CONTINUOUS REINFORCEMENT

This is the method used when setting up the conditioning procedure. Each response is reinforced, but if reinforcement is ceased extinction occurs fairly quickly.

FIXED-RATIO REINFORCEMENT (FR)

The subject's behaviour is reinforced only after a fixed number of responses. Pigeons in a Skinner box have been known to respond to an FR of 1:1,000, or 1 reinforcement for 1,000 responses – commonly written as FR 1,000. This gives a fast rate of response and fairly rapid extinction.

FIXED-INTERVAL REINFORCEMENT (FI)

The subject's behaviour is reinforced only after a fixed period of time, provided at least one response has been made during that period. This method provides a slow rate of response, often only one response per period; for example in an FI 2 schedule, reinforcement is provided every 2 minutes. Often the animal makes a response only in the last few seconds of each 2-minute period. This has a fairly rapid rate of extinction.

VARIABLE-RATIO REINFORCEMENT (VR)

Reinforcement is given after an average number of responses; for example, a VR 10 schedule is one in which, on average, every 10 responses gain a reinforcement. The actual reinforcement does not arrive on every tenth response, but there will be three reinforcements given for 30 responses (as in Figure 5.3 below).

Figure 5.3. Responses

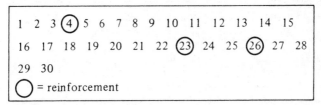

This method provides a steady rate of response which is resistant to extinction: the animal makes many responses before extinction occurs.

VARIABLE-INTERVAL REINFORCEMENT (VI)

Reinforcement is given, say, every 5 minutes on average, but not on every fifth minute. A VI 5 reinforcement schedule would look like this, with three reinforcements per 15 minutes:

Figure 5.4. Minutes

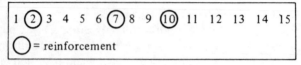

1 ②3 4 5 6 ⑦8 9 ⑩ 11 12 13 14 15

◯ = reinforcement

This provides a steady rate of response, but not as high as with the VR schedule. The response becomes very resistant to extinction: the animal continues to respond for a long time after the reinforcement ceases.

It is obvious that we cannot switch suddenly from a continuous reinforcement schedule to, say, an FR 1,000 schedule; the process has to be a gradual one. For example, to obtain an FR 1,000 schedule the intermediate stages might be FR 5, FR 10, FR 20, FR 50, FR 100, FR 200, FR 300, FR 500 and so on up to FR 1,000.

Table 5.1. Effects on Response and Extincton Rates

Schedule		Effect per minute on Response Rate	Effect on Extinction Rate
	Continuous	Steady – 5 per min.	Fast
FR	Fixed ratio	Fast – FR 5 gives 20 per min.	Fast
FI	Fixed interval	Slow – FI 1 gives 2 per min.	Fast
VR	Variable ratio	Fast – VR 5 gives 15 per min.	Slow – many responses
VI	Variable interval	Steady – VI 5 gives 10 per min.	Very slow – long time

Successive Approximation or Behaviour-Shaping

All the schedules of reinforcement detailed above are generally used, and are only applicable to a single response. This response, however, can be far more complex than a simple lever-pressing reaction.

Skinner, for example, taught – or more properly, conditioned – pigeons to play ping-pong, and to act as pilots in rockets.

Such feats are achieved by *successive approximation*. Operant conditioning selects particular actions and by reinforcing them ensures that they are repeated. Once an animal has been conditioned to perform a particular action it tends to use this as the basis of its behaviour and elaborates on it. If, for example, we want a pigeon to turn round and to walk in a left-hand circle, we first reinforce any movement the pigeon makes to the left. It repeats this and elaborates on it, maybe by pecking at the floor, fluttering its wings, and moving its head further to the left. We reinforce only this last response, so that we now have two conditioned acts of behaviour – one the pigeon's turning perhaps 15 degrees to the left, the second a turn of another 20 degrees or so. With two reinforcements we have therefore conditioned the pigeon to turn 35 degrees to the left. If we continue to reinforce only movements that take the pigeon further to the left, eventually the pigeon will turn full circle. The whole process may take as little as five minutes or so. Each successive behavioural action *approximates* – becomes closer – to the final type of behaviour required.

Extinction, Generalization and Discrimination in Operant Conditioning

In classical conditioning, extinction could be produced by removing the UCS, which was the reinforcer. The same procedure applies in operant conditioning but takes time. Removing reinforcement completely after, say, a VR 5 schedule will not extinguish the response as quickly as removing the reinforcer after an FR 5 schedule.

Generalization can also occur: a response to stimuli similar to, but not identical with, the original can be made. The rat in the Skinner box, for example, may have been conditioned to press the left-hand lever but may occasionally generalize the lever-pressing response to the right-hand lever.

Discrimination in a subject can be achieved, and can overcome generalization if desired, using the same principles as those employed in classical conditioning. We could, for example, teach the animal to discriminate between a situation in which it will be reinforced for pressing the lever, and one in which it will not; for example, we could condition the animal to press the lever only when the light above the lever is on, by giving reinforcement only if the animal presses the lever when the light is on.

Positive and Negative Reinforcement

You will remember that the formula for operant conditioning is:

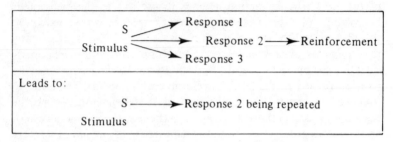

By giving the animal something it wants, such as food, we reinforce response 2. Giving the animal something it wants, needs or likes is called *positive reinforcement*.

The negative-reinforcement formula, however, looks slightly different:

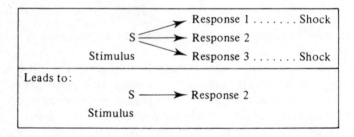

Here, the reinforcement occurs when we stop something which the animal does not like. Thus the presentation of something which the animal wants or needs (positive) and the removal of an unpleasant stimulus (negative) are both reinforcers, because they both strengthen the required response.

SECONDARY REINFORCEMENT

In the examples of operant conditioning discussed above, food is involved as a reinforcer; it is the main or *primary reinforcer*. It might be argued that operant conditioning could not be used as an explanation of normal human development because we do not go around reinforcing our children with food everytime that they produce an appropriate piece of behaviour. Food, however, is by no means the only reinforcer that can be used to strengthen behaviour. If we pair another stimulus with the primary reinforcer the second stimulus also acquires reinforcing properties. For example, when the animal makes a correct response in the Skinner box, a food tray may click into position with an audible sound. This clicking noise can thus become associated with food because every time the animal hears the click, food appears. In time the animal will perform the requires responses while accepting the clicking noise alone as a reinforcer: the sound becomes a *secondary reinforcer*. Something which has been associated with primary reinforcer – for example food – can thus become a reinforcer too.

You will remember this idea of pairing or associating from the earlier description of classical conditioning; the above case is also an example of this. Consider how much more flexible secondary reinforcers can make operant conditioning. The reinforcer need not always be a primary one so that the range of possible reinforcers can be greatly extended; more or less anything that has been paired with a primary reinforcer can become a secondary reinforcer. Perhaps the most obvious case with humans is that of money, which in the past was associated mainly with primary reinforcers: you can use money to buy food and drink. Thus it is now possible to reinforce and induce repetition of behaviour with money. Although money can be a motivator or reinforcer for people at work it is by no means the only possible one; social reinforcement such as attention and praise from other people is also a very powerful reinforcer. Yet some social reinforcers may be an entirely separate kind of reinforcement and perhaps innate; Harlow's experiment concerning love in infant monkeys (see page 43) suggests that this might in fact be the case.

Behaviourists such as Skinner believed that the rules of operant conditioning, discovered in the study of laboratory animals, could be directly applied to human development. According to Skinner, behaviour develops because some responses lead to reinforcement and others do not; the simple behaviour of young babies is *shaped* into the complex behaviour of older children. That is not to say that parents spend their time deliberately deciding when to reinforce and when not to; reinforcement often occurs as a normal part of social behaviour. For example when a baby first babbles 'Da' adults become excited, reinforcing the child with attention; after a while the novelty of this will wear off and the child may have to produce 'Da Da' and later 'Daddy' to gain the same reinforcement. Even though the adults haven't planned it the child's behaviour is being shaped.

BEHAVIOUR THERAPY – A CASE STUDY

The principles of conditioning are used in *behaviour therapy*, or *behaviour modification*, to treat children who behave in an abnormal or anti-social fashion. The basic idea is to change the child's behaviour by reinforcing that which is desirable and ignoring or punishing abnormal behaviour. The case study of Clifford shows how it works in practice.

Clifford was seven years old, an only child of bright, professional parents. At school he was disruptive and at home he threw tantrums and would break toys and damage furniture. When the teacher worked on her own with Clifford he was attentive and his work suggested that he was of above average ability. After these individual sessions he would work for a while but soon started disturbing those around him; the teacher found that she spent a great deal of time calming Clifford down and was concerned that the rest of the class was missing out.

The Education Psychologist to whom Clifford was referred felt that his behaviour was largely a matter of attention-seeking. Clifford was supplied with as many toys and games as any youngster but he had no other children to play with during his early years and although his parents did play with him their work made it difficult to give up a lot of their time. Attention from other people is pleasant for most of us but if we are deprived of this it can become a very powerful reinforcer (like food for a hungry rat). The Educational Psychologist explained that when Clifford quietly got on with his work or with playing with his toys he was largely ignored but once he became disruptive an adult would come to intervene; in other words Clifford was being reinforced for his 'bad' behaviour, and his 'good' behaviour was being ignored. For you or me the sort of attention that Clifford was getting might seem quite unpleasant but for him it was reinforcing; this is similar to the effect that real hunger can have in persuading us to eat food that we might otherwise ignore.

To alter Clifford's behaviour his parents and teacher were told about the basic principles of behaviour modification and asked to pay attention to Clifford only when he was behaving in an acceptable manner. When he was being disruptive Clifford was either ignored or, if this was not feasible, would be taken for 'time out'. In 'time out' Clifford was taken to a small room in the house or to the back of the classroom where he had to stay for five minutes and where he was completely ignored; unacceptable behaviour during time out was punished by extending the five-minute period. It could not be expected that Clifford's behaviour would transform overnight and so to wait for an extended period of 'good' behaviour before applying reinforcement was not likely to be successful; the technique of shaping was used so that at first quite short periods of acceptable behaviour were reinforced and gradually these periods had to be longer before an adult would go over and talk to him.

The treatment sounds simple enough but it is very difficult in practice. The adults concerned needed to think constantly about their own behaviour and when to give reinforcement, it was very difficult to ignore Clifford when he was being disruptive and the tantrums during his first periods of time out were particularly distressing. In many cases the treatment fails because it asks too much of the people trying to help the child. In this case a classroom assistant was appointed to help with the treatment and Clifford's behaviour improved greatly over a period of six months. In his later school life he was regarded as a happy, well-adjusted boy.

Social Learning Theories

Social Learning Theorists have taken the work of the behaviourists and applied it to human development. They are particularly interested in the development of social behaviour.

The human infant may be born into any of an uncountable number of different societies, all of which have different expectations of the way that he or she should behave. In most societies men and women are expected to behave differently; they have *sex roles* which, although they are rarely written down, have a great effect on behaviour. The sex roles differ from one society to the next so we couldn't expect the young infant to be born with this knowledge.

Although there may be a lot of agreement that actions such as taking another person's life are wrong, the agreement is by no means universal and at times of war it seems to be possible to modify even this attitude. How is a new-born baby expected to pick up all the subleties of morality? During the first few months of life it is quite acceptable to demand food and drink in the most outrageous manner whenever the child feels like it; this is not so acceptable later on and an individual whose behaviour is governed only by his or her own immediate motivations is one who becomes a social outcast.

The process by which we learn the patterns of behaviour which are expected of people in different positions in a society is known as *socialization*. It is how the values, attitudes, beliefs, and acquired behaviours of a society, institutions or group are passed on to individuals.

The social learning approach to the explanation of socialization, as taken by writers such as Mischel, emphasizes the effects of the consequences of our actions on our later behaviour. In other words it applies the rules of reinforcement and conditioning that we discussed above. Unlike Skinner and the early behaviourists, who were only interested in observable stimuli and responses, Mischel and other social learning theorists such as Bandura are quite happy to take into account the *expectations* of reward and punishment that the individual may have. The individual is not a passive recipient of all this reinforcement and punishment; Bandura emphasizes the extent to which individuals modify their environment and choose to do particular things so that they have a greater expectation of pleasant rather than unpleasant outcomes. In addition to reinforcement to guide behaviour, the social learning theorists also stress the role of observational learning or *imitation*. This form of learning can result in the production of complex patterns of behaviour without the need for an extended period of shaping.

One of the classic experiments demonstrating imitation was performed by A. Bandura. Nursery-school children were allowed to watch an adult performing aggressive acts towards a large rubber doll, such as hitting it with a hammer, kicking it and picking it up and throwing it. The children were then tested individually in a room containing the rubber doll and other toys; the experimenters noted the total amount of aggressive behaviour shown, and in particular the amount of aggressive behaviour which was copied from the adult model. The children who had been allowed to see the adult model performed a large number of aggressive acts towards the doll, about a third of these being direct copies of his behaviour. The other children, who had not been allowed to see the adult model, demonstrated notably fewer aggressive responses, and of these actions very few resembled those of the adult model. This suggests that the childen who saw the model were copying him, because the behaviour of the control group did not resemble his. Imitation can therefore take place; but this is something most of us already know from our own experience.

Some Studies of Imitation

It is not enough simply to observe that imitation can take place; we must make some attempt to define under what circumstances it occurs.

Many conditioning theorists tried to explain imitation in terms of operant conditioning and it is true that imitation will be increased if the child is reinforced each time an imitatory response is produced. The traditional forms of reinforcement are applied to the learner directly but in many situations where imitation occurs it is the model that is reinforced for particular behaviours and we tend to imitate behaviour which we have seen reinforced in somebody else. This has been termed *vicarious reinforcement*. It may be that seeing someone else reinforced leads the child to believe that he will be reinforced for the same actions.

Bandura, Ross and Ross tested the idea that vicarious reinforcement was responsible for imitation in the following manner. First the children used as subjects were split into three groups; all the children saw a film in which a model behaved in a most bizarre and aggressive way but the end of the film was different for each of the three groups.

Group A saw the model punished for his behaviour.

Group B saw the model rewarded.

Group C saw the model neither rewarded or punished.

Conditioning theorists or behaviourists would expect that Group B, who saw the aggressive behaviour rewarded, would show the most aggressive behaviour when tested; that Group A who saw the model punished would show the least; and that the behaviour of Group C, whose model was neither rewarded nor punished, would be somewhere in between.

The actual results of this experiment *did not* uphold this prediction. Certainly the group of children who observed the punished model behaved less aggressively when they were tested, but there seemed to be no marked difference between the group whose model was rewarded and the group whose model was neither rewarded nor punished. From these results we can say that although the sight of the model being punished seems to have prevented the children's imitation of his behaviour, the sight of the model being rewarded for his aggression (vicarious reinforcement), did not increase the likelihood that the children would imitate him.

Vicarious reinforcement, therefore, is not necessary for imitation to occur.

The children who saw the model punished did not imitate as much as the others but does this mean that they hadn't *learnt* as much? Bandura, Ross and Ross tested the idea that the vicarious punishment had simply led the children to hide what they had learnt. The three groups of children tested earlier were thus put back into the test situation and were then given rewards each time they produced a piece of aggressive behaviour. All three groups showed approximately the same levels of aggression and, more importantly, roughly the same numbers of their aggressive acts were ones that the model had produced in the initial part of the experiment. In other words, all three groups must have learnt the model's behaviour equally, because they were all able to demonstrate the same number and type of aggressive acts in the second test. The group whose model was punished had presumably shown less aggressive behaviour than the other two groups in the first test because of the inhibitory effect of having seen the punishment of their model. They had nevertheless learnt as many aggressive acts as the other two groups, and were willing to demonstrate them when rewarded.

The study of the effects of vicarious punishment shows that we should make an important distinction between learning and performance: an individual may have learnt something by observing a model but may not necessarily show by his behaviour or performance that he has learnt it. A piece of behaviour that has been learnt but inhibited in this way may never show itself. On the other hand it may suddenly appear when the inhibition is removed. On pp.85–7 we discuss the effects of the use of physical punishment to control children's behaviour; one effect of this is that the child may learn that violence is one method of getting your own way. The violent behaviour may be inhibited in the presence of adults but show itself when the child is in the company of other, weaker, children.

Bandura has shown a range of factors which affect whether imitation is likely to occur. Imitation is most likely when:

(1) The model is similar to, but of slightly higher status than, the subject.
(2) The model is *not* punished.
(3) The subject is in an unfamiliar situation.
(4) The subject is rewarded for imitating.

We can increase the extent of a child's imitative behaviour simply by reinforcing it when it occurs; but this does not really help us to understand why we imitate in the first place. Reinforcement is not the cause, because even without it children still imitate. Why should this be? Babies show imitation very early in life. They appear to be able to copy an adult pulling their tongue out before they are an hour old (see page 47). It is quite likely that this predisposition to imitate is an innate characteristic of ourselves and other mammals. The ability to imitate would obviously have survival value simply because it enables one to learn adaptive behaviour more quickly and efficiently than is possible through trial-and-error learning or behaviour shaping.

Sex Role
Mischel and the other social learning theorists believe that children pick up the appropriate sex role by imitating the same-sex parent and being reinforced for behaving in a manner which the particular culture expects of a boy or girl. Bandura showed that imitation is most likely to occur if the model is perceived as similar to the imitator. This makes it most likely that little boys will imitate the behaviour of their older brothers or their father rather than the behaviour of females.

Most children have a close adult of the same sex that they can imitate in order to pick up the appropriate sex role, but even in single-parent families social learning theory can explain the development of sex role by the process of operant conditioning. By reinforcing masculine behaviour in a boy, both or either of his parents could ensure that he showed masculine behaviour, and that, similarly, feminine behaviour would be developed in a girl. It thus follows that the presence of either parent is sufficient to promote the development of appropriate sex-role behaviour in a child. So in the case of a woman living without a husband and rearing her son, provided that she has an idea of normal male behaviour she should be able to reinforce any behaviour in her son which corresponds to this idea and non-reinforce any feminine behaviour that the boy might show. According to the Law of Effect we should therefore expect the reinforced masculine responses to be performed more often than the non-reinforced feminine responses. Summarized in table form below are the principles by which behaviour – including sex-role behaviour – can be shaped. Remember that behaviour which is not reinforced tends to be extinguished.

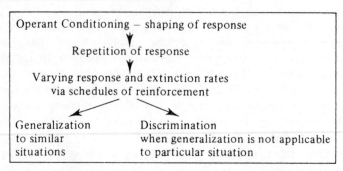

Note also the use of positive reinforcement here: desired behaviour is given positive reinforcement – such as a smile for saying please when asking for something. Negative reinforcement can also be used – for example, if a child has a temper tantrum he can be shut up in his room and only allowed out again when he calms down and apologizes.

Some people object to the social learning explanation of sex role on the basis that they don't believe that the sexes are treated differently. There is, however, a considerable amount of evidence that adults do behave differently to boys and girls.

Smith and Lloyd (1978) watched adults playing with children. The adults were all mothers of children less than a year old and were asked to play with a baby boy or girl for ten minutes. Smith and Lloyd noted that the first toy offered to the baby boys was usually a hammer-shaped rattle and the girls were offered a soft pink doll. When talking to the children the boys were more often encouraged to play vigorously and the girls were more often praised for their cleverness and attractiveness. If the babies became very active they were often imitated by the adults and encouraged if they were boys but the adults tried to calm down the same sort of behaviour in girls.

It is often argued that *if* adults do behave differently to boys and girls it is because the children themselves behave differently; this argument assumes that sex differences in behaviour are grounded in biological differences between the sexes. The interesting thing about Smith and Lloyd's work was that they had controlled for any possible sex difference in the behaviour of the babies by fooling the adults about the sex of the baby. They used male and female babies but sometimes it was a boy who was dressed in pink and called Jane when it was handed to the adult, at other times it was a girl. The 'male' babies were dressed in blue and called John but some of them were actually girls. The adults did not realize this deception was going on and their behaviour was shown to depend on the sex they *believed* the baby to be.

Lloyd points out that the play of two-year-olds reflects the stereo-typed view of the behaviour of the sexes that is held in our society. She argues that this may result from the way that adults play with the children during the first year.

Parents have been shown to display disapproval when older children play in a sex-inappropriate fashion. Langois and Downs (1980) asked boys and girls between three and five years old to play with 'boys' toys' such as cars and cowboy sets in the way that boys do. None of the children had any difficulty doing this. Neither did any of the children asked to play with 'girls' toys' in the way that girls do. The children were quite aware of the differences between boy and girl behaviour. Langois and Downs were interested in the reactions of the children's parents when they came into the room after the children had been playing for some time. Most of the parents either joined in the play or were supportive in some other way, but some showed disapproval. It was interesting that nearly all the disapproval came from fathers whose sons were playing with girls' toys.

When it comes to aggressive behaviour Rothbart and Maccoby showed that mothers were more likely to tolerate this from their sons than from their daughters (see page 87).

Aggressive Behaviour

Bandura's work illustrates how aggressive behaviour can be either increased or decreased by imitation learning in the laboratory, and the same factors can influence aggression in the real world.

Aggression is also affected by reinforcements and punishments. If a child has gained from aggressive behaviour in the past it is more likely that the child will become more aggressive generally and particularly in situations similar to those of his or her previous successes. Patterson, Littman and Bricker (1967) observed children over a period of ten weeks, recording the outcomes of any aggressive interactions that they had. Their results showed clearly that children who had been successful in defending themselves by counter-aggression were less likely to remain passive in a new situation of attack than those who had been unsuccessful. Those who had been ignored by their victims when they attacked them were less likely to attack again than those who had been reinforced by the crying of their victim.

Sears, Maccoby and Levin (1957) examined the relationship between parents' use of punishment and aggression in children. They distinguished between two forms of punishment – physical punishment, which involves such things as spanking or withdrawal of physical objects such as pocket money; and psychological punishment, which involves, for example, telling the child that he has disappointed his parents or simply becoming less affectionate, looking sad and being quieter then usual. They studied six-year-old children and found that those who were most punished for aggression were almost as aggressive as the children whose parents were highly permissive; these particular children were usually punished by physical rather than psychological means.

Why should a child who is often physically punished be so aggressive? There are several possible interpretations of this finding. A likely explanation is that the physically punishing parent acts as a model for aggressive behaviour (see p.81). The child sees that when his parents become frustrated they hit out, and he may then decide to imitate them. Such punishment might succeed in preventing aggression towards the parent, which would only result in further punishment, but it might also teach the child that he can get what he wants if he is aggressive towards others, such as weaker children who cannot hurt him. On the other hand, the child of a parent who uses psychological methods, distracting the child's attention from the object of aggression or simply telling him not to hit other people, has to learn to cope with frustration by means other than aggression.

The above explanation assumes that the parent's behaviour causes the children to become aggressive. But it is possible that some children are naturally aggressive and frustrate their parents to such an extent that they have to resort to physical punishment; in other words it is the children's aggression that causes the parents to behave in the way they do. The results of a study in 1961 by Bandura, Ross and Ross refute this second explanation. They interviewed the parents of hyper-aggressive boys and argued from their findings that parental rejection and punishment occur before the child shows aggressive tendencies; this suggests that parental behaviour causes a child's aggression rather than the other way around.

When Sears examined the development of the children of the Sears, Maccoby and Levin study six years later, he found that although the children of permissive parents were still aggressive, those of the parents who had used physical punishment to combat aggression were much less aggressive than they had been at the age of six. It seems that by the time the child is twelve, continual physical punishment has been successful in inhibiting violent tendencies; however, the children who had thus been made more peaceable often showed great anxiety about aggression.

Boys usually show more aggression than girls; social learning theorists argue that this is caused by differences in the way they are treated by other people, especially their parents. In 1966 Rothbart and Maccoby tape-recorded the spontaneous behaviour of parents towards their children rather than using the more usual interview technique. They found that mothers were usually more permissive towards aggressive acts committed by sons than towards those committed by daughters; fathers tended to be more permissive with daughters. Since it is often the case that the mother spends more time with the child than the father, at least in the early years, these findings may provide one explanation of why boys are often more aggressive than girls.

The View that Behaviour Depends upon the Situation

Mischel argues that the socialization process does not produce an individual with set characteristics that will be displayed in all situations. Rather, the resultant personality is largely controlled by the situation that the person is in; it is as though the person asks the following questions before deciding what to do:

Is this situation similar to one I have been in before?

What did I do last time?

What was the outcome?

Is the outcome likely to be the same this time?

Since people's experience will have been slightly different in different situations, their answers to these questions will vary and their resulting behaviour will be *situation specific*.

The classic study by Hartshorne and May (1928), which we described on pages 14–15, demonstrates how behaviour such as honesty is situation-specific even though many people think of it as a personality trait that is a characteristic of an individual irrespective of the particular situation.

Mischel argues that the consistency that we notice in people's behaviour across many situations is largely in the eye of the beholder. He puts forward a number of reasons why this false perception is maintained.

(1) The general characteristics of perception and memory which try to see patterns in the world and ignore exceptions.
(2) We usually see people in the same sort of situation or role and then attribute the consistency of their behaviour to their personality rather than their role.
(3) There is a tendency to believe that personality is consistent because other characteristics such as physical appearance have this quality.
(4) Once we form an impression of somebody we are reluctant to alter it.

Conclusion

The behaviourists and social learning theorists have produced valuable explanations of development, backed up by a lot of research evidence, but no one theory can hope to explain everything. The behaviourist's concentration on observable stimuli and responses was a very useful contribution to the study of psychology but in recent years the cognitive psychologists have shown that it is possible to study processes such as perception and decision-making in reliable ways which add to our understanding of behaviour. The behaviourist and social learning theories tell us a lot about the role of learning in development but ignore the roles of genetic and maturational factors.

It can be useful to consider the interaction between learnt and innate factors. Any slight difference between individuals at birth might be amplified by environmental experiences. For example, children seem to vary in temperament from the moment of birth; parents are likely to react differently to a baby that continually cries than to a more docile child. The resulting differences in experiences will make the two children even more different than they were at birth.

The assumption that the rules of learning are the same for all species has been questioned over recent years. Animals have different predispositions that make some things easier to learn than others; for example children learn language far more quickly, and with greater ease, than they learn the rules of mathematics. There is evidence that they are predisposed to notice the sounds that make up language and that they are able to pick these out from the surrounding noise. Writers such as Chomsky have argued that children possess an innate language-acquistion device which facilitates the learning of the rules of grammar.

Piaget has shown the value of considering maturational factors in development (see pages 1–3). There is no need to accept one type of theory and reject another; a full understanding of child development will come by drawing material from a range of theories which should be recognized as different, but not necessarily contradictory, explanations.

Summary

1 Behaviourists emphasize the role of learning in the development of behaviour. They study observable behaviour, often that of laboratory animals, in order to discover general laws of behaviour which can be applied more widely.

2 Learning is a relatively permanent change in behaviour as a result of experience.

3 Classical conditioning (Pavlov) is probably the simplest form of learning, and is based on reflexes. The organism can be conditioned to make a reflex response to a different stimulus by repeated presentation of this new (conditional) stimulus with the original (unconditional) stimulus. If the conditional stimulus is continually presented alone, the conditional response will gradually become weaker and stop; this is known as extinction. The organism will generalize the response to stimuli similar to the conditional stimulus, but generalization can be overcome by discrimination conditioning.

4 Classical conditioning may provide an explanation of the development of human emotions and phobias.

5 Operant conditioning (Skinner) is based on Thorndike's Law of

Effect, and shows that responses which are reinforced by something an animal wants, needs or likes, are repeated. Negative reinforcement involves the removal of unpleasant stimulation when the correct response has been made. Schedules of reinforcement and successive approximation or behaviour-shaping make it a very flexible technique.

6 The social learning theorists believe that the socialization process can be explained in terms of reinforcements and imitation learning.

7 Bandura found that children will learn to imitate actions from their observations of a model, and that although seeing the model punished affected the extent of their imitative behaviour, seeing the model rewarded did not. Rewarding the child for imitative behaviour showed that even when the child had seen the model being punished it had still learnt the behaviour of the model; the punishment observed had simply inhibited the child's performance.

8 Mischel argued that behaviour depends more on the situation and the role that an individual adopts than upon stable personality characteristics.

9 No one theory can hope to fully explain human development. The blindspots of the behaviourist and social learning theories include the role of genetics and maturation, as well as cognitive factors such as perception and thinking. The assumption that the rules of learning are the same for all animals has been questioned.

Further Reading

Brown, H. and Stevens, R., *Social Behaviour and Experience* (1975, OUP), Chapter 19.

Child, D., *Psychology and the Teacher* (3rd edn, 1981, Holt-Blond).

Hill, W., *Learning* (3rd edn, 1980, Methuen).

Miller, G.A., *Psychology: The Science of Mental Life* (1970, Penguin), Chapter 13.

Mischel, W., *Personality and Assessment* (1968, Wiley).

Chapter 6

Freud's Theory

Sigmund Freud was the founder of the *psychoanalytic* school of psychology. He developed his theories of personality and development whilst working as a therapist and his work has had a huge effect on the development of psychology through the psychoanalytic movement which followed and modified his theories and also through other strands of psychology which disagreed with him but made many discoveries whilst attempting to disprove Freudian ideas. Freud's academic career started in 1885 and continued almost up to his death in 1939.

Freud was one of the earliest writers to emphasize the importance of the first five years in determining the personality for the whole of life. The first five years' experiences were thought to have a dramatic effect on adult behaviour as different as nail biting, obsessive cleanliness and problems with relating to members of the opposite sex. This emphasis is much greater than that of many others such as the Social Learning Theorists (see Chapter 5) who would agree that early life is important, because we learn some of our basic behaviours then, but who argue that the effects of the early years may be changed by later experiences.

Freud argued that development through the first few years followed a particular pattern for all children. As the pattern unfolds the child pays attention to and receives pleasure from different parts of its anatomy. The pattern takes the form of a series of what Freud called *psychosexual stages*. The stages are as follows:

> *The oral phase.* During the first year or so of life, children gain satisfaction from putting things into their mouth and sucking. The objects may range from the feeding nipple to anything which happens to be in reach. Smoking and nail biting in adult life were

seen by Freud as evidence of frustration or overindulgence during this stage.

The anal phase. During the second and third years the child becomes capable of more control over its bowels and obtains great pleasure from the retention and expulsion of faeces. It is during this period that potty training starts and if parents approach this in too strict a manner or try to force the child too early into the socially acceptable methods of coping with defecation Freud argued that this could result in the formation of the anal personality in adulthood. Individuals with 'anal personalities' are excessively concerned with order and cleanliness and cannot bear unpredictability or untidiness.

The phallic phase. Between roughly the ages of three and five the genitals become the area of the body from which the child derives pleasure. It is during this stage, according to Freud, that sex role and conscience develop as a result of the process of *identification* (see below).

These three stages are the most important in personality development and socialization and are followed by a *latent phase* which has no particularly important features for Freudian theory and the adult *genital phase*, which starts at puberty.

Freud sees the adult personality consisting of three elements which interact with each other. The part which other people interact with directly is known as the *Ego*. Behind the Ego is a part of the personality that contains all our unconscious needs and wishes, the *Id*. The Id is the unsocialized part of our personality which wants to satisfy all our basic urges without waiting or being polite about things. If the Id were allowed out on its own it would be arrested in no time because as soon as it was hungry it would grab the first bit of food that it saw whether it was from the fridge or in someone else's hand; if it fancied a member of the opposite sex ...! (Of course, since the Id is simply one system within the personality and not something that could exist alone it could not in fact be 'let out.') The other part of the personality is the *Superego*, which is the socialized part of the personality and which contains the conscience and an image of how the individual ought to behave. The Id and the Superego are often in conflict and the Ego is sometimes seen as a sort of referee. The behaviour and personality which is shown is a result of the interaction of these three systems.

It is important to note that Freud regarded the majority of factors which affect behaviour as having an *unconscious* origin. The Id and the Superego are largely in the unconscious, as are many of the memories of early life that have such a strong effect on our conscious personality. We are not aware, according to Freud, of most of the motives that drive us. Take an example of a woman who finds it difficult to get on with men. There are many possible reasons for this but one might be that as a young girl she was sexually assaulted, perhaps by a man that she knew well. This memory would cause great anxiety to the young girl and so, Freud would argue, it would be *repressed*; that is, the memory would be blocked in the unconscious and the older woman would not know of its existence. Although the memory itself is not available to conscious thought, it can still have an effect on behaviour, causing the adult woman's problems with men. The techniques of psychoanalysis including the analysis of dreams are designed to explore unconscious motivations and bring them to a conscious level in a therapeutic situation where the individual may be able to come to terms with them. Once the repressed memory of the sexual assault is brought to consciouness it can be seen for what it is and the woman will be more likely to cope with relationships with men.

Freud said that one principle governing the personality was that the Ego should be protected from anxiety and this is one reason that most of our motivations are unconscious. In the example above we talked about repression, which is one technique by which the Ego can be protected from unpleasantness. Repression is just one example of a *defence mechanism*, which is a technique used to reduce Ego anxiety.

The Ego has an image of the sort of person that it thinks you are. If the image is unrealistically prim and proper it may be difficult to cope with the basic urges of the Id. The Ego will be protected in some way from recognizing this crude part of your personality but it may not be possible to bottle it up totally. In this type of situation the defence mechanism which helps avoid Ego anxiety may be *projection*; that is, rather than accept your own basic aggression and sexuality, these characteristics are projected out onto the rest of society causing the individual concerned to notice these aspects of society much more than other people. Using this defence mechanism the individual can pay attention to sexuality and aggression without disturbing the Ego because the Ego can interpret the world as being full of sex and violence and can criticize other people rather than having to accept his or her own unconscious motives.

The defence mechanism of *identification* is an important factor in the development of the Superego and is central to Freud's ideas about child socialization.

Identification

Identification involves the adoption of another person's whole range of attitudes, values and behaviour. After identification, a child may act as he thinks the other person would in a new situation.

Freud first used the concept of identification to explain the way that children acquire their sex role – masculine behaviour in the case of boys, feminine behaviour in the case of girls. He put forward the idea that a boy's love for his mother increases greatly at around the age of four or five, to a point when he wishes to possess her sexually. The boy sees his father as a rival for his mother's love and develops a fear that his father will castrate him (*castration anxiety*). Freud called this unpleasant situation the *Oedipus Complex*; according to him all boys, regardless of culture, go through this. Understandably, young boys would like to escape from the Oedipus Complex, and to do this they use the oldest trick in the book: 'If you can't beat them, join them'. Boys therefore identify with their fathers, becoming as like them as possible. Girls go through a similar process, known as the *Electra Complex*, which results in identification with the mother, though even Freudian psychologists admit that his theory of female identification is unsatisfactory and unclear.

Freud's description of the Electra Complex varied over the years of his writing and he admitted that he had problems with his theory of female socialization. At one point he suggested that his problem reflected the fact that women were actually less well socialized than men! Most studies suggest that if anything the opposite is true. In one of its less confused versions the description of the Electra Complex goes like this:

At some time during the phallic stage and young girl realizes that she has not got a penis and develops what Freud called *penis envy*. She realizes that her mother is also without a penis and believes that mum is responsible for her own loss. This produces a conflict between mother and daughter which is too much for the young child to cope with and so she identifies with the mother in order to reduce this tension.

Many of the later followers of Freud (the Post Freudians) accept the concept of identification but don't go along with the notion that it develops from a *fear* of the same-sex parent. For example, Whiting agrees that boys develop love for their mothers and girls for their fathers, but argues that identification occurs due to envy rather than anxiety. The child identifies with the same-sex parent in order to achieve the same status and control over the mother (in the case of boys) or the father (in the case of girls). This is known as the *status envy* theory of identification.

Bandura, Ross and Ross have managed to define more clearly what status envy means. They believe that the major factor behind it is that the person who is envied has *control* over resources; simply to be in possession of resources is usually not enough. Thus in an experiment a child saw two adults involved in the following sequence of behaviour:

(1) Adult A, who was in apparent control of a large number of expensive and elaborate toys, gave some of these to adult B.
(2) Adults A and B then performed certain different striking patterns of behaviour which would be easy to recognize in the child if it imitated them.

Then the child's behaviour was observed.

If it is merely possession of the wanted objects which prompts imitative behaviour in the child then we might expect him to imitate the behaviour of both A and B. If, however, it is A's control of resources which is the major motivator then only A's behaviour would be imitated. Observation of the child's behaviour showed that while he imitated some behaviour demonstrated by A and some demonstrated by B, recognizably more of A's behaviour was imitatated. This finding suggests that both control of resources and possession of resources act as motivators for imitative behaviour, but that control over resources is probably the more important of the two factors.

We could apply these principles to male sex-role identification:

(1) A boy's father is seen by the child to control a valuable resource, namely his mother.

(2) The boy envies his father's control of this much-desired resource.
(3) The boy identifies with his father.

It is evident that a child is liable to find adults' presence, attention or praise reinforcing, and will imitate or perhaps identify with them if he can see that they control resources which he himself wants.

Many psychologists find Freud's theory of identification difficult to accept, for a variety of reasons. The theory would, for example, find it difficult to explain how the children of one-parent families can grow up to develop normal sex roles.

Criticism of Freud's Theories

Source of evidence. Freud worked as a therapist and gained most of his insights into behaviour from his patients. These were a very limited and biased sample of the population in general. The sample has been described as consisting of middle-aged, middle-class, mid-European, neurotic women. He did study some males such as the famous *little Hans* whose father wrote to Freud over many years recording the boy's behaviour in great detail (see below). Given that so many of his patients were women it is surprising that his theory of female socialization is so weak. This has led some people to suggest that his theories are based on his own childhood.

Since Freud was working as a therapist his main concern was the treatment of his patients rather than the strict control of variables that is found in the laboratory. In this situation it is very easy to lead patients into saying things that fit in with the theory that you hold, and when writing up the case afterwards memory is likely to be distorted in a way that fits the 'facts' to the theorist's existing ideas.

Freud's theory is unscientific. Eysenck has argued that Freud's theory 'explains everything and predicts nothing'. It is a bit like the man who sits in pub on Sunday lunchtime and can explain exactly why a particular horse won the race yesterday but is never any good at telling you which horse will win next week's race. To be scientific a theory must make testable predictions in such a way that if the prediction proves false the theory would be discarded.

Some argue that it doesn't matter that the theory is unscientific and point to other important theories such as the existence of God which have had a far greater effect on people's lives and the history of civilizations than most scientific theories. Following this line the strength of Freudian theory lies partly in the fact that it helps people through the process of psychoanalysis.

Eysenck questions the effectiveness of the psychoananlytic method. He compared the recovery rates of two groups of patients, one who had psychotherapy and one who had no treatment and claimed that after six months there was no difference between the recovery rates of the two groups.

Too many hypothetical notions. If there is no other way to decide between two theories the last resort is to accept the one that makes the least assumptions. Freud's theory is full of things like the Id, Ego, Superego, Oedipus complex and so on which are not directly observable and are supported by questionable evidence.

The nature of conscience. Freud saw conscience as a quality of the individual that was fairly similar from one situation to the next. The work of the Social Learning Theorists on the situation-specific nature of conscience directly contradicts this (see page 87).

Little Hans – an Example of a Case Study

In many, probably most, pieces of psychological research an individual subject's behaviour appears relatively unimportant since it is usually brief, often performed in unusual surroundings and once recorded is mixed in with that of many others so that a generalized conclusion may be made. The case study is one method that puts individuals back in focus and records aspects of their own behaviour and conversations, rather than putting them into the constraints of the experimental set-up.

The 'little Hans' case study consists of a written record of the behaviour and conversations of a young boy taken down by his father, who was a pupil of Freud. When Hans was about five years old he developed a phobia of horses which, since they were the predominant mode of transport at the time, had a disruptive effect on family life. A behaviourist psychologist might treat this problem with systematic desensitization (see page 69) and, if he was interested in the cause of the phobia, would assume that it was related to some traumatic experience with horses. To a Freudian, or psychoanalytic, psychologist the problem is seen in a different light; the fear of horses is regarded as a mere symptom of an underlying, unconscious problem and the treatment lies in finding and dealing with the more deeply rooted disorder.

An analysis of much of Hans' conversations revealed evidence to suggest that the horse was a symbol for Hans' father (something that might be expected since Hans was at the age of the Oedipus Complex). An example of some of the evidence was that Hans was most afraid of white horses with blinkers and 'something black around the mouth'. It was pointed out that Hans' father had a dark moustache and wore glasses and that in records of his conversation he had used phrases such as 'Daddy you are lovely! You are so white!' and that at another time when his father was leaving the table Hans had said 'Daddy don't trot away from me'.

This sort of case-study material is often used as evidence of the validity of Freud's theories but it seems very much like finding the facts to fit the theory and ignoring the rest. It is unlikely that a recorder without a Freudian bent would have bothered to record what many would simply regard as a slip of the tongue (don't *trot* away from me). But to a psychoanalyst, of course, it is these mistakes which reveal unconscious motivations.

In other parts of the case study, Hans' father seems to lead Hans into saying things that fit in with Freudian theory. For example, when he asks Hans if he would like to be married to Mummy and the boy says 'Yes', this can hardly be taken as evidence for the Oedipus Complex. It is difficult enough to avoid these 'experimenter effects' in the brief, planned encounters of an experiment but in the prolonged close relationship that often develops between the recorder and the subject in a case study it is much more difficult to control.

Play Therapy

Adults often find it useful to talk through their problems and anxieties with a sympathetic listener. The other person doesn't have to say much, simply show all the signs of listening and perhaps ask questions from time to time to allow the talker to explore their own feelings. During these sessions, which may be with a trained counsellor but more likely with a friend or spouse, unconscious conflicts may come to the surface and be resolved. For children, play may serve the same function.

Play therapy is a range of techniques designed to help psychologically disturbed children. The child may be unable to control feelings of aggression and may be disruptive or they may be withdrawn as a response to a specific event such as a death in the family or for unknown reasons. Play therapy is a process in which a child, with the help of a therapist, works to relieve anxieties and conflicts through play activities. Toys are used to encourage the child to act out inner conflicts or role-play a situation which has or may cause stress in real life. The relationship with the therapist is probably more important than the toys themselves. The child must feel secure and uninhibited. Most play therapists prefer to be relatively non-directive, i.e. they allow the child to decide what form the play will take.

Like the adult finding relief in working through internal conflicts by talking, the opportunity to release conscious or unconscious anxieties, desires, or motives in an unthreatening and supportive environment is thought to be therapeutic for children.

Behaviour-therapy techniques based on conditioning theory tackle the undesired behaviour of these children head on. They examine the behaviour performed by the children and arrange things so that acceptable/desirable behaviour is encouraged by reinforcement and other types of behaviour are discouraged by removing reinforcement. Play therapy, with its roots in Freudian psychology, does not concern itself directly with the immediate behaviour of the child. Rather it assumes that the aggression or withdrawal is the result of deeper emotional problems and that, when this has been worked through, the aggression or withdrawal will disappear.

Both play and behaviour therapists can point to many clinical examples of children who have been helped by their techniques. Some children may benefit more from one technique than the other, depending upon their particular personality or problem. But ultimately the success of the therapy may depend less on the background theory and much more on the social relationship that can be built up between the child and the therapist.

Summary

1 Freud believed that children develop through a series of psychosexual stages (oral, anal, phallic, latent and genital) and that the first five years of life were most important for later adult personality.
2 There are three main parts to the personality: *Id* – present at birth, motivated to satisfy basic urges as soon as they arise. *Superego* – contains the conscience and an image of how the individual ought

to behave. *Ego* – interacts with the world, a referee between the Id and Superego.

3 We are not consciously aware of all the reasons for our behaviour; unconscious motivation has a huge effect. Defence mechanisms work to protect the Ego from anxiety.

4 Sex role is developed as a result of the process of identification with the same-sex parent. Freud's idea that boy's identify with their fathers in orders to reduce the fear of his aggression was modified by Whiting, who believed that identification is motivated by the boy's envy of his father's status.

5 Freud's ideas about the role of play have led to techniques designed to help disturbed children

Further Reading

Miller, G.A., (1970) *Psychology: the Science of Mental Life* (1970, Penguin), Chapter 15.

Miller, J. (ed), *States of Mind* (1983 BBC), Chapter 13.

Chapter 7

Sex Differences in Behaviour

A small girl was watching a cartoon on television. In the story, a tug boat captain was in the galley, cooking fish. His wife, said the narrator, was up on deck, painting the funnel. The four-year-old giggled and turned to her mother. 'They just said that to make it funny', she remarked, 'It would be the other way round really.'

What makes a little girl think in this way? Do such differences between the sexes really exist? and if they do, from where do they stem? Are they there, fixed, biologically at birth, or are they due to learning, that 'relatively permanent change in behaviour due to experience?'

Like most other aspects of our behaviour, any difference in the behaviour of the two sexes depends on biological, social and cultural factors. Before looking at these in detail it is useful to define some of the terms used by psychologists in studying this topic. The words 'sex differences' applies to biological differences, but the word 'gender' is used for behaviour and psychological differences. 'Sex,' or 'gender roles' applies to a set of external behaviour patterns that our society regards as appropriate, whereas *gender identity* refers to our inner sense of being male or female, and being able to label ourselves and others correctly. 'Sex-role behaviour' is the exhibiting of behaviour that matches the culturally defined sex role such as choosing sex-appropriate toys, wearing appropriate clothes, etc.

What factors contribute to differences between the sexes?

Constitutional (i.e. Biological) Factors

A few of these, it seems, can date from even before birth (the pre-natal period).

(a) Boys secrete a hormone called testosterone during the early pre-

natal months which affects the brain so that the correct male
hormones are secreted at the right time later on.

(b) Girls' skeletal development tends to be 3–4 weeks ahead of that
of boys.

(c) Boys tend, however, to be larger and heavier at birth, but still
they are more vulnerable to disease.

After birth, there are differences in physical development but these
become magnified after puberty. Until then girls' development seems
to be slightly faster and more regular and predictable than boys.
Because these physical differences exist, it seems likely that some of
the early behavioural differences between the sexes might be due to
biological factors such as genes or hormones. For example, Malina
(1987) points out that girls spend more time in small motor co-
ordination (e.g. bead threading) and boys spend more time in large
motor movement such as climbing. Boys, in general, show larger
'grip strength' from an earlier age than girls, whereas girls' general
development seems to be slightly earlier than boys, so the baby's
change from grasping things with the finger pressed against the palm
to finally using the thumb in opposition to the finger probably occurs
slightly earlier in girls.

Maccoby and Jacklin (1974) noted that young males are more
active and assertive then females. Boys of 2–3 years old engage in
more rough and tumble play than females, and at five years old they
are more likely to respond aggressively to attack, or give verbal
insults. Maccoby and Jacklin noticed similar results cross-culturally,
in Switzerland, India, Ethiopia and Mexico, and these findings were
also reported by Harlow (1962) on rhesus monkeys. This seems
to suggest that this earlier difference in activity and aggression is
constitutional in origin, especially as the effect was enhanced in
monkeys when they were given extra male sex hormones.

Various investigations have also suggested that there are cognitive
differences between the sexes which could be biological in origin.

Witkin (1962) studied the perceptual abilities of young children
using the 'embedded figures test'. A child has to find a simple figure
hidden in a more complex figure by ignoring the other features of
the drawing. Children generally become better at ignoring the 'field'
or background as they grow older. Witkin found that age for age,
young girls were more 'field dependent' than boys.

Maccoby and Jacklin suggested that male children are slightly better at spatial ability than females in IQ tests, whereas males do less well with verbal reasoning than females. This may have something to do with the pattern of hormones. Geschwind has linked spatial ability with the presence of large amounts of male hormone during pregnancy, and Waber (1977) has noted a hormonal connection. In young girls, those who develop later, i.e. have less female hormones present at the time, are better at spatial tasks than those who develop early.

These studies suggest that there is a biological pre-disposition to behave in a certain way, but social and cultural factors have also been found to play an important part in determining behaviour.

Social Factors

Although Maccoby and Jacklin's cross-cultural study (see page 102) suggests that the early tendency for males to be the rougher sex is biological, social factors increase the difference.

Parents tend to reinforce the gender role behaviour they believe to be appropriate to their particular culture, by approval and attention (see page 70), and even the structure of a child's family can affect this later behaviour.

Several studies have suggested that parental reinforcement is important. In Chapter 5 we described the study of Smith and Lloyd (1978) who watched adults playing with children. The adults were all mothers of children less than a year old and were asked to play with a baby boy or girl for ten minutes. Smith and Lloyd noted that the first toy offered to the baby boys was usually a hammer-shaped rattle and the girls were usually offered a soft pink doll first. When talking to the children the boys were more often encouraged to play vigorously but the girls were more often praised for their cleverness and attractiveness. If the babies became very active they were often imitated by the adults and encouraged if they were boys but the adults tried to calm down the same sort of behaviour in girls.

It is often argued that if adults do behave differently towards boys and girls it is because the children themselves behave differently; this argument assumes that sex differences in behaviour are grounded in biological differences between the sexes.

The interesting thing about Smith and Lloyd's work was that they had controlled for any possible sex difference in the behaviour of the babies by fooling the adults as to the sex of the baby. They used male and female babies, but sometimes it was a boy who was dressed in pink and called Jane when it was handed to the adult, at other times it was a girl. The 'male' babies were dressed in blue and called John, but some of them were actually girls. The adults did not realize this deception was going on and their behaviour was shown to depend on the sex they believed the baby to be.

Lloyd points out that the play of two-year-olds reflects the stereotyped view of the behaviour of the sexes that is held in our society. She argues that this may result from the way that adults play with the children during the first year.

Soames (1957) found that parents will allow a higher degree of aggressive behaviour in their sons than in their daughters, although Snow, Jacklin and Maccoby (1983) found that, in general, boys received more punishment than girls from their fathers.

Even with children as young as one year old, the toys we provide for children and the ways in which we encourage them to use the toys also tend to differ for the two sexes. Rheingold and Cook (1975) listed the toys in the rooms of children aged one month to six years and found that the boys' rooms had more sports equipment, vehicles and shape-sorting toys, whereas girls had more dolls and floral decorations. Since these children were so young it seems that parental choice was at work here rather than simply children's preferences.

Many psychologists agree that the male stereotype is stronger and develops earlier than the female one, i.e. it is less acceptable for boys to play with dolls than it is for girls to play with cars. Fathers, in particular, seem to disapprove of 'girlish' behaviour in their sons. This was demonstrated in a study by Langlois and Downs (1980). 3–5-year-old children were given 'girls' and 'boys' toys such as dolls and nurses' outfits, and cars and cowboy outfits, respectively. Half the girls had boys' toys, the other half had girls' toys, and the boys' group was divided in the same way. Those who had boys' toys were told to 'play with these toys the way that boys do', and vice versa.

After the children had been playing for some time, a mother or father would be allowed into the room, and Langlois and Downs observed parental behaviour to see whether it was supportive or disapproving. They found that fathers showed some disapproval 11 per cent of the time when sons played with girls' toys, but only 1 per cent of the time when they were using boys' toys. Fathers did not mind which toys daughters used, and to mothers it made little differences which toys either sex were given.

This therefore suggests that reinforcement from parents is important in shaping behaviour. A study by Carlsmith (1964) shows that the lack of a suitable model during the early years may affect later behaviour and even cognitive interests. Carlsmith studied boys who had grown up without a male model, usually because the father was on military service. At maturity these men tended to be less 'masculine' in their interests and they scored higher in verbal than in mathematical ability.

The effect of parenting can also magnify any cognitive differences that might already exist between the sexes. In spite of recent attempts to provide sexual equality in schools, as late as 1982 Parsons, Adler and Kaczala found that parents of 5th to 11th grade children (age 6–11) thought that their daughters were less good at maths than their sons, despite the fact that their achievements did not differ. They believed that their daughters had to work harder to achieve the same results.

Paulsen and Johnson (1983) showed that children of both sexes who had a positive attitude to maths did better on maths tests. So it seems that, to some extent at least, children's intellectual performance is shaped by parental and teacher attitudes and expectations as well as their own. These serve to exaggerate any small intellectual differences which may already exist.

Other evidence demonstrating the importance of social factors in the production of sex differences comes from sex-reassignment cases. Hermaphrodite children are rare cases who possess both male and female sex organs. Sometimes they are re-labelled after having been categorized male or female. Money and Ehrhardt (1972) report on a child who was genetically male (he had XY chromosomes) and was reassigned to female at 17 months old. According to the parents, there was an immediate change in the way in which the 'girl' was now treated, even by her 3-year-old brother.

Another case study by Money and Ehrhardt (1972) involved two normally born identical male twins. One twin had a surgical accident at seven months, and sex-reassignment was agreed on. From that time on, the twins were treated very differently, and by $4\frac{1}{2}$ years they also behaved very differently, according to their sex roles. Money and Ehrhardt report that the girl sat in front of the mirror, and the boy was very sloppy and wanted to be a fireman! However, it is also reported that the genetic male blueprint did have some effect – the girl twin was unusually active compared to girls of that age.

It seems, therefore, that environment as well as heredity can have an important effect on sex-role behaviour. The environmental influences discussed so far have been social influences from family or teachers, but there is a more unusual kind of environmental influence which could occur before birth and could therefore be mistaken for a genetic factor. Goy (1968) reports that girls who are accidentally exposed to high amounts of the male hormone androgen during pregnancy are often unusually large and active compared with age-mates. Female monkeys who have been given doses of androgen experimentally, engage in more aggressive behaviour than normal.

However, most environmental factors do tend to be social in nature and due initially to the expectations that family or friends have of different sex-role behaviour.

Cultural Factors

In a wider sense, expectations about sex-appropriate behaviour come from the culture in which we live, and there are many societies where the behaviour of males and females differ from ours. The studies of Margaret Mead suggest that, far from being uniform, there are many variations of the sex roles in different cultures, and that the behaviour we can expect from boys and girls depends largely on the way they are treated as children.

Mead studied three groups of people in New Guinea – the Arapesh who live on hillsides; the Mundugumor who live by the riverside; and the Tchambuli who are lakeside dwellers. She found the following differences in the way in which they were brought up to fulfil the sex roles.

THE ARAPESH
Both males and females of this tribes are brought up to act in what our society might call a feminine way, and in adulthood are gentle, loving and co-operative.

THE MUNDUGUMOR
Both men and women are self-assertive, arrogant and fierce. They continually quarrel, and Mundugumor mothers have little to do with their children apart from teaching them to taunt their parents.

THE TCHAMBULI

Girls are encouraged to take an interest in the economic activity of the tribe whereas boys are not. The result of this style of child-rearing is that men's and women's roles might be seen as the reverse of our traditional roles, the women taking care of trading and food-gathering and the men, who are considered sentimental and emotional and not capable of taking serious decisions, spending much of the day in artistic pursuits or gossiping.

It can be seen, then, that gender or sex-role behaviour is a result of both biological factors and socialization. Three theories of socialization have been examined elsewhere (see Chapter 5 and 6), and it is interesting to compare how the theories of Freud, Bandura and Kohlberg account for the development of our sense of being male and female.

Theories of Sex Typing

Freud's psychoanalytic theory maintains that the child identifies with the same-sex parent in order to become like him or her. Identification is the end-product of the Oedipus and Electra complex. Around five or six years, for example, the boy feels 'If I am like him, he won't hurt me, and she will love me.' Therefore he incorporates much of his father's personality, particularly that regarding sex role.

The social learning theory of Bandura, unlike Freud, maintains that gender role and identity do not arise from the sex drive. Children are rewarded when they behave in a way appropriate to their sex, and often punished by ridicule when they do not. They learn by imitation rewarded by attention, due to cultural pressures on their parents.

Kohlberg based his theory of social and moral development on the cognitive stages suggested by Piaget (see page 11). He believes a child's understanding of his gender depends on his level of intellectual development; in particular Kohlberg believes that just as a child in the early pre-operational stage cannot conserve number, mass and volume, so he has no idea of conservation of gender even though children as early as 2 years have the ability to recognize their own gender.

Thompson (1975) says that if children aged 2 are shown one same-sex picture and several opposite-sex pictures and asked 'which one is you', they can pick out the same-sex picture correctly. By 3 years they can identify 'which one is a boy', etc., and yet true gender constancy does not develop until about the age of 5 or 6.

This was demonstrated by Katcher (1955). He presented children with figures of clothed and unclothed men, women and children which were cut into head, trunk and below-trunk sections. The children were asked to put the figures together and identify their gender. 3–4-year-olds did well with the clothed figures, but the unclothed figures confused them, and they seemed to think that girls could be boys if they wore boys' clothes and hairstyles.

The three theories are summarized in Table 7.1.

Table 7.1

	Freudian Theory[1]	Social Learning Theory[2]	Cognitive Development Theory (Kohlberg)[3]
Gender role stems from:	Erotic and emotional feelings	Cultural forces and parents shape child's behaviour	An idea of self develops. What is 'me' and 'not me'.
	↓	↓	↓
	Directed to opposite-sex parent (Oedipus or Electra)	Reinforcements and imitation of models	Basic idea of one's own sex (2 years)
	↓	↓	↓
	Identification with same-sex parent	Gender identity	As the constancies develop (e.g. number, mass, volume) so the idea of gender becomes stable. The child chooses to model those who reinforce his basic idea of his own gender.
	↓		↓
	Gender role behaviour		Gender constancy (5–6)

[1] Based on the child's level of emotional development.
[2] Based on the child's ability to learn.
[3] Based on the child's level of intellectual development.

Summary

1 Studying sex-role behaviour illustrates what true socialization involves. It shows the importance of the social and cultural environment in which the child grows up, but it also illustrates that this takes place within the limits imposed by our biological make-up.

2 There are three theories which try to account for sex-typing.

Freud's theory is based on his theory of emotional and personality development, i.e. the child behaves in an appropriate way due to identification with the parent of the same sex.

Social learning theory maintains that cultural forces shape the parents' behaviour and then the parents influence the child directly, so that the child learns appropriate behaviour by a process of reinforcements and imitation of models.

The third theory, that of *Kohlberg*, suggests that development of gender identity is closely related to the child's cognitive development. As he becomes able to conserve number, mass and volume, so he also becomes aware that the gender of a person is also stable and he chooses to copy models who reinforce his basic idea of his own sex.

Further Reading

Bee, Helen, *The Developing Child* (1985, Harper and Row).
Maccoby, E.E. and Jacklin, C.N., *The Psychology of Sex Differences* (1974, Stanford University Press).

Chapter 8

The Development and Expression of Aggression

Psychology has an important role to play in trying to understand the causes of behaviour. It is a sad fact that we live in a violent and aggressive culture and perhaps, as many people maintain, this trend towards hostility is increasing.

Psychologists have studied this question and tried to understand the causes of aggression by looking at the relationship between factors during early development and the expression of aggression in children. This helps to identify processes that may lead to aggression and violence in adults.

Another key area is the study of *pro-social behaviour*, i.e. what makes one person behave in a positive way in a situation which may easily lead to aggression by another?

This chapter will attempt to summarize some of the views on this topical issue.

What is Aggression?

Aggression in some cases has a clear biological function. Animals will fight to maintain a territory, to defend their young, or when catching and killing prey. Humans, too, may be aggressive when doing these things, or when simply 'standing up for themselves'. This kind of aggression, which is carried out in order to gain something (for example territory, defence of the young, or food) is called *instrumental aggression*.

Aggression which takes place without an apparent motive is called *hostile aggression*. Both instrumental and hostile aggression can involve physical or verbal attack, so a working definition of aggression could be: 'Aggression is behaviour which is intended to physically injure or verbally attack another person.'

In many cases aggression is difficult to understand. For example, many studies have shown that a mild electric shock given to an animal can cause it to be aggressive towards another non-hostile animal. In human terms if you hit your thumb when knocking in a nail you may be more likely to shout at a friend nearby.

Some psychologists think of aggressive behaviour as an innate (inborn/inherited) response; that is, animals acquire the ability to behave aggressively due to their genes. It is not a learned response. A good example of this can be seen in cases of the selective breeding of some animals, for example Siamese fighting fish. These fish have been artificially bred for their aggressive behaviour, and even fish reared in isolation will display aggression when given the opportunity. These theories are called *biological theories of aggression*.

Other psychologists (the social learning theorists) feel that aggressive behaviour is a process like operant conditioning. This may have important implications for child-rearing, as a significant amount of human behaviour may be learned through the process of imitation and reinforcement.

Biological Theories of Aggression – Freud's Theory

(See p.91 for a full description of Freud's theory of personality.)

According to Freud, the child's Superego (in children aged 3 or over) has to try to control the aggressive urges of the Id. (Freud calls these urges the Death Instinct, or *Thanatos*.) If the child's Superego has not developed strongly (see p.94), aggressive urges can become conscious aggressive behaviour. The energy for behaving destructively is continually being built up in the Id, and Freud therefore regarded human aggression as inevitable. One way of relieving aggressive energy is through a process of *catharsis*, expressing this energy in non-destructive ways; for example in work, or in aggressive sports (playing or watching!).

Remember that on page 96 Freud's theories were said to be able to explain everything (after it had happened), but were unable to predict what was likely to happen. Freud's theory on aggression suffers from the same problem, and there is very little evidence to support it (see p.14 for Hartshorne and May's study).

Biological Theories of Aggression – the Ethologists' Theory

Ethology is the study of animal behaviour in the natural environment of the species being looked at. Lorenz (1963) believed that aggression is innate. It has evolved because it has a survival function; it is a behaviour that has helped animals to survive and to reproduce. The biological energy for aggressive behaviour builds up in the nervous system and is released by external stimuli in the environment. For example, a male robin will attack another male that has invaded his territory (or even a stuffed model, for that matter); the aggressive behaviour is 'released' by the sight of the red breast feathers of the rival. Such stimuli are therefore called 'releasing stimuli' or 'releasers'.

This viewpoint, like the Freudian approach, sees aggression as inevitable. Aggression can be 'released' through exercise (i.e. discharged like electricity from a battery) but Lorenz believed that aggression would eventually build up and be shown in behaviour even if no stimulus was present. He also believed that humans were the only species which killed its own members. Later research on animals (for example lions) has shown that this claim is not in fact true. Other researchers have found that even with highly aggressive Siamese fighting fish, preventing them from being aggressive (by taking away all aggressive releasers) reduces aggression rather than increases it.

The Frustration-Aggression Hypothesis

This theory assumes that frustration leads to aggression. Frustration is a drive that is produced by external factors such as having goals or aims blocked, being thwarted in some way or meeting externally raised barriers. As an example, imagine how frustrated and aggressive you might feel after queuing for 20 mintues at a supermarket checkout, only to have it close just as your turn came!

Dollard et al. (1939) went on to say that aggression (caused by frustration) can be *displaced*; that is, aggression is not always shown towards the person or object causing the frustration. For example, it would not be wise to be aggressive towards your teacher or your boss. So aggression may be displaced towards another object or a less powerful person, e.g. smashing a plate or shouting at a friend.

There are some problems with this theory. Sometimes people cry in response to frustration or behave aggressively without being frustrated. It seems that aggression is only one possible response to frustration.

The Brain and Aggression

Researchers on animal behaviour have found that by injecting chemicals into the brain, or by electrically stimulating parts of the brain in an area called the limbic system, aggressive behaviour can be triggered. Brown electrically stimulated part of the hypothalamus in cats, and the animals showed 'rage' responses – biting, spitting and scratching. But aggressive behaviour can also apparently be stopped by electrical stimulation of the brain. Delgado implanted a micro-electrode (a very thin electrode) into an area of a bull's brain called the septum. This electrode could be stimulated by a radio transmitter which Delgado held in his hand. As the bull charged towards him, Delgado pushed the button which electrically stimulated the bull's septum (apparently a very unpleasant experience for the bull). The bull screeched to a halt and walked away! Presumably, the stimulation either stopped the bull's aggression directly, or created such unpleasant effects that the bull stopped its charge. (What might have happened if the batteries in the transmitter had run out, we leave to your imagination ...)

At first glance, this physiological evidence seems to support the biological theories of aggression put forward by Freud and Lorenz. It may be that there are innate brain mechanisms for aggression (this idea is also supported by the fact that animals can be specifically bred to be aggressive, doberman dogs for example. But notice that these results do not say anything about whether aggression is inevitable or not. Note also that we cannot automatically apply findings from other animal species to humans.

Aggression – the Social Learning Hypothesis

Social learning theorists view aggressive behaviour as a learned response influenced by reinforcement and punishment (see Chapter 5). The frequency of aggressive behaviour depends to some extent on an individual's past reinforcement history – the more they have been reinforced for aggression in the past, the more likely they are to show aggression. For example, factors like reward and punishment by others, the success of aggression to relieve frustration and the presence of aggressive models which can be imitated, all influence the frequency of aggressive behaviour.

The social learning approach to the explanation of socialization, as taken by writers such as Mischel, emphasizes the effects of the consequences of our actions on our later behaviour. In other words it applies the rules of reinforcement and conditioning that we discussed earlier (see p.85). Unlike Skinner and the early Behaviourists, who were only interested in observable stimuli and responses, Mischel, and other social learning theorists such as Bandura, are quite happy to take into account peoples' expectations of reward and punishment. Bandura emphasizes the extent to which individuals modify their environment and choose to do particular things so that they have a greater expectation of pleasant rather than unpleasant outcomes (see the discussion of Bandura's work on p.81). In addition to reinforcement to guide behaviour, social learning theorists also stress the role of observational learning or imitation. This form of learning can result in the production of complex patterns of behaviour without the need for an extended period of shaping.

Age-Related Factors and Aggression

It seems that individuals who commit aggressive acts often have a history of aggressive behaviour. A longitudinal study (see page 198) carried out by Huesmann and colleagues in 1984 showed clearly that the aggressive thirty-year-olds of today were yesterdays' most aggressive ten-year-olds. This leads to the alarming hypothesis that aggression is established in childhood and remains stable from that point. This finding does not throw much light on the establishment of aggressive behaviour but demonstrates the persistence of these behaviours over time.

The section below looks at the effects of the mass media on childrens' socialization. In particular, it examines two questions: first, Do the mass media maintain sex-role stereotypes? and secondly, Can violence on television make children behave violently?

The Influence of Mass Media on Socialization

The mass media (newspapers, television, radio, books, etc.) can affect people's attitudes and opinions – that is why some advertisers pay a great deal of money (up to £250,000) for a thirty-second slot on prime-time television for their adverts, and it is why politicians of all parties have become much more aware of their media image – especially near election time! One area in which developmental psychologists have been interested is the effect of the media on childrens' socialization.

The mass media have often been accused of sex-role stereotyping – that is, showing male and female roles in an oversimplified, stereo-typed way. An example of how subtle stereotyping can be was shown in a study by Goldberg in 1968. Female students were given articles on professional topics to read, and asked to say how well they were written, how persuasive they were, how technically correct, and so on. Unknown to the students, the names of the authors had been slightly changed, so that some students received an article written by 'John T. McKay' and others received the same article written by 'Joan T. McKay'. Articles supposedly written by female authors received significantly lower ratings than exactly the same articles when it was thought that the author was male. The subjects seemed to believe that women could not be as good at professional matters as men. Since this study in 1968, however, other researchers in the 1970s have found that the effect has become weaker, presumably because people are more aware of the dangers of sex-role stereo-typing.

Children's books have frequently been criticized for supporting sex-role stereotypes, and a study in 1973 by Saario, Jacklin and Tittle in North America shows how widespread the unspoken assumptions about sex roles were in the elementary-school books of the 1960s which they examined. They found:

Females appeared in books much less frequently than males.

Females tended to follow orders rather than to give them.

Females were more likely to be involved in fantasizing rather than problem-solving.

Females were more conformist than males.

Females were more verbal than males.

Females spent much more time indoors than males.

Positive events (e.g. success) were often attributed to the actions of males.

Positive events which happened after female actions were attributed to the situation or to the goodwill of others, rather than to the female's actions.

These differences in behaviour between the sexes increased with the age of child towards which the books was aimed.

Similar themes and attitudes have been displayed in television programmes – females being physically passive and emotional; males being physically active, aggressive and generally being 'in charge'. Although a television cartoon series *She-ra – Princess of Power* and police series such as *Juliet Bravo* and *Cagney and Lacey* feature heroines who defeat male characters in battle, or overcome male criminals, such programmes are still very much the exception rather than the rule.

The Mass Media and Aggression

Both laboratory studies and studies in real-life situations support the idea that the influence of the media (particularly television) is strong in the development of aggression. Television executives often claim that they only produce violent programmes because that is what viewers want to see. However, a study of Diener and Du Four (1978) suggests that this claim is not actually true.

Half of the subjects of Diener's study watched an uncensored version of an episode of an American TV series called *Police Woman*. This uncut version contained several scenes of violence, for example a man's hand being plunged into boiling water and a car jack being removed so that the car fell on the mechanic underneath. The remaining half of the subjects saw a verison of the episode from which all the violent scenes had been cut. Both groups were then asked to rate the episode on two counts: (i) how violent they thought the film was, and (ii) how much they had like the film. Not surprisingly, the group who had seen the violent version rated it as being more violent, but both groups showed an *equal* liking for the film.

This study suggests that viewers do *not* choose programmes because of the violence contained in them.

Nevertheless, TV programmes and films do contain large amounts of violence. In the USA, for example, Liebert has estimated that by the age of 16 years, the average American child will have seen 13,000 killings on TV! But does watching violence on TV make children more violent themselves? Bandura's studies suggest that children can learn violent acts from live, cartoon and filmed models, but Bandura himself pointed out that these laboratory studies may not reflect real-life situations. Other laboratory studies had suggested that children were more likely to imitate violence if:

- the aggression in the film is justified (i.e. it is against a 'baddie').
- the viewer can identify with the aggressor.
- the viewer is already aggressive before watching the film. (Eron found that children who were more aggressive were more likely to watch violent TV programmes.)

Eron also carried out a longitudinal study, in which children from the age of about 8 years had the amount and type of TV programmes they watched monitored, and observations made of the amount of aggressive behaviour they showed, until the age of 18 years. A positive correlation was found between the amount of TV watched at age 8 and the level of aggression shown at age 18. This suggests that TV has some effect; but since 'correlation does not imply causation' (see page 213), experimental evidence is needed to show that TV can *cause* aggression.

Leyens, Camino, Parke and Berkowitz (1985) in Belgium set up an experimental study of the possible link between TV and violence at a boys' boarding school. The boys, all teenagers in four dormitories, were studied for a week, and their levels of aggression and violence were observed and recorded. Two of the dormitories (1 and 2 in Table 8.1) were rated as high in violence, and two were found to be low in violence. For the next week, the TV sets in all four dormitories were fed by video recorders showing films specially chosen by the experimenters.

Leyens et al. noted that the violence shown by the boys who saw the violent films was similar in type to the violence they had seen in the films. (Note also, however, that in the low-violent group who saw the violent films, although physical violence increased, verbal

Table 8.1. Results of the study by Leyens et al.

| | Dormitories | | | |
	1	2	3	4
Level of violence before TV films	High	High	Low	Low
Type of film shown	Violent	Non-violent	Violent	Non-violent
Level of aggression after film week	Increased	No change	Increased	No change
Level of verbal aggression	Increased	Stayed the same	Decreased	Stayed the same

aggression actually *decreased*.)

The results of Leyens' study show clearly that violence on TV increases the levels of violence shown by both previously violent and low-violent groups. Violence on TV can therefore be said to increase violent behaviour. A similar type of study, this time in the USA, by Leyens and others, on juvenile delinquents also supports these findings.

Can anything be done to reduce the effect of TV on violent behaviour? TV organisations themselves have begun to try to reduce the amount of violence in their programmes (aided and perhaps triggered by complaints from government leaders and members of the royal family!) Some findings from the USA also suggest that it may be possible to make children less likely to imitate violence on TV. Hicks found that if a child's parent watches with the child, and condemns the violence in the programme, the child is less likely to be aggressive. Eron gave children a three-hour training session which emphasized the fictional nature of the violence and explained how (through special effects, for example) the violent actions did not actually hurt anybody. Children who had had this training session were significantly less aggressive than a control group of children who had not had the training. Murray tried to use television to encourage pro-social behaviour in children. Children who watched TV programmes which emphasized kindness and helpfulness (for example, episodes of *Lassie* and *Sesame Street*) showed more helpful behaviour than similar children who had not seen the programmes.

Such schemes are in their infancy, but show signs of being useful ways of reducing the effects on children of TV violence and of promoting pro-social behaviour.

Summary

1 Aggression can be divided into two types – instrumental aggression (aggressive acts performed in order to gain something) and hostile aggression (where there is no obvious gain to the aggressor).

2 Freud's psychoanalytic theory argued that aggression is innate, and that the Id is the seat of aggression. Although it may be controlled by the Superego, aggression energy in the Id will always find a way out.

3 The ethologists also believed that innate aggression energy builds up in an individual and must eventually cause aggressive behaviour.

4 The frustration-aggression hypothesis argues that aggression is due to something frustrating a person's or animal's attempts to get what it wants.

5 Physiological psychologists have found that certain parts of the brain (notably the limbic system and areas near the hypothalamus) seem to be involved in aggression.

6 Social learning theorists believe that aggression is not innate – aggression occurs because it has been reinforced in the past, or as a result of imitation.

7 In addition to providing aggressive actions for people to imitate, the mass media also help to maintain sex-role stereotyping. There is some evidence that the mass media could be used to reduce aggression, by providing models of non-aggressive behaviour which can be imitated.

Further Reading

Manning, A., *An Introduction to Animal Behaviour* (3rd edn, 1979, Arnold), Chapter 5.

Sparkes, J., *The Discovery of Animal Behaviour* (1982, Collins/ BBC).

Miller, G., *Psychology – the Science of Mental Life* (1970, Penguin).

Chapter 9

Play

No book on child development would be complete without some mention of play. The aim of this chapter is firstly to attempt to define play, and discover in what ways it differs from other forms of behaviour. Secondly, some of the theories which have been put forward regarding play are examined to see if this apparently useless behaviour has a purpose. Different types of play are discussed, and finally some of the ways in which the research findings have been used are considered.

What is play, how can we define it? Are the same mechanisms at work when elderly people play bridge as when children play hide and seek or build with Lego? Climbing trees would be regarded as hard work by most adults, but many small children spend a large proportion of their waking lives doing just that. What then is the distinction between work and play?

A small boy of two years old had been given a simple jigsaw for his birthday. His mother noticed that he did not 'play' with the jigsaw very often. One day the child took the toy, put it on a table with great determination and announced 'Johnny do bit of work now'. Obviously this child's distinction between work and play was not the same as that of his mother.

There are certain characteristics of play which are widely accepted, but even these do not make a complete distinction between play and other activities, as some of them can be applied also to behaviour which is 'not play'. For example:

(1) Play is pleasurable. (This is also true of some work.)
(2) Play is voluntary and usually spontaneous. (This can also be said of some voluntary work, which is undertaken with no expectation of financial reward.)
(3) Play has no extrinsic (external) rewards; such rewards are mainly

intrinsic (internal). The enjoyment of the activity is more important than an external reward.

(4) Play is not an isolated area of behaviour; it has many links to
areas which are 'not play', e.g. social behaviour, language, creativity, learning. (This is also true of some work.)

So it can be seen that a simple definition of play is hard to find and
maybe it is foolish to attempt it. Perhaps, like many other words in
the English dictionary, play has many shades of meaning, and it is
only researchers who feel it necessary to reduce it to a single sentence
and a rigid definition.

Mary Sheridan (1977) suggests that three definitions may be useful
to the researcher; these are: play, work and drudgery.

Play is the eager engagement in pleasurable, physical and mental
effort to obtain emotional satisfaction.

Work is the voluntary engagement in physical or mental effort to
obtain material benefit.

Drudgery is the enforced engagement in distasteful physical and
mental effort to obtain a means of survival.

Sheridan says that play and work can merge into what she calls
as 'ploy'; and work and drudgery can merge into 'slog'. An example
of 'ploy' would perhaps be school children who learn to measure by
making models, whereas 'slog' would be learning to measure by
simply drawing hundreds of lines of prescribed lengths.

PLAY	PLOY	WORK	SLOG	DRUDGERY

Thus play, ploy, work, slog and drudgery are here on a con-
tinuum – perhaps this is a more realistic than making a clear distinction between what is play and not play.

Does Play have a Purpose?

Does play have a purpose? Several theories suggest that it does.
Children, the young of higher animals and sometimes adults play.
This has been observed since the time of Plato and Aristotle, and
many of the educational reformers such as Froebel believed that

education should take note of the child's natural interest. These writers merely made observations. The first theories of the function of play did not appear until the mid-nineteenth century. Some of these are entertaining, but none managed to explain all aspects of play.

Spencer's surplus energy theory said that play uses up surplus energy. Spencer argued that the lower an animal is on the evolutionary scale the more of its energies are used up in finding food and escaping from its enemies. Higher animals have more spare time because they have more skills, hence play 'evolved' to fill this extra time, and use the surplus energy.

Spencer's theory does explain the behaviour of children who are suddenly let out into the school playground, but it fails to explain how children who are exhausted at the end of the day will carry on playing and refuse to give in to their obvious need for sleep. Hence the theory seems applicable to some forms of play but not all.

Hall's recapitulation theory. This theory is based on the idea that children are simply a link in the evolutionary chain between animals and man. Because some of the stages through which a human foetus passes before birth are similar to the developmental sequence from fish to man, this seemed to Hall to suggest that individual development repeated the development of the race. Hall extended this idea and said that the child also relives the history of its race, and re-enacts the activities of primitive man in play.

According to Hall, children's enjoyment of water play could be connected with the fact that humans originally evolved from fish. Climbing trees shows the connection with our monkey ancestors, and the fishing and canoeing activities which are typical of many boy-scout troups would no doubt, according to Hall, be based on the experiences of early tribal man.

Like Spencer's theory, this theory, however, does not explain all play – riding bicycles is hardly an ancient experience, and the ability to do this is certainly not passed on genetically. It also fails to account for the way in which children played at 'Spacemen' before men had actually travelled into space.

Groos's theory – play is the practice of skills. Groos was interested in the play of young animals, arguing that play allows the animals to practise skills such as fighting in a non-threatening situation, so that the animal is competent at these before a serious situation arises. He regarded play as an 'instinct to practise instincts'. In a modified form, without involving 'instincts' this idea that play is practice is still commonly held. But, again, this theory is insufficient to cover all forms of play. If Groos's theory were correct, many more old people would be found playing the harp, rather than cards or bowls!

These early theories tended to assume a special function or impulse for play. Later theories, for example those of Freud and Piaget, saw play as part of total development. As a result Freud's and Piaget's theories are rather more successful at explaining play than some earlier ones.

Although Freud and Piaget see play as part of total development, they do stress different aspects of that development. Not only did Freud believe that the way a child played was affected by his level of emotional development but also that play could actually help that emotional development.

Freud's Ideas Regarding Play

Freud's views on development of the personality have already been outlined, and it is against this background that his ideas on play must be seen. Freud suggests that the child's level of emotional maturity will be shown in the way he plays, and also, at the same time, playing can help the child's emotional development.

Freud's theory begins with the *pleasure-pain principle*. This means that each individual wants to gain pleasure and avoid pain, and this motivates all of a child's behaviour and thinking unless other people make demands on the child. Freud noticed that in play, as in dreams, there are no restraints. The child in play can organize events to please himself, even though he might use objects and situations from reality to help him in his play. Freud says the libido (life energy) goes through a series of stages until maturity, and is rather like a stream that must find an outlet. If not, it is likely to be repressed, and cause problems later in life.

Several outlets can be found through play. Freud says *sublimation* can occur – when for example the young child's urge to play with faeces can be reduced by making mud pies and doing finger painting. *Projection* is another defence mechanism which can be used by young children, when bad feelings and behaviour are attributed to other children, to imaginary friends and even objects. Adults can occasionally be heard to encourage this – if a child trips over a chair, for example, the adult may say: 'give it a smack then, the naughty chair' and this seems to soothe a small child's distress.

Freud also suggests that *substitution* can occur during play, for instance if a child is unkind to a baby doll the real jealous wishes against a new sibling can be made relatively harmless. In a severely disturbed child, anxiety may be so great that all play is inhibited. But in a normal child the conflicts and wishes of each stage of development can be seen in child's play (see 'play therapy' on page 98).

When the child is in the oral phase, play often involves the mouth, e.g. the child sucks objects and often blows bubbles with saliva. The later anal phase (around 2 years) can be indicated by the child's interest in water and sand play, mudpies and primitive attempts at painting. Later on during the phallic phase the child may make a pretend penis from plasticine; and in the 'identification' period which follows this, boys and girls typically play games, which indicate they are filling a role e.g. a boy might play at being a bus driver.

One aspect of Freud's theory was his idea of *homoeostasis*. This means that the child needs to keep the level of nervous tension constant and that children often repeat distressing events over and over again in play in order to gain control over the event and reduce nervous tension. Freud believed that repetition reduced the excitement that had been aroused by the original distressing event.

Freud's theories have been challenged many times (see page 96), but his view of play as wish-fulfillment and projection has led to techniques of using play as a therapy for disturbed children.

The Theory of Jean Piaget

Piaget's theory of play is related to his ideas on intellectual development: the level of intellectual development is often demonstrated in the child's play; also, some play can aid that intellectual development.

Piaget believed that it was by two processes, assimilation and accommodation, that a child builds up his schemata which give him his internal idea of the world (see Chapter 1).

Although play sometimes involves accommodation, according to Piaget there is always more assimilation. Some play is pure assimilation. He distinguishes between play as a repetition of an action already mastered, and repetition of an activity in order to understand it. The latter involves some accommodation. Suppose a child is given a magnet. At first a four-year-old might play with the new object using old schemata. He might suck it, throw it, or tip it from the back of his tipper truck (assimilation). Then he finds that whilst it slips from the plastic truck it refuses to slip from a certain metal one. This presents a problem – the child has no schema to cope with this. So now he plays with the magnet in a different way; he might walk around the room touching it on different objects to see which it sticks to. He is building up a new schemata, i.e. his play now involves some accommodation.

Piaget observed childen and noticed different kinds of play which he believed corresponded to the stages of cognitive development.

SENSORIMOTOR STAGE

According to Piaget, play at this early age is mainly *mastery play* or *practice play*. Play at this stage of development involves the reproduction of sensorimotor acts. For example, spontaneous fist waving and spontaneous vocal babbling. This is pure assimilation, a skill newly mastered is repeated at every opportunity. At four months a child learns to push a suspended rattle, and then repeats this. At 7–12 months a child will remove covers to discover hidden objects. The early grasping reflex can later be used voluntarily as the child deliberately picks up objects. Later still he learns to 'ungrasp' or let go of articles on purpose; and around one year old, the child will systematically empty his pram of toys then call loudly for them to be returned to him.

PRE-OPERATIONAL STAGE (2–7 YEARS)

Repetition of motor acts continues throughout this stage, and the child's competence at exploration and manipulation increases enormously. At this stage the child also delights in verbal play, using newly acquired words. One of the most interesting developmental characteristics of the stage is the introduction of *symbolic or make-believe play* into the child's repertoire. This is pure assimilation and it repeats and organizes images and symbols (schemata) that the child already has. It helps to consolidate the child's emotional experiences because anything important can be produced in play but it can also be distorted – reality does not matter as the child is very egocentric at this stage, i.e. he finds it hard to view a situation from any viewpoint other than his own. Egocentricity is less important as the child grows older and, towards the end of this stage, play moves closer to reality. Play is then more constructive and ceases to be so 'playlike'.

CONCRETE OPERATIONAL STAGE (7–12 YEARS) AND FORMAL
OPERATIONAL STAGE (12 +)

At these stages, play often consists of games with rules or codes of
honour, such as rounders or football, or games where the children
invent their own rules, such as hide and seek. After the age of eleven,
which Piaget's cognitive theory describes as the formal operational
stage, children cease to play quite so much – except for games
which include rules. The child's understanding of the origins and
application of rules varies with age, as Piaget's investigations into
the games of children showed (see page 7).

Co-operation and reciprocity can now be seen in the child's play.
Just as the child now de-centres and realizes that others have their
own view of the world, so he also develops social reciprocity which
makes him realize they too have feelings, they also like him to share
toys, etc. Now the child is more altruistic, ready to take part in a
way that ensures the enjoyment of other players as well as himself,
and ready to take part in team games. For the sake of the team he
is more willing to pass the football in order for the team to succeed.
Previously, he regarded a 'good' game of football as one where he
himself had control of the ball as often as possible.

There are some difficulties with Piaget's theory. It suggests that a
child will tend to play at whatever activity he has just learned and
that during the play reality will be distorted to suit the child's needs.
Piaget says little about the amount of distortion that occurs and
whether this can be modified by experience or interaction with adults.

However, in spite of this criticism, the theory has something to
offer. Assimilation and accommodation continue throughout life, so
this theory could be used to describe the 'play' of adults as well as
children; it can explain activities as different as indulging in hobbies
and playing whist.

Different Types of Play

Most psychologists would agree that play is best seen as part of the
total development of the child. Simply watching children bears out
that their development in the following areas is helped by play:

Physical
Intellectual
Linguistic

Emotional
Social

Psychologists have tried hard to categorize play and there are many different ways to do this. Mildred Parten in the 1930s observed children aged 2–4 years and noticed the following types of play according to age.

Table 9.1

	Type of play	Example
Solitary Play	Child plays alone.	Child plays with toy car.
Looking-on Play	Child watches activities of another	Young child watches older children with train set.
Parallel Play	Young children of same age play side by side with same materials but little interaction.	Children around $2\frac{1}{2}$ years in sand pit.
Associative Play	Children interact doing similar things but not actually helping each other.	Two small cyclists use same route and same tree as a petrol pump.
Co-operative Play	The children interact together and help each other.	One child might act as petrol pump attendant, another act as driver of the cycle.

Parten said that play changed gradually from solitary to co-operative with age. Piaget also categorizes play according to age but he makes a second distinction between play which is pure assimilation and that which contains some accommodation.

Obviously some play activities benefit some areas of development more than others, for example riding a bicycle or using a climbing frame can help physical development, but often the areas of benefit can overlap. Climbing on a frame with other children needs a certain amount of consideration for others and self-control. What begins as one kind of play may change into another kind, and the child may be developing cognitive schemata at the same time as he seems to be involved in, for instance, make-believe play. The following example demonstrates this.

A 3-year-old boy known to the authors was engaged in make-believe (symbolic) play. He had placed an old chair horizontally on the floor, with the high chair back uppermost. He then climbed into the 'racing car' and sat, turning an imaginary steering wheel and making car noises. He later put a collander on his head for a helmet. The adult who was with him asked why he kept rotating the helmet. 'I'm making glogs (goggles)' was his reply. He persevered in vain, trying to move the collander so that both handles were covering his eyes simultaneously, and eventually gave up, having presumably undergone some kind of cognitive development regarding the properties of circles and collander handles – even though his original play was purely imaginative.

Classification of play is useful when trying to design a nursery school or playgroup. Garvey (1977) suggests that play can involve:

> Language
> Motion
> Objects
> Social behaviour
> Rules

It is useful to look at the scientific studies that have been done in these different areas of play, as well as remembering that play can be helping development in many ways at the same time.

PLAY INVOLVING LANGUAGE
This can involve primitive baby babbling, nursery rhymes and rhyming games.

Ruth Weir recorded the pre-sleep monologues of Anthony (2:10). He seemed to be carrying out a solitary practice of making nonsense sentences and playing with words that sounded the same (e.g. That's office, that's office, Look Sophie, That Sophie) and saying phrases he had obviously heard often, e.g. 'good boy'.

Catherine Garvey points out that social play using language tends not to appear until after the age of three, when it tends to be more similar to an adult conversation than the solitary babblings listed above.

Work by P. and I. Opie on rhymes and games amongst children throughout England suggests that once a child can communicate, rhymes are transmitted from child to child without the involvement of adults. An example of this is that once language is established, children in what Piaget calls the pre-operational/concrete operational stage take delight in using the schemata they have learned, perhaps for Christmas carols, and adding alternative words ('We three Kings of Orient are, One in a taxi one in a car'). They also enjoy primitive jokes and puns at this age.

PLAY INVOLVING MOTION

This is one of the earliest amusements offered to infants. Piaget gives an example of a child discovering a voluntary head movement which was at first done to gain a new view of a familiar object and later this was carried out playfully. Other examples are young children who peer at the world upside down through their legs, or older children who swing on a gate, at first accidentally and later deliberately for pleasure.

It is interesting that play involving motion is one aspect of play which animals also enjoy. Young monkeys peer through their legs to see the world differently. Ethologists believe that play increases the chances of survival for the individual and for the group. Ethologists try to study animals in their natural habitat, but sometimes they are able to carry out controlled experiments to test hypotheses developed from their naturalistic observations. From these they have concluded that animals which are well adapted to a single environment do not play (e.g. ants) and that those animals that do engage in play have a relatively long period of maturation, an increased reliance on learning behaviour by observation and usually some kind of peer-group structure within their social group. Young monkeys will copy one another and repeatedly climb along a particular branch to jump into a pool, much in the same way that children will run and jump into a paddling pool, queue for the slide in the park, or take turns swinging on a gate.

An observational study by West on domestic kittens showed that they tended to practise specific kinds of movements, e.g. the pounce, the side-step etc. These occurred first when the animal was alone, and were practised alone until five weeks when the play became mainly social, until four months when it declined. West concluded that this physical play contributes to the social life of the kitten and keeps the group together at an important time when they are all dependent on the mother. Beckoff came to a similar conclusion having studied beagles and coyotes.

Harlow noticed similar behaviour in groups of rhesus monkeys. The solitary play patterns of the individual monkey are used again and again when the monkey plays socially later on. Harlow noticed that rhesus monkeys who are deprived of play with other young have difficulty joining adolescent groups, being too aggressive and generally awkward.

Compared to the detailed ethological studies of West and Beckoff there are few detailed studies of rough and tumble play in children. However, Smith and Connolly report that boys tend to take part in more rough and tumble play than girls and that the younger children in a nursery school tend to spend more time watching than their older peers. Usually, the rough and tumble play is the last activity in which children new to the nursery tend to join. Smith and Connolly also note that first-born children spent more time watching and wandering than do later offspring. This perhaps suggests that rough and tumble play is social rather than aggressive, as the animal studies also showed.

Cross-cultural studies, e.g. Maccoby and Jacklin (1974), have shown similar patterns, with boys engaging in rough and tumble play more than girls. Active social play, however, seems to occur earlier in societies where the babies are cared for by older siblings, for example Samoa.

PLAY INVOLVING OBJECTS
This can help with physical development, e.g. grasping and pulling, it can help with intellectual development because exploration will extend to give children more knowledge of the physical world. Talking about objects with adults can aid language development. Objects can also be used to express the child's feelings and concerns, thereby helping his emotional progress; and finally objects can be used as currency, i.e. they are things to share. This is very important for the social development of young children.

Objects can be articles that the child encounters accidentally, or 'toys', i.e. articles specifically provided by adults to amuse and stimulate the child.

PLAY AND EXPLORATION – IS THERE A DIFFERENCE?
An important part of play with objects is their value as a source of exploration to the child. Piaget distinguished between play that was pure assimilation and play that involved some accommodation. In a similar way, Corinne Hutt (1966) regards some behaviour with objects as exploration rather than play. She designed an experiment where children were carefully observed whilst they investigated an

object they had never seen before. The amount of attention the child paid to the object was noted and also different kinds of behaviour towards the object were recorded.

Hutt constructed a box with a movable lever, whose movements were recorded by four counters which could either be covered or visible. A bell and a buzzer were also connected to the apparatus. The complexity of the response from the box, obtained from working the lever, could be pre-set and varied to give four different effects.

(a) bell and buzzer sounding, counters in view
(b) bell and buzzer sounding, counters covered.
(c) bell and buzzer switched off, counters visible.
(d) bell and buzzer switched off, counters not visible.

The subjects in the experiment were 3–5-year-old children. Each individual child had several ten-minute sessions in a room which contained this box along with several conventional (i.e. not novel) toys.

Hutt found that the more complex the response from the box, the more children remained interested in the particular object, and she also found that their behaviour with the box could be divided into two types or categories, exploratory behaviour and play.

Exploratory behaviour – when engaging in this, the children gave the box their full attention, they looked directly at it and felt and touched it carefully.

Play – this differed from exploratory behaviour in that the behaviour was more diverse. The children did not gaze so intently or directly at the object – for instance they would lean on the lever whilst gazing around the room, or even race around the room giving a ring on the bell each time they passed.

Hutt noted that sometimes the child would use the object for some other function altogether, e.g. sitting on it or climbing over it. This 'transposition of function' is reminiscent of Piaget's view of play – an old 'climbing' schema is being used for a novel object.

As well as Hutt, Kathy Sylva et al. (1980) also regards the distinction between exploration and play as important. She carried out at investigation to discover whether children's ability to use tools in a task would be affected by whether their previous experience with those tools had been playful or exploratory. The task was to get a piece of chalk from a box that opened by operating a latch. The tools provided were two sticks and two clamps. The box was out of reach, even when using one stick, so the solution involved clamping the sticks together to create a longer implement. Before attempting the solution, four groups of children were given different experimental conditions.

Group I	Group II	Group III	Group IV
These children saw an adult construct the tool.	These children were allowed free play with sticks and clamps.	This group saw a dramatization of the tool construction where a 'Mr Clamp' put his teeth round the sticks.	This group was given specific training into how to construct the tool.

All children were given standardized hints if they could not solve the problem. The results were surprising. The previous experience of groups III and IV seemed to have little effect. Group II performed slightly more systematically and efficiently than group I.

Sylva concluded that the free handling was more efficient because the children could find solutions for themselves. The fact that many of the children had used transformation of function on the clamps and sticks (i.e. using them to shape houses and other items) suggests that the children *were* playing with the objects and not simply exploring them. Sylva believes that these results show that play can help to foster creative problem-solving.

So, play with objects can help cognitive and linguistic development and also problem-solving. It can also contribute to socialization.

PLAY INVOLVING SOCIAL BEHAVIOUR

Although good social development depends to a large extent on early relationships with other people, experience with objects is also thought to help with socialization, in animals as well as humans.

Harlow points out that young monkeys play with objects. He noted that play with playmates of the same age does not occur until after the monkey has played with objects on its own – perhaps the monkey views his peer group as 'moving parts' of his environment. Harlow noticed that monkeys approach the agemates later than animals who mature quickly, e.g. cats and coyotes, and that rhesus monkeys deprived of play with agemates had difficulty when included in a group of adolescents. They behaved awkwardly and were more aggressive than normal.

Young humans begin by playing with adults and enjoying the

mutual games of the early attachment process (see page 45); then they must progress to playing with other children. This can follow on from playing with objects. Perhaps the child sees an agemate as a moving part of his environment, and therefore more interesting than static toys or objects. However, playing with another child is more difficult than playing with an adult because another child is less predictable and less controllable.

Mueller and Eckermann both report that interaction between children increases after twenty months. This, at first, takes the form of playing side by side with objects, or perhaps riding tricycles with little interaction. Later they might toot horns at each other, and later still, one might change role and act as petrol-pump attendant, i.e. co-operative social play is developing. Objects can later be used as currency – things to share.

Social expertise is founded on experience with adults and it is noticeable that groups of children of varying ages often play more amicably than similar aged children. This is seen in make-believe play. Perhaps this kind of play bridges the gap, for the young child, between play with adults and play with agemates whose social behaviour is no better developed than his own.

We have seen that play with language, motion and objects can all offer opportunities for social behaviour to develop. Make-believe play also offers opportunities for social developments, but this has been dealt with already, in the context of the theories of Piaget and Freud; likewise play with rules which begins to develop around the age of eight years.

Play in Pre-School Groups

It is now time to look at some of the ways in which psychologists' knowledge about play has been put to use in the various organizations that offer provision for the pre-school child. This aspect of child care and development has been studied extensively by the Oxfordshire Pre-School Research Project (Sylva, Roy and Painter (1980); Garland and White (1980); and Bryant, Harrison and Newton (1980). Some of their observations are summarized below.

Parents who try to find pre-school provision for their children may run into difficulties. Depending on the area in which they live, they may find very little provision; or at the other extreme they may be completely overwhelmed by the variety and quality of the different organizations on offer. A list of possible sources of information is provided at the back of this book (page 217). In some of the institutions the emphasis is on health and physical care; in others, educational considerations are of the first importance.

Day nurseries, private day nurseries and workplace nurseries all place emphasis on physical care, as do childminders. Children are likely to stay there for full days rather than attend part time. On the other hand, playgroups, private nursery schools and those run by the local authority place more emphasis on education and enjoyment, and children may well attend for only part of the day.

CHILD-MINDERS

Child-minders usually look after other people's children in their own homes. They often have children of their own or have had children of their own. Some have had training, i.e. they may have been trained as nursery nurses, but it is usual for them to have had no specific training other than their experiences looking after their own children. Child-minders should be registered with their local Social Services Department, but enforcing registration is very difficult because so many child-minders are neighbours, relations or good friends of the parents of the children they are minding. Although child-minders have to be paid for in the same way as day nursery care, they have some distinct advantages not offered by other venues: they are often very local and work very flexible hours (some including weekends and baby-sitting). Unfortunately, the image of child-minding is still tainted by the notions of drudgery and wet-nursing from an earlier time despite the efforts of the National Association of Child Minders to improve their image. Recent surveys and an investigation as part of the Oxfordshire Pre-School Project have not been very complimentary about the quality of physical care and play facilities offered by child-minders, although they admitted that it was a difficult area to research and therefore to come to firm conclusions (Bryant, Harris and Newton (1980)).

LOCAL AUTHORITY AND PRIVATE NURSERY SCHOOLS

Some local authorities provided education for pre-school children which is staffed by trained nursery teachers. In private nursery schools also, the emphasis is on education which should be as good as in the maintained sector. The difference is cost. Many are individually run, usually by trained teachers. Others belong to groups who run schools according to certain well-defined educational principles; for example, the Montessori Nursery Schools where children learn through activities and movement and are encouraged to be independent although part of a group. In a Montessori school the young children's ages vary within a class, and the younger children learn from the older ones.

Nursery schools are usually led by a teacher who has been specifically trained, and who is well acquainted with the theories of play and all their implications. She will realize the value of many different activities and will have a permanent well-equipped room, often with access to a garden or playground. Probably there will be students or assistants to train, and the wise head teacher will make the most of their individual gifts as well as passing on her own insights regarding the children in their care.

Having trained specifically for the task, the nursery-school teacher will be well aware of the necessity for encouraging development in all five areas: physical, intellectual, linguistic, emotional and social. For instance, she will know that provision of items such as dressing-up clothes will encourage children's social skills. In dressing up the children tend:

(a) To play in groups instead of alone.
(b) To discuss in a friendly way which child shall fill a particular role.
(c) To hold imaginative conversations.
(d) To imitate the behaviour of adults.

All these items contribute to social development. The teacher will also recognize that many activities can help intellectual (cognitive) and linguistic development – for example, play with water, or dry sand, where the child can pour these materials from one container to another helps the child develop concepts such as conservation (see pages 4–5). Sinclair-de-Zwart (1969) found that children who had not yet developed volume conservation tended not to understand the meaning of such words as 'more', 'less', etc. as well as children who had ability to conserve volume even when they were given specific training in the use of these words, showing that intellectual and language development are closely related. The wise nursery teacher will be able to supply appropriate items such as 'new words', suggestions for games or novel objects to ensure that the child has ample opportunity to both assimilate and accommodate and so develop his schemata. In the magnet example noted earlier (p.124) it might be an adult who suggests that the child tries touching the magnet against other items.

Another area in which the nursery teacher's understanding of child behaviour is demonstrated is in the actual arrangement of the room. Smith and Connolly's suggestion that new children take time to join in the rough and tumble play of a group means that it is often wisest to keep this activity away from the door and to place some inviting quiet tasks such as plasticine or crayoning just inside the entrance. Then as each new child arrives he or she can be handed from mother to a parent substitute (which Bowlby recommends). Later he can use this adult as a safe base from which to progress to the more adventurous nursery activities.

PLAYGROUPS

These are staffed by leaders, assistants and volunteers, often parents. Playleaders have often attended some form of training course. The groups must be registered with the local Social Services Department, and about 75 per cent are also members of the Pre-School Play-group Association. Most of these groups meet in community accommodation or church halls. Although some playgroups are privately owned and organised, many are run by a committee of parents for their children. The quality of playgroups varies enormously, and the emphasis is certainly on play, since playgroup staff are not allowed to teach directly. Even so, children learn a lot incidentally, without being given instructions, if the environment is stimulating.

A good playgroup could be providing almost as good an environment as nursery school and previous descriptions of play in the nursery are applicable here. Playgroups are at a disadvantage in that most do not have a permanent room, so the equipment has to be put out afresh for each session, nor is the head of the playgroup usually so well trained in the theories of learning and play as the nursery teacher. However one advantage of a playgroup is that parents are usually involved, fathers as well as mothers, and hence parents can learn a lot about the value of activities which can later be used at home. By belonging to the playgroup movement many parents find that *they* develop as well as their children.

What then does a good pre-school group provide? Bearing in mind that children develop physically, intellectually, linguistically, emotionally and socially, suitable equipment should be provided for each of these areas of development.

Sensory development can be helped, and experience can be gained from dry and wet sand, clay and water play, encouraging children to listen to different sounds, e.g. drums, shakers and bells; to look at different objects and sometimes, as a game, the leader might introduce a blindfold sniffing game, with such things as lavender, coffee, Vick, etc.

Motor development. The development of small precise motor activities might be encouraged by providing the child with large beads to thread, sturdy pieces of cloth with many buttons and buttonholes, a large screw with a quantity of coloured plastic nuts and bolts, etc., as well as the usual jigsaws. The development of large motor activity may be encouraged by climbing frames (indoors or out) sometimes with rope ladders, footballs, ropes, tricycles, etc.

Linguistics and intellectual development may be stimulated by objects. The leader may sometimes provide a table containing pleasant pebbles, shells, flowers and even live specimens such as caterpillars and tadpoles. Games or construction kits such as Lego help intellectual development. Opportunities to sort objects into categories, e.g. colour or shape categories, are very useful too. A table where cutting, glueing and sticking are available is very popular. Crayons for the youngest children should be of a suitable size to be grasped in a fist, until the child's motor development allows him to hold a thinner crayon correctly. Wax crayons keep frustration to a minimum at this stage.

As well as being given the opportunity to discuss objects as an aid to intellectual and mental growth the child's development will be greatly helped by children's rhymes and stories. These also encourage the child to sit and listen, and a quiet time is usually set aside each day when the group gather together for songs and stories.

Another useful activity in playgroup or nursery is the mid-session drink. By insisting that this is done in a controlled and organized fashion with consideration for their neighbours, children become accustomed to conforming with the group, taking turns in the queue and so will be more prepared to deal with infant school later on.

Social and emotional development. A very popular activity for both boys and girls which helps social and emotional development is dressing up, and a clean selection of dressing up clothes is essential. Some kind of Wendy House or adapted clothes horse is also valuable is also valuable as children love to get into a miniature space, even if it is only a 'tent' beneath the table.

The arrangement of the room is just as important in the playgroup as in the nursery school, with 'noisy' activities being placed well away from the quiet tables and paints. The children should be taken by the hand as they arrive, so as to give new arrivals a 'safe base' from which to explore.

Pre-School Play and its Relation to Learning

What do children learn at a pre-school group? Do they learn anything or are they just filling in time?

Bearing in mind that playgroup leaders are not permitted to teach directly, any learning that goes on in this situation will be due to trial and error and also sometimes due to the 'short cut' of imitation.

Joe, for example, has just arrived at playgroup. He is 3 years old, and he comes into the room and sits at a table which contains waste materials and glue. On investigating the boxes he finds a date box. He explores its possibilities and announces 'It's a boat!' With the middle of a toilet roll he adds a funnel and then, feeling more secure due to his success, he leaves his chair and goes to a new piece of equipment. He climbs the ladder to the top of the small climbing frame and slides down the slide on the other side. Because climbing up was followed by pleasant consequences, the action is repeated several times (Law of Effect). Joe might then notice that Tim is wearing cardboard 'binoculars' round his neck, so Joe once again approaches the 'glue' table and asks the adult there if he can join in and stick toilet-roll centres together. He now has binoculars too; imitation has occurred. Making the boat involved initial exploration of the materials but imitation of Tim provided a short-cut to learning.

It is interesting to observe that once children have made a particular object, e.g. binoculars from toilet rolls or goggles from egg boxes, they delight in using these schemata over and over again – in Piagetian terms they use the schemata because they have them.

If learning is a 'relatively permanent change in behaviour due to experience,' children *are* learning in pre-school play situations, and will learn best when the environment is as rich and stimulating as possible, i.e. when there are plenty of opportunities to take part in trial-and-error and imitation activity.

During the Oxfordshire Pre-school Research Project, Bruner,

Sylva and their colleagues (1980) were very interested in materials, events and social interactions that would encourage concentration and complex activity. They suggest that children can play at two levels – one only keeps them amused but the other contributes to their educational development. The first type of play offers little challenge to the child, the second offers a high level of challenge. For instance, a challenge is met by children who use Sticklebricks or Lego to construct a building or machine, compared with some children who will only make simple guns with these materials.

The Oxfordshire study was carried out over three years, and it took the form of observation of different forms of pre-school care and interviews with minders, leaders and teachers. The findings were interesting. Sylva observed 120 children aged 3–5, taking two 20-minute observations of each target child. The features that were noted were:

(a) Type of task.
(b) Conversation.
(c) Whether the child was alone or not.
(d) Was the activity taking place in free play time or not.
(e) Was the child concentrating, i.e. looking intently or frowning etc.

Jerome Bruner had already questioned the value of a 'laissez-faire' approach to children's play situations – a more structured approach is more challenging than leaving the children to play with materials with no structure. For example, Sylva found that although free play with sand or clay can be emotionally satisfying it is not challenging. If these materials are presented carefully, and if objects such as moulds, sand combs etc. are included with them, then creativity can be enhanced. The Sylva study showed that the child benefits most from having a healthy balance between free play and structured activity and that it is important to have some structured activity that encourages concentration in every session. The findings of the Oxford Study could be summarized:

(1) Children learn most from activities with a clear goal which encourages them to concentrate e.g. Lego, puzzles, pretend play.
(2) Children work well in pairs and this inspires the intellectual level of the play.

(3) Extra adults, e.g. helpers, parents etc., can help to encourage and stimulate language.

Another study also carried out observations and interviews amongst pre-school establishments. This took place in Cheshire and Staffordshire under the supervision of Corrine and John Hutt and their colleagues at Keele University. One of the results of this study was the Keele Pre-school Assessment Guide.

By answering a simple questionnaire, and ranking the child on seven-point scales for such abilities as concentration and creativity, it is possible for the nursery teacher to draw a profile of the child's level of development in four areas – physical skills, socialization, language and cognition; and hence to check after several months whether the child is progressing or not.

It seems then, that a child has a lot to gain from attending a well-run pre-school group. Unfortunately some groups are good and some are not so good. Recently there have been attempts by organizations such as the Thomas Coram Foundation to investigate and find a way through the jungle of pre-school provision, but as yet there is no clear 'best path' for parents to take.

Many teachers of reception classes in infant schools would agree that children who have never attended a pre-school group might take a little longer to settle down at school than those who have attended a good playgroup or nursery. On the other hand, teachers have been known to complain that children who have been allowed to 'run wild' in an unstructured playgroup have more difficulty adjusting to school life than anyone else.

Perhaps the best advice to parents is to recommend that they select an establishment with care, if possible visit several of them, and at the same time bear in mind that play goes on throughout development, and that parents can do a great deal within the home to ensure that each child has a varied, stimulating environment in which to blossom.

Table 9.2. Play Categorized According to the Child's Age

Average age at which certain play is common	Parten's classification	Piaget's description
6 mths – 2 years	Solitary play	Sensorimotor stage: mastery or practice play
2 years	Looking-on play	
2–3 years	Parallel play	Symbolic or make-believe
4 years	Associative play	play
5 years	Co-operative play	
7 years and older	Co-operative play	Play with rules begins

Table 9.3. Other Classifications of Play

Piaget	Play that is pure assimilation		Play that involves both assimilation and accommodation		
Hutt	Play		Exploration		
Sylva & Bruner	Simple play		Complex play (contains exploration)		
Garvey	Play using motion	Play using objects	Play using language	Social play	Play with rules

Summary

1 Play is hard to define; most of the characteristics of play either fail to apply to all types of play, or they also apply to activities which are not playful.

2 Several theories have suggested that play has some purpose. One early theory suggested that it was a means of using up surplus energy. Another that it involved practising skills for later life, and a third that it was a recapitulation of our own evolution. These theories failed to explain playful behaviour successfully, largely because they did not consider play within the context of the child's total development.

3 Freud and Piaget both attempted to explain play as part of the total development, although they viewed the topic from different angles. Freud saw play as both an illustration of the level of the child's emotional development and a means of helping their emotional growth to continue. Piaget extended his theory of cognitive development to cover play and concluded that play was any activity where the amount of assimilation exceeded the amount of accommodation by the child.

4 There have been several attempts to classify play. Freud and Piaget classified by stage and approximate age, as did Mildred Parten. Others have looked at what the play involves – motion, objects, language, etc. It is important to remember that most of these divisions are for the convenience of observers and theorists, and that activity in any one play area could aid development in many spheres at the same time.

5 Interesting distinctions have been made between play and exploration (Hutt), and simple and complex play (Bruner and Sylva). It is possible that these are similar to the distinction made by Piaget between play that is pure assimilation, and play that contains some accommodation.

6 There are three types of pre-school group where play and education are the prime consideration. These are state nursery schools, private nursery schools and playgroups. Parents who are thinking of sending children to one of these would be well advised to arrange a preliminary visit, to check that the facilities provided will allow healthy progress in all five domains of a child's development.

Further Reading

Millar, S., *The Psychology of Play* (1968, Pelican).

Sheridan, Mary, *Spontaneous Play in Early Childhood* (1977, NFER-Nelson).

Garvey, Catherine, *Play* (1977, Fontana).

Chapter 10

The School as a Social and Cultural Environment

Social interaction seems to be fundamental to human existence – cities, pyramids, Stonehenge, cave paintings and golf clubs – all testify to human beings' desire to collect together in groups and mix.

In our society the family, nurseries, play schools, infant classes and child minders are a part of this social process and the adult–child, teacher–pupil, child–child relationships are all important influences in social learning, or what psychologists call socialization. By socialization is meant the way in which we come to take in, or internalize, socially acceptable behaviour, often described as our values, attitudes and beliefs.

So necessary to human development is social contact that humans have long used its absence as a punishment, for example solitary confinement in prison. Similarly, as Chapter 4 suggests, children who have suffered great deprivation in infancy, for example being deprived of normal physical and social contact with caregivers, find difficulty in socializing with adults and peers. Skuse (1984), for example, reported the case of two sisters, Mary and Louise, who had spent the early part of their life with a mother who was mentally retarded and possibly suffering from a severe psychiatric illness. On discovery, the children were described as 'very strange creatures indeed'. On encountering strangers they would scamper up to them and sniff them, at the same time grunting like animals. Since discovery and subsequent removal to a small children's home, both sisters have made an attachment to a caregiver but their ability to mix in groups is still severely restricted.

The beginnings of socialization are found in babyhood, particularly in early attachment behaviour to parents. This is followed closely by a spread of attachments to significant others: older siblings, grandparents, regular baby-sitters, and neighbours and friends (seen on a regular basis). Mary and Louise are an example of where this natural development did not take place, leading to disastrous consequences. Most babies enter the world with some social skills, however simple. Babies are able to communicate socially through crying, smiling, eye contact and other behaviours referred to as attachment behaviour. Through these behaviours both baby and adult are able to seek out and retain social contact. Throughout childhood these behaviours become re-formed and extended and eventually become the complicated sets of social behaviour shown by adults through, for example, verbal and non-verbal behaviour (body language). We must always remember when thinking about children that we are observing a person with a developing brain. As children grow physically so, too, do their powers of thinking and in turn their ability to understand the environment in which they live which, of course, means their social environment as well.

Anyone who has watched two toddlers pull faces, laugh, scream, point and jabber at each other cannot help but be struck by their degree of awareness of each other. Similarly, watching two 2-year-olds scream, hit and spit at each other while arguing over a toy one must concede that this is social interaction. Much of this behaviour is peer imitation – one child screams and the other follows suit. But it will eventually become more refined as the child goes through childhood until it develops into the more sophisticated social behaviour of the adult which we would call sharing or co-operation. What exactly, however, is social behaviour and socialization, as defined by psychologists, and how does it happen? How do children convert aggressive behaviour to the more measured and controlled responses of the adult?

If you were to stand outside your local playschool or nursery and ask parents what they felt social behaviour was, you would probably find that they would mention the following: 'independence'; 'sharing and getting along with other children'; 'learning to behave properly'; 'having good manners'; and 'knowing how to help others'. Many rule-of-thumb methods of assessing behaviour used by all of us in our daily life are a product of our social and cultural upbringing. For some people, social behaviour is concerned with etiquette; others see it as concerned with discipline and self-control, and others see moral development as most important. Such aspects of social growth and behaviour have interested many of the great names in psychology and education. Maria Montessori, Freud, Eric Erikson, Piaget and John Bowlby, to name just a few, have expressed interest in and have tried to explain how children develop social behaviour, in particular aspects of socialization such as independence, altruism (i.e. unselfish and helpful behaviour), sex role behaviour, attachment to others and conformity. Unfortunately, a text book of this length does not allow a detailed discussion of all aspects of social behaviour currently under review by a wide variety of psycholoists and sociologists. Instead, we will take a more general look at the role of schools and schooling in the shaping of social behaviour in children.

It is very noticeable that in cultures which are planning changes in the social structure of that society, the family and schools and schooling are used as the main instruments of change. Those of us who have lived through recent history have seen a number of governments, political regimes and revolutionary groups use schooling as a means to change society. The Khmer Rouge of Cambodia recognised what a powerful social instrument a school was both in terms of bringing about social stagnation as well as change. They destroyed, or tried to, both the family unit and schools in order to effect a radical change in Cambodia. On the other side of the world and in an earlier decade President Lyndon B. Johnson and his predecessor, President J. F. Kennedy, saw the need for social change in American society. Both saw schools and schooling as a means to integrate rich and poor in society, but more particuarly to integrate black and white in America. The American Head Start programme, a massive pre-school programme of compensatory education, was seen in part as helping to bring about changes in American society, particularly within the poor immigrant minorities. What is it, then, that is so important about schools and schooling that governments feel they can bring about fundamental changes in people?

Schools are complex social institutions. They have social status; they have rules; they provide education; they care for young children; in many countries attendance at school is compulsory and society at large has expectations as to what a school should be like. In this respect therefore, they are a reflection of our culture.

Culture and Multicultural Education

Culture, as a psychological term, is very difficult to define. Suffice it to say that as far as we are concerned it is what one might call the 'Englishness' of being brought up in England or the 'Jewishness' of being brought up in a Jewish community. Schools, to a greater or lesser extent, enable society to transmit to children socially acceptable norms of behaviour. Through assemblies, religious instruction and at a more subtle level through drama, history and English lessons, schools impart the cultural norms and values of society. So although all morning assemblies may look the same, the content of a Christian school assembly would be different from that at a Jewish school or a school for Muslim children.

Multi-cultural education is a direct result of the changes immigration and emigration have brought about in our society. Schools (including pre-schools) now comprise children of many ethnic and culturally dissimilar backgrounds. Unfortunately, too, the issue of multi-cultural education has produced much antagonism between those on the far right of politics who wish to see the predominant Englishness of English culture reign unopposed in schools, and those on the left who wish to see a very positive approach to the teaching of multi-cultural education. Although this is a very general assessment of the situation, at ground level the reality of one culture meeting another head-on is much more tortuous. Indeed, recently in the LEA of Kirklees in the north of England, a group of parents refused to send their children to a state school. They felt that, because of the high number of children of Asian origin attending the school, their own children would not get an 'English' education, i.e. the traditional English curriculum would perhaps become absorbed into a multi-cultural curriculum. The episode has been viewed with sadness by community leaders on both sides. Asian community leaders feel very disappointed having spent many years building up good relations with their English neighbours. Similarly leaders of the local education authority feel that their efforts to integrate the two communities by implementing a multi-cultural curriculum in their schools has not worked, at least in this instance.

The Effects of Schools and Playgroups

It is instances like Kirklees which bring into sharp focus just how powerful a school is in transmitting social and cultural values. Schools present to children powerful role models: both real and imaginary. As well as meeting real people in the form of teachers, nursery nurses, volunteers and peers, the child meets characters in fairy tales, stories, plays and in educational television programmes.

Similarly opportunities to learn in groups in order to facilitate socialization are encouraged in schools through assemblies, group work, drama, competitive sport and games, pair work and house systems. Teachers actively implement such teaching techniques as group work in order to encourage character traits such as co-operation, tolerance and leadership in the knowledge that the child's peers can be role models too, because children often learn from watching each other. By the age of 5 years, when a child enters full-time compulsory schooling, he or she will be spending approximately 30 per cent of their week, for about 38 weeks in every year, in the company of people other than their parents and siblings. For the pre-school child this is much less, but even here, by the age of 5 years the DES estimates that about 40 per cent of children are attending some form of pre-school provision, the biggest proportion attending playschool. The figure could be higher, as some child-care facilities are not registered with any local government agency. It is this latter group we shall look at more closely now before continuing with our discussion on socialization.

Just exactly what facilities exist in the United Kingdom that cater for the pre-school child? As a result of the Oxford Pre-school Research Project under the direction of Jerome Bruner (1980) (as mentioned in Chapter 9 on p.133), we now have some very detailed information on pre-school provision including playgroups and nursery schools, child minders and day nurseries. Each in turn to a lesser or greater extent helps the growth and development of social behaviour in children. The Oxfordshire Pre-School Research Project certainly seems to indicate that the child-minder with her limitations in terms of space, expertise and time cannot offer the same opportunities that the day nursery or playgroup can. It would seem that the extra stimulation offered by nurseries and playgroups and the way in which they present this stimulation in an organized way is very beneficial in developing children both intellectually and socially.

By three years of age the average child has developed language, albeit simple. His overall proximity-seeking behaviour (wishing to be with his Mum all the time) declines, possibly because now the child is a reasonably effective communicator he can keep in contact with Mum over a distance through speech. The child can now be left on his own to play in another room while mother attends to something else. Overt attachment to parents declines and we begin to see attachment behaviour to significant others such as baby-sitters and regularly seen neighbours. This makes leaving the average three-year-old with, say, a child-minder or nursery nurse easier – although, as many parents will testify, the first few separations can be quite distressing to both child and parent.)

School (including nurseries and playgroups) presents to the child role models to imitate in the form of both adults and his fellow peers. Let us first consider the adult as a role model.

The Effects of Leadership

In 1939 Lewin, Lippitt and White conducted an experiment which has now become a classic study. It provided an insight into how young people react to different kinds of leadership – authoritarian, democratic and laissez-faire. In the study, 11-year-old boys, all members of a model-making club, were randomly allocated to three groups. Each group had a leader who adopted a different style of leadership. The authoritarian leader behaved in a manner we would describe as 'strict', i.e. critical, distant, formal and dictatorial. The democratic leader on the other hand encouraged dialogue between himself and the boys and between the boys; he allowed choice and was helpful. In contrast, the laissez-faire leader gave no guidance or support and provided no information in terms of the quality of their work.

The boys responded very differently to the three styles of leadership. The boys in the authoritarian's class showed more tension and aggression although output was higher when he was there. In the class run by the democratic leader there was more group satisfaction and enthusiasm for the model-making and much less hostility amongst members of the group. Output was lower than that of the authoritarian's class but quality was better. The group led by the laissez-faire teacher did worst of all. Their work was poor and productivity was low. The boys were not happy and seemed perplexed by the lack of direct input from the leader.

Although this experiment has had its critics and as a scientific experiment it may be of limited value because no control group was used, it certainly seems to agree with similar experiments in the same vein. If you remember, earlier in this book we discussed the work of Sears, Maccoby and Levin whose research seems to show that parents who physically punish their children for acts of aggression seem to have children whose aggressive behaviour increases. We also discussed the work of Bandura and Walters (1963) who showed in their experiments that children will copy aggressive acts that they have seen adults commit on a previous occasion.

Child-Child Relationships

Let us now turn our attention to child-child relationships. Is there any evidence that children watch and learn from each other?

For some time now it has been suggested that young children are too egocentric to indulge in social interaction in an effective way. The reasons for this are that children (i.e. those under 3 years) lack sophisticated language and are not sufficiently well-developed mentally. This hypothesis has been contradicted somewhat in recent years thanks to the use of the video camera. Social contact between infants is often very quick and brief and as a consequence is easy to miss if observing by more traditional methods, for example pencil and pad methods.

Children spend a lot of time with each other either as brothers and sisters or as friends. Moreover, in our schools we usually place children of similar ages together; therefore it is quite likely that social relationships between peers will be very different in quality to child-adult or child-teacher relationships. We know from having been brought up in families that siblings often copy each other. Dunn and Kendrick (1982), two researchers very interested in young children's interests in their brothers and sisters, found that this sort of imitation was frequent and appeared to be a pleasing and exciting activity. But what about social interaction outside the home?

Psychologists, sociologists and anthropologists have taken a keen interest in this area, and a large amount of work has been completed in recent years. Their research methods have ranged from formal experiments conducted in university research laboratories to participant–observer recording of social interaction between members of street gangs.

Rather than summarize the vast wealth of information now available we shall look closely at one experiment conducted by Lewis and his associates in 1975 into peer relationships amongst infants of 12–18 months of age. Lewis placed two mother-infant pairs in a playroom together. The four had not previously met. The observers watched to see who the infants touched and looked at the most. Their results were quite surprising. As one might assume from studying attachment theory, the infants touched their own mothers the most. However, they looked at their fellow peer twice as often as at their own mother. Taken in conjunction with other research on a similar vein we can say that infants are very interested in each other and that maybe this forms the basis of social behaviour seen in older children as friendship.

Children's Friendships

Friendship and friendship groups are yet another very important aspect of social learning for children. As adults we are often shocked by the way children can make and break friends so easily and without apparent feelings of guilt or regret. In this respect we are measuring children by *adult* norms of behaviour, in terms of character traits such as trust, loyalty and discretion. Such qualities of behaviour cannot always be seen in children's friendship behaviour because children do not perceive relationships in the way that adults do.

Cognitive Theories of Social Relationships

The study of how children understand and develop understanding, as regards social relationships such as friendship, has come to be known as *social cognition* – a very new branch of social psychology and heavily influenced by cognitive psychologists such as Piaget, Kohlberg and Bruner. At its simplest, social cognition theorists believe that social relationships help to shape thought and in turn thought helps to shape social relationships. Their research methods have included:

(a) Direct observations, e.g. video recordings of children at play.
(b) Interviewing parents, teachers and others involved in the care of young children.
(c) Participant-observer, i.e. becoming part of a group in order to study it yet trying not to influence it, as used to study street gangs.
(d) Interviewing children using open-ended questions favoured by cognitive psychologists such as Piaget and Kohlberg (see Ch. 1).

By recording on video tape the actions of children playing in a group, one can produce a map of their social relationships with each other. Sociologists and social psychologists use this method, which is sometimes referred to as *sociometry*. The resultant map is called a *sociogram*. An example of a very simple sociogram is illustrated in Figure 10.1.

A sociogram (as in Figure 10.1) can be constructed by making a series of 30-second observations of each child in a group over a number of hours. By noting which children are interacting together, it is possible to build up a picture of their social relationships. If the observations include the number of contacts made, and who initiated them, then the sociogram would indicate which children interact with each other regularly and frequently, and conversely those who have little or no interaction with their peers. We are able to see in Figure 10.1, for example, that boy 3 seems to be quite popular in the group, whereas boy 5 is isolated and seems to have no interaction with his peers. Girl 8 on the other hand seems to interact with a number of her classmates, yet none of them initiate contact with her.

Figure 10.1. Sociogram Showing Relationships Between a Small Group of Children in a Classroom

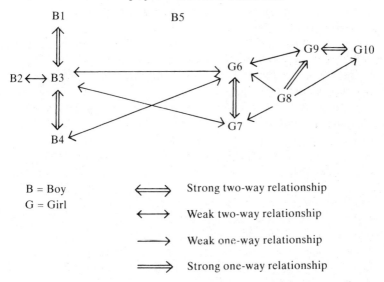

A sociogram may be very revealing in terms of how a group of children, for example in an infant class, interact with each other. But it tells us very little about how children perceive relationships such as friendships. In this respect the data obtained from observations like this are only descriptive; that is, they show us who is associating with whom, but we cannot assume that this association is the same thing as friendship. If we return to the sociogram in Figure 10.1, we could say of boy 5 that he is a solitary child or an isolated child and therefore has no 'friends'. This presupposes that by friendship we mean a close association between people. But it is possible to interact with lots of people yet have no close relationship with any of them that we would commmonly recognize as friendship: girl 8 seems to fit this description. In order to investigate the nature of children's concepts of friendship we need to use the fourth research method from the list above. We would need to interview the children and ask them questions such as: What is a best friend? What do you like the most about your best friend?

Children's Ideas about Friendship

One cognitive psychologist, Robert Selman (1977), was interested in this aspect of children's social relationships and how they change over time. His investigations were heavily influenced by Piaget and he used a similar open-ended method of investigation to that used by Piaget. Selman devised a series of short stories, each one dealing with a typical problematic situation which might occur within a friendly relationship between two children. In this respect his research is also very similar to the work of Lawrence Kohlberg, another cognitive psychologist who researched children's under-standing of right and wrong (see Chapter 1). Children would read or have read to them a short story dealing with a situation such as how far should you help a friend who has lost something very important to them. By analysing the children's responses to those stories, Selman was able to see how children's social awareness changes as they develop. He was able to see, for example, that at the earliest stage of understanding, between the ages of 3 and 6 years, children are rather egocentric in their understanding of people's relationships. They can recognize upset when they see it but are unable to link the symptom with the inner thoughts and feelings of the person being observed. By the onset of puberty Selman noted that most children were able to appreciate that human beings are complex, and are products of their upbringing and the society in which they live. Obviously this shift from the self-centred notion of relationships to a more detailed and appreciative view must influence a child's notion as to what friendship is.

One way Selman went about trying to explore children's notions of friendship was to ask children various open-ended questions about specific aspects of friendship, namely:

(a) What makes a 'good friend'?
(b) How do you make friends?
(c) How are 'best' friends different from other people you know well?

Obviously he could not ask these questions in the form they are presented above, particularly to young children, so he presented to his subjects questions such as:
Why is X your best friend? Is it easy to make friends? Can friends have a fight or an argument and still be friends afterwards? Why do you like your friend? As a result of his researches he hypothesized that there were five levels of understanding of friendship, as set out in Table 10.1

Table 10.1

Level	Approximate age (years)	Brief description
0	3–6	Close physical interaction – whoever the child is playing with at the time will be considered as a 'close/best' friend.
1	5–9	One-way assistance – other children fulfil needs, e.g. a good friend is someone who shares his sweets with you.
2	7–12	Fair-weather co-operation, i.e. friendship is understood as being two-way but only as long as they keep on pleasing each other.
3	10–15	Adolescents begin to understand that friendship is concerned with behaving in ways that will maintain a relationship, e.g. intimacy, and emotional rather than just physical support.
4	12–Adult	Older adolescents begin to realize that friendships, as relationships, change and that there is a need to be an individual as well as a member of a close-knit group.

Selman therefore sees children's friendship awareness as following a ladder-like development moving from the concrete to the abstract. There is a gradual shift in focus from seeing friends in purely physical and immediate terms to seeing friends as part of a wider social environment. This progression in social awareness is made possible by the fact that the child's intellectual growth also moves from the concrete to the abstract.

Summary

1 Social interaction seems to be universal; socialization is the way we internalize socially accepted behaviour which is often referred to as our values, attitudes and beliefs. Severe deprivation can severely retard this development.

2 Socialization begins in infancy and has its roots in attachment behaviour.

3 Schools reflect culture, which in turn influences the way in which socially accepted norms are transmitted to children. Multi-cultural education is a way in which educators are trying to deal with cultural changes in school as a result of immigration and emigration.

4 The Oxfordshire Pre-school Research Project has been very important in outlining the various childcare facilities currently available, and the influence they have on young children.

5 Evidence points to the fact that adults, other children and siblings act as powerful role models in the development of social behaviour.

6 One aspect of children's social behaviour which has recently come in for extensive study is that of friendship, which has been investigated through observation, interviewing adults involved with children, participant observer, and interviewing children.

7 Direct observation resulting in a sociogram may be informative insofar as it presents a map of social interaction. In this respect it is decriptive rather than analytic.

8 Cognitive psychologists like Robert Selman have been more interested in children's ideas of friendship. He maintains that a child's concept of friendship follows a similar progression to that described by Piaget, i.e. the child's understanding moves from the concrete and immediate to the abstract.

Further Reading

Blatchford, P., *Playtime in the Primary School* (1989, NFER-Nelson).

Carrington, B. and Short, G., *'Race' and the Primary School* (1989, NFER-Nelson).

Dunn J. and Kendrick, C., *Siblings: Love, Envy and Understanding* (1981, Grand McIntyre).

Sylva, K., Roy, C. and Painter, M., *Childwatching in Playgroup and Nursery School* (1980, Grant McIntyre).

Chapter 11

Discovery Learning versus Programmed Learning

If you have ever waited outside an Infant or Junior School for either your own child or maybe a younger brother or sister you might have heard the following comments made by some of the more sceptical parents.

'I don't think they can be learning anything. All they seem to do is play with toys.'

'They ought to be learning the 3Rs, not playing around with computers.'

'He/she loves it here, they let them do as they please. Mind you, I can't see what they can be learning.'

In a sense all of these comments represent a debate in educational psychology that has been going on almost as long as there have been schools and psychologists. The kernel of the debate is this: Should children be allowed to learn how and what they please, or should we structure their experiences?

Translated into psychological topic areas the debate is centred around the two opposing theories of learning, Behaviourism and the Cognitive Theorists. The debate relies heavily on the work of Skinner's theory and its application in the form of programmed learning on the one hand, and the work of Piaget and discovery learning on the other. Before we decide on the merits of each method let us see exactly what is meant by discovery learning and programmed learning.

Discovery Learning

Piaget believed that children actively try to understand the world they live in because they are motivated to by their own natural curiosity. The idea is not completely new – others before Piaget such as Maria Montessori and Frederick Froebel had similar ideas about children, but it was Piaget who perhaps provided the most convincing theory for this. As we learned in Chapter 1, Piaget based much of his theory about children learning on his clinical observations of them solving problems. He noted the way in which children of different ages tried to solve the puzzles he gave them. This led him to believe that children should be free to explore their environment and learn about it.

On the surface, discovery learning looks like play. In a structured environment, however, such as that presented in infant classrooms, children are encouraged to discover things about themselves and their environment by experiencing it as first hand. Play may well the vehicle used by the child as a means of learning but Piagetians would argue that play combined with curiosity helps the child to 'discover' his environment and in turn to form concepts, for example the concepts of singleness and pairedness. The Piagetian teacher would say that you cannot teach concepts of singleness, pairedness, triadness (threeness) in a traditional way, by having children learn information about the world they live in as facts given to them by their leaders. Piagetians would claim that for a child to 'realize' the difference between pairedness and singleness she must be allowed to experience them in a concrete way such as through dressing-up games. To the layman this may seem as if the child is simply playing with old clothes and shoes. But in the hands of the informed parent or teacher this situation can be used to help children discover for themselves the mathematical relationships which exist between single and pair, long and short, left and right, as well as many other more subtle aspects about themselves.

Programmed Learning

In contrast there are those who prescribe more structured learning. They criticize the discovery method on the grounds that, to quote an old proverb, 'You can take a horse to water but you can't make him drink'. In other words you can place a child in an enriched and planned learning environment but do you know that she/he is learning? Some would say that Piaget's belief that children's minds quite naturally organize and process incoming stimuli converting them into schemata, which in turn helps them to understand new information, is not proved. Many feel that Piagetian theory cannot explain many areas of human learning behaviour – in particular the wide variation which exists between individuals and within groups and cultures.

Teachers who see Piagetian theory as allowing children too much freedom advocate a more structured approach. One such approach is that advocated by the Behaviourist school. Explanations of learning theory as presented by people such as Pavlov, Thorndike and Skinner might seem to be too remote to be applied to the infant and junior school classroom. In fact they have been and still are being used in a number of teaching situations such as in the teaching of foreign languages, dealing with children with severe and moderate learning difficulties, and children with emotional disturbance. Indeed, many of the very recent developments in educational technology such as computer aided learning (CAL) and educational games and tutor packs using interactive video base much of their organization and format on programmed learning. So what is it and how does it work?

At its simplest level a programmed learning text involves small packets of information (called frames) presented in such a way that the response they elicit is always correct – the child is reinforced by knowing he got the answer correct. Through a series of successively more difficult stimuli – response frames – the student may be taken from simple to more complex information. Such a programme is sometimes known as a *linear programme* because if you were to represent it diagrammatically it would look something like this:

START → Step 1 → Step 2 → Step 3 → Step 4

You would move in a line through frames, 1, 2, 3 and 4.

Translated into school learning this could well be a CAL programme to teach a child to count from 1 to 10. This first frame shows a teddy-bear with the figure 1 beneath it. The second frame shows the same teddy-bear with the figure 1 and another figure beneath it. In order to progress to the third frame the child must press 1 on his keyboard. Pressing any other key returns him to the first frame again. Pressing the correct key also makes the teddy-bear laugh.

Linear programmes by virtue of their simplicity can often be boring. Successive reinforcement, as Skinner demonstrated in laboratory animals, often leads to satiation and a reduction in performance. Modern educational technologists are now able with the aid of the computer to build into simple programmes for children other reinforcers; for example, five correct responses means you are able to press Key D and made the teddy-bear dance all round the screen. This use of schedules of reinforcement rather than relying totally on continuous reinforcement has been used very successfully by designers of educational software to help children learn what has traditionally been seen as quite tedious information such as the letters of the alphabet, the times tables and simple spelling rules.

A complex but more flexible programme is known as the *skip technique*. This enables the programmer to place remedial frames within a total programme. So, for example, in a programme to teach simple addition the child might see a teddy place one box on top of two others. Beneath this appears:

$$2 + 1 \rightarrow \begin{array}{ll} \text{(a)} & 1 \\ \text{(b)} & 2 \\ \text{(c)} & 3 \end{array}$$

A choice of (a) or (b) refers to child automatically to a remedial frame which helps her to understand her error. The choice of (c) means she proceeds to the next level of complexity in the programme, thereby 'skipping' the remedial frame.

In order for you to appreciate more fully the differences between the two teaching methods the main points about them have been summarised in Table 11.1.

Which Method Works Best?

To try and decide which method of teaching is the better would be very difficult and would present an experiment designer with masses of extraneous variables to try and control. Learning, like other complex areas of human behaviour, is affected by our state of health, our levels of motivation and the type of person we are, to name just three factors. The truth, as in so many other disputed issues in psychology, lies not so much at the extremes of the debate but somewhere in the middle. Most practising infant and junior school teachers would probably agree that many things have to be learned by directly experiencing them, whereas other aspects have to be learned off by heart. It is difficult to see how one could 'teach' through programmed learning perceptual skills related to smell and taste. Similarly, no amount of free play with a wooden alphabet would bring the child to realize some of the more complex abstract concepts formed in algebra. The skilled teacher knows that he needs both styles; the skill comes in knowing how and when to use them, and in what combination.

Table 11.1 The Differences between Discovery and Programmed Learning

	Discovery learning	**Programmed learning**
Influences	Piaget and others with a nativistic view.	Skinner and the behavourist school.
Vocabulary	Discovery learning Discovery play. Experiential learning.	Programmed learning. Programmed instruction. Directed learning.
Style	Informal/free experience within a planned environment.	Formal/mechanistic – behaviour-shaping by reducing complicated information to a series of simpler frames or 'chunks'.
Use	Concept learning.	Subject- or fact-centred learning.
Time	Determined by child's neurobiological maturity plus opportunity to interact with a rich environment.	Mainly determined by the programme.
Implementation	Educational toys and games – learning environments designed for children.	Programmed learning texts, CAL, interactive video.

Summary

1 Programmed learning relies heavily on the work of B.F. Skinner. Discovery learning relies heavily on the work of Piaget.

2 Piaget maintains that children 'discover' their environment through their natural curiosity. This is often observed as play but Piagetians would maintain that as well as playing children are learning concepts about the world they live in.

3 Behaviourists criticize this method on the grounds that it is too free and not structured enough.

4 Skinnerian learning theory can be translated into practice through educational technology such as CAL, computer games, tutor packs and interactive video.

5 At its simplest, programmed learning involved presenting small packets of informaton (frames) in a way that the response they elicit is always correct. By graduating the level of difficulty students may be successfully taken from the simple to the complex.

6 By introducing a system of variable reinforcement, programmed learning texts and games can be made more interesting.

7 Modern classroom teachers usually use both discovery and programmed learning nowadays.

Further Reading

Rachlin, H., *Introduction to Modern Behaviourism* (1970, Freeman).
Donaldson, M., *Children's Minds* (1978, Fontana).
Boden, M., *Piaget* (1979, Fontana).

Chapter 12

The Nature/Nurture Debate on Intelligence

The Nature/Nurture Problem

At conception every animal is provided with a mix of genetic material from its parents which governs much of its later development, such as whether the new being will develop into a frog or a toad, a male or a female; many other major or minor physical characteristics are also genetically determined. For some animals these hereditary factors determine most of the behaviour performed during a lifetime.

For example, a digger wasp lives for only a few weeks, during which it has to hunt, dig a nest hole, mate, lay eggs and provide next year's generation with a store of food. The wasp then dies; there is no adult to teach complicated behaviour patterns to the young, nor time for them to learn by trial and error. Life is very different for the human infant, but to what extent are we controlled by inherited factors?

The nature/nurture debate is about the relative importance of inherited and environmental influences on human and animal characteristics.

The debate is not just of academic interest, since presumably if it was decided that human intelligence was limited by inherited factors this might affect educational policy in a different way than if environmental experience was considered to be most important. Extreme right-wing political parties have selected some of the studies that we will quote later, to argue that some races are genetically inferior to others. If the selection of evidence is biased in a different way, studies show that the way we treat people is the most important determinant of behaviour. It is not surprising that, superficially, studies appear to give contradictory results, since the question 'is nature more important than nurture?' is rather like asking whether the length of a rectangle is more important than the width in determining its area.

If either the width or the length is taken away you have no rectangle; keep the length constant and variation in the width will change the area, just as the length will determine the area if the width is constant. Human behaviour and characteristics are an interaction of nature and nurture. Even in the very rare cases where we know the hereditary factors associated with a particular human quality, as with Phenyl-ketonuria (PKU), it is not possible to separate nature and nurture.

PKU is a genetic disorder which occurs when an individual receives a particular pair of genes at conception. Genes are small elements of the genetic code that are carried in their thousands on each of the string-like chromosomes contained within the nucleus of every cell in the body. Most people have a pair of genes that successfully control the breakdown of phenylalanine, a protein contained in many everyday foods, but the PKU sufferer has a pair of genes which cause phenylalanine to be broken down into a substance which is poisonous to the developing nervous system, resulting in mental retardation. Surely this is an example of genetic factors controlling intelligence since we can trace the problem back to the pair of 'defective' genes? The controlling factors, however, are not so clear, for if the disorder is detected by a routine blood test soon after birth, and the child is raised on a diet free of phenylalanine, he develops normally and may have an IQ anywhere in the normal range.

The PKU example shows how the effect of genetics depends upon the environment; it is not possible to say that genetic factors *caused* the low intelligence of a particular person with PKU since we know that given a different environment, in this case a simple change of diet, his IQ would be different. It would be equally foolish to claim that environment had *caused* the retardation. The intelligence of the PKU patient and the rest of us is a result of an *interaction* between genetic and environmental factors.

The nature/nurture problem has been discussed for centuries. Once the question of whether genetics *or* environment causes particular qualities or behaviour has been disposed of, there are a number of more sensible questions that can be asked: do babies perceive the world in the same way as you and I, or was William James right in saying that the newborn baby's world is 'one blooming, buzzing confusion'; are there any particular experiences that infants need in order to ensure a properly functioning adult perceptual system, or do they have a fairly inflexible system which is relatively unaffected by environmental factors? In the area of intelligence, to what extent are the *differences* between people in a particular population due to genetics?

The major contributions that psychologists have made have been in the field of practical studies performed to test the hypotheses that result from taking particular positions in the debate. At its simplest, the argument is between the *empiricists* who stress the role of learning and environmental influence on human characteristics, and the *nativists* who stress genetic (hereditary) influences.

In this chapter and the next we shall look at some aspects of the nature/nurture debate as they apply to the areas of intelligence and perception. In the area of intelligence, psychologists from different sides of the debate became very aggressive with each other because, at first, both camps took up extreme positions – intelligence was either inborn *or* it was due to the effects of the environment.

The Contribution of Nature and Nurture to Intellectual Development

D. O. Hebb in 1949 argued that much of the misunderstanding about intelligence arose because two separate facts were not recognized:

(1) Humans have brains and brain cells for whose structure and function there must be some genetic blueprint. Presumably also encoded in the genetic blueprint is the ability of these cells to join together to form cell assemblies which allow us to store memories and solve problems. In effect, we have an innate ability to form cell assemblies.

(2) Although we may have the potential for forming such brain connections, we may not necessarily actually do so to the fullest extent: the environment may help or hinder their formation.

In other words, not only must we have brains and potential neural connections within the brain, but we must also actually make these connections. Therefore, according to Hebb, we ought to recognize two distinct types of intelligence.

INTELLIGENCE A

This means potential intelligence – the genetically-determined structure of the brain and the potential ability of the brain neurons to connect. This potential intelligence is laid down in an individual's genetic blueprint. The fertilized egg has the genetic blueprint or potential for the development of the ten thousand million brain neurons and their ablity to connect. What happens to the organism after conception can either help this potential to be realized, or hinder it; it cannot alter the potential itself.

INTELLIGENCE B

This describes the extent to which this genetic potential has been realized as a result of the interaction of an individual's genetic makeup with the effects of his environment.

To indicate how complex the interaction between heredity and environment is, consider what happens to the newly fertilized egg. In minute one it is immediately affected by the environment – the conditions of implantation in the womb, and food and oxygen supply, for example. It is now no longer a simple reproduction of genetic information: some of the genetic blueprint has been reproduced, but some has either not been reproduced at all or has been reproduced imperfectly. The organism at minute two no longer shows only genetic potential: it is the result of the effects of the environment at that time on the structures which are currently developing. It is a different organism from minute one. But at minute two this new organism is still being affected by its environment, to produce yet a different basis at minute three, on which the environment will have further effects. At minute four it will be different again, and so on.

Intelligence B is thus, according to Hebb, the way in which the brain functions after the environment has helped or hindered its development from the genetic blueprints of its cells; it is the average level of performance or comprehension on the part of the developing individual that we infer from his or her behaviour.

We cannot directly study intelligence A: how can you study a potential until it has been realized? We could perhaps devise systems for measuring the neural 'connectablity' of an individual's brain, but because we could not do this until neurons had formed, the environment would already have had an effect. Nor is intelligence B measurable. Hebb regards intelligence B as the normal functioning of the brain; thus although it is theoretically possible to monitor separately the activity of each brain neuron, the complete process for an entire brain would take roughly fourteen million years. Even then we should not know what connection each of the neurons had with intelligent behaviour.

Intelligence tests, Hebb says, measure only a sample of intelligence B, so that it is impossible for them to give us reliable information about the nature of intelligence A.

INTELLIGENCE C

Philip Vernon, a British psychologist, has proposed a third type, intelligence C. This, he says, is an unknown amount of intelligence B which can be measured with IQ tests. IQ tests cannot measure the whole of an individual's intelligence B, as we have seen, because intelligence B is the way the individual responds to the environment as a whole. Vernon therefore argues that because intelligence C is an unknown proportion of intelligence B, and B is an unknown proportion of A, it is most unwise to use IQ – intelligence C – scores to find out about intelligence A; we do not know anything about the relationship between intelligence C and A (see Figure 12.1).

Figure 12.1. The Hebb-Vernon Model of Intelligence

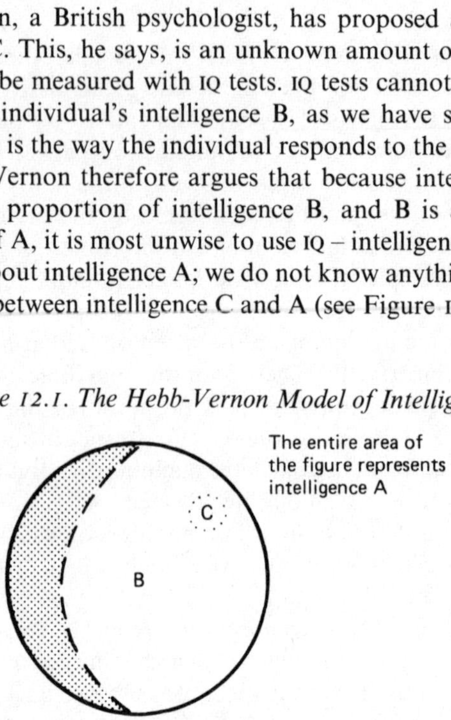

The entire area of the figure represents intelligence A

Family Studies

Towards the end of the last century, Francis Galton performed a series of family studies. He found that intelligent (high-IQ) parents tended to have offspring with high IQs and that tracing a family over a series of generations showed a remarkable consistency in the type of people in each generation.

At first sight many people might take this as evidence of the importance of heredity in characteristics such as intelligence. A longer consideration makes us question this. Intelligent parents may pass on 'intelligent' genes to their children, but their environment may also differ from the kind provided by less intelligent parents: a child may see more books, have a different kind of conversation with his parents, and so on. However, precisely because of this, we cannot use family studies alone for valid evidence in the nature/nurture debate: the child's IQ may be a result of either nature, or nurture, or both.

Twin Studies

Ideally, a study which attempted to separate the effects of genetics and environment would compare people with the same genetic makeup but different environmental experiences, or it would do the opposite, comparing individuals who have different genetic makeup but the same environmental experiences. The use of twins allows both these kinds of studies since there are two types of twin. Monozygotic (MZ) twins develop from the same fertilized egg which splits to produce two individuals with the same genetic makeup; these are identical twins. Dizygotic (DZ) twins develop from two separately fertilized eggs and are not genetically identical; they are only as genetically similar as any set of brothers and/or sisters, but since they are the same age their environments are likely to be more similar than is usual for separate individuals.

As we argued earlier, an individual's IQ results from an interaction of environmental and inherited factors and it is not logically possible to say which is most important. The twin studies do not attempt to tackle this logical impossibility – they are designed to produce a *heritability estimate*, an estimate of the extent to which inherited factors are responsible for *differences* between the IQs of people in a particular population. If the heritability estimate for IQ in this country was 90 per cent it would mean that 90 per cent of the differences between people's IQ scores was due to inherited differences passed on through the genes, and only 10 per cent of the variation was due to environmental factors.

COMPARISON OF MZ TWINS REARED TOGETHER WITH MZ TWINS SEPARATED IN EARLY CHILDHOOD

MZ twins brought up together have very similar IQs. This is not surprising since they share the same genes and environment. To get an idea about what effect the environment can have on IQ differences we could look at MZ twins who are separated at birth and brought up in very different environments; if the twins also have very similar IQs then it could be concluded that environment has very little effect on IQ differences. In other words, the heritability estimate would be high. If the twins brought up separately had very different IQs this could only be due to environmental differences, and so the heritability estimate would be low.

In theory this sort of study sounds ideal, but in practice not many MZ twins are separated at birth, and many of those who were have been reared by relatives in the same town – hardly a totally different environment.

COMPARISON OF DZ AND MZ TWINS

Another sort of twin study tries to counter these problems by comparing the similarity of IQ of MZ twins brought up together with that of DZs brought up together. The theory behind this is that if DZs brought up together are as similar in their IQs as are MZs then the important factor must be the similarity of environments, since DZ twins do not have identical genes. If, however, DZ twins reared together are not as similar as MZ twins reared together this would suggest a high heritability factor, since it must be genetic rather than environmental similarity that causes the MZ twins to have nearly the same IQs.

Unfortunately, this type of study also has problems: can we be sure that DZ twins are treated as equally as MZ twins who look the same and may often be mistaken for each other? Many people argue that boys and girls are treated differently by adults; yet both members of an MZ pair will be the same sex, but half of all DZ pairs consist of one boy and one girl. To improve the likelihood of DZs having an environment as similar as MZs, studies should not include mixed-sex pairs – though many have failed to exclude them.

In the early days of twin studies many mistakes may have been made in identifying twins as MZs or DZs. Twins are often thought to be identical because they look the same. A large number of physiological tests are required to be sure that twins are MZ; looking the same is not enough because even unrelated people can look identical if they happen to have a relatively small proportion of similar genes, those affecting external physical characteristics of the face and head.

Although MZ twins are regarded as genetically identical it is now known that there are very small genetic differences between them.

The correlation coefficients shown in the results of C. Burt in 1953, H.H. Newman, F.N. Freeman and K.J. Holzinger in 1928 and Bouchard and McGue (in a summary of studies published in 1981) indicate the degree of similarity found between their subjects: the nearer to one the correlation coefficient is, the more similar are the individuals in terms of IQ. Thus the correlation of 0.9 between the IQ of monozygotic twins shows that if one twin has a high IQ then the other is very likely also to have a high IQ. You will notice that the IQs of dizygotic twins and siblings (or brothers and sisters) have lower correlations: the lower the correlation, the less similar are the IQs of the individuals in each pair.

Study of	Correlation Coefficient		
	Burt	Newman, Freeman & Holzinger	Bouchard & McGue
Monozygotic twins reared together:	0.92	0.91	0.86
Monozygotic twins reared apart:	0.84	0.67	0.72
Dizygotic twins reared together:	0.53	0.64	0.60
Siblings reared together:	0.49	No figures available	0.47

All these problems reduce the value of what originally looked like a very valuable method for investigation of the nature/nurture debate.

Some of the most influential studies in this field were those performed by Sir Cyril Burt, who concluded that 80 per cent of the differences between the IQs of people in Britain were due to inherited factors and only 20 per cent were due to environmental differences. Many psychologists used Burt's data in producing their own heritability estimates and there was some degree of agreement that an average eight out of every ten IQ points of difference between people in white Western European and American populations were due to genetic variation. It is now generally accepted that Burt falsified at least some of his results and so any heritability estimate produced from them must be re-evaluated. The Newman, Freeman and Holzinger studies produced heritability estimates of about 50 per cent, and other researchers have produced even lower figures.

Even if the twin studies were perfect it would not be surprising if different studies came up with different results, since the heritability estimate is an average for a *particular* population. For a group of people who stress conformity and treat their children as similarly as possible, any differences in IQ are more likely to be due to genetic differences, but if their culture promotes independence and the treatment of children as individuals then there is much more room for environmentally induced differences; the heritability estimate that you find will depend on which group you study.

Adoption and Fostering Studies

Imagine this situation: a man and woman who both have low IQs, have a child. This child is adopted at birth (or fostered from birth) by a high IQ couple. When the child is older, its IQ is measured and is compared with its real (biological) parents' IQs, and also with its adoptive parents' IQs. If heredity is the most important factor in IQ, the child's IQ should be similar to its biological parents' IQ. However, if the child is found to be more similar to its adoptive parents in IQ, then this suggests that environment is more important in determining IQ.

Early studies which followed the above procedure found an average correlation of 0.44 between the child and its biological mother (the figure for children who are brought up by their biological mother is approximately 0.50). This figure of 0.44, however, masks some evidence: although the correlation looks as if the children's IQs are similar to their biological mothers, if you look at the actual IQs involved, the children made big gains in IQ after being fostered or adopted. For example, Scarr and Weinberg (1976) studied disadvantaged black children who were adopted or fostered by white families. The black parents were usually poorly educated and below average in IQ. By 4–7 years old, the children's IQs were 110–112 – much higher than their biological parents, and much more in line with their adoptive or foster parents.

Similarly, Schiff studied children who were moved (before the age of six months) from low-status families to families of a higher social status. Schiff compared the adopted children's IQs with brothers and sisters who had stayed with the biological parents. The average IQ of the adopted children was 111, whilst the average IQ of the children who had stayed with their natural parents was only 95.

Fostering and adoption studies seem to suggest that environment can have a large effect on the development of children's IQs, but a recent review of this area by Locurto (1988) finds that such improvements are not obviously caused by the child moving to a more stimulating environment. Locurto believes that what is also important is that the adoptive parents are more sensitive to the child's particular needs – it is not *more* general stimulation which the child needs, but the right specific stimulation, and sensitive adoptive parents can find and provide this stimulation.

Race and IQ

From the early days of IQ testing there has been an interest in the comparative scores for different races. R. Lynn has recently shown that Japanese schoolchildren score about four and a half points more on IQ tests than do Americans.

In a controversial paper in the *Harvard Education Review* in 1969, Arthur Jensen looked at reasons why American negroes score, on average, 15 points less than whites on IQ tests. Before discussing these reasons it is worth emphasizing that we are only talking about averages and that there is a great deal of overlap between the scores of the different races, many negroes having a greater IQ than many whites. Remember also that the discussion is about IQ, a very limited definition of intelligence.

Jensen argued that the 15 points difference between whites and negroes was too great to be explained by environmental factors; he backed this up by quoting heritability estimates of 80 per cent for intelligence. He felt that specialized education programmes for children of different ability groupings should be devised, to allow the full development of each child. This idea was seized upon by many white Americans in the southern states as an argument to continue segregated schooling of black and white children, which was a hot political issues at the time; it was conveniently forgotten that Jensen was talking about average scores and that many negro children have greater measured IQs than many whites.

Jensen's position has been heavily criticized. Leo Kamin has demonstrated problems with a lot of the studies used to produce the heritability estimates, including the fact that some of the work originated with Burt and therefore cannot be relied upon.

Hebb put forward the following analogy to show the difficulty in using heritability estimates to look at the differences between populations. Suppose we kept all baby boys in barrels from birth and fed them through the bung-holes until they were mature. If we then tested their IQs and compared then with the IQs of the girls who were reared normally, we should probably find that the girls' IQs were much higher than those of the boys. Because all the boys had been brought up in identical environments, any differences in their IQs should be caused by genetic factors. Could we then say that the boys were less intelligent than the girls, and therefore that, because the differences among the boys' IQs were largely created by genetic factors, the differences between boys and girls were also caused by genetics? Of course not. Firstly we would be comparing IQs, not intelligence as a whole. Also we could not compare the role of heredity in determining the boys' and girls' IQs unless both groups had been reared in identical environments.

If we apply this analogy to the race and IQ debate, we cannot compare the effects of genetics in the determination of negroes' and whites' IQs unless we are sure that they have been brought up in identical environments. Jensen claimed that because he compared middle-class negroes with middle-class whites, and working-class negroes with working-class whites, he had held the environmental variable constant. We do not yet know enough about the effects of the environment to be certain which factors are important in IQ, but there is considerable doubt that using social class as a yardstick is a sufficiently sophisticated way of ensuring that the environment is constant.

I. I. Gottesman has shown that large differences in IQ can result from environmental differences: in one study of identical twins the average IQ difference was fourteen points. J. R. Flynn (1984) compared IQ scores of different generations and showed that today's white American children score 15 points more than did their equivalent in 1928, something that is most likely due to changes in education.

Kamin and many others have pointed out that IQ tests are *culturebound*, i.e. they favour people from particular backgrounds, using language and setting problems that reflect white middle-class educational and other experiences. The discrepancy between different races in IQ score may simply reflect this, and so there have been attempts to produce *culture-free* tests though none has been unanimously accepted.

A. and E. Hendrickson (1980) have shown a close relationship between IQ and brain-wave patterns shown on an electroencephalograph in response to a series of tones. C. Brand (1982) has shown a similar relationship with inspection time; people with higher IQs take less time to make simple decisions such as which is the longer of two lines presented to them. Brand argues that these techniques may be used as fairer measures of intelligence.

The arguments about heredity, race and intelligence rage on because there are no definite answers and may never be. It is important, however, to be aware of the shortcomings and counter-claims in this area, if only to be able to rebut the claims of those with extreme views who carefully choose the evidence which supports their case.

Environment and Intelligence

What aspects of the environment have an effect on intelligence? We have already said that schooling can change measured intelligence, and studies of Learning Sets suggest that the more experience of different types of problem, the more likely we are to be able to 'grasp the essentials in a situation and respond appropriately to them'. Remember that environment includes the food we eat and the air we breathe, and the chemical nature of these can have an effect (as it certainly does with PKU patients – see p.163). The environment has an effect before birth: smoking and drinking during pregnancy are known to have some effects on the unborn child, as are particular maternal illnesses such as German measles. Environmental effects which cause strong emotions in the mother or child can have lasting effects which seem out of proportion to the original event. A programme to devise the best environment for development of intelligence would have to take all these factors into account, and it might be that what is best for one aspect of intelligence is detrimental to another. The optimum environment for one individual with a particular genetic makeup may not be best for us all.

We now turn to examples of procedures in this field of study. One obvious need for a developing human being is food, and in particular protein, which is necessary to build brain cells. If an adult is starving to death the last area of the body to lose weight is the brain; any other organ will be sacrified first. But in babies this is not the case: if during the period of brain development the baby is deprived of protein, the brain suffers along with the rest of the body. Although the genetic potential for development might exist, the material with which the body's structures can be built is absent, so that it does not develop properly. J. Cravioto, in studies of protein- and stimulation-deprived children in Mexico, has found that such children show impairment not only of intellectual functions but also of physical development. Moreover, even such simple forms of behaviour as coordination between hand and eye – in catching a ball, for example – are affected adversely. Studies are continuing to attempt to distinguish more clearly between the effects of protein deficiency and stimulation deficiency. Early results suggest that both factors can have separate detrimental effects on the development of intelligence.

At the University of California M. R. Rosenzweig and D. Krech have devised experiments to investigate the effects of a lack of environmental stimulation on normally-fed rats. Rats reared with several other litter-mates in a stimulating environment – with treadwheels, ladders, swings, roundabouts, and daily changes in these toys – showed marked differences in both brain structure and behaviour compared with litter-mates who were reared in an unstimulating environment with one rat to each sound-proofed cage and no toys. The differences were that 'enriched' rats showed a significantly larger brain size with more transmitter molecules – in other words, larger and more active brains – than the 'deprived' group, and that 'enriched' rats were significantly better at solving discrimination-learning tasks than were 'deprived' rats. A stimulating environment, then, seems to help the intellectual development of rats. Hebb's daughter reared rats as household pets, and these animals performed significantly better on maze-learning tasks than litter-mates housed in normal rat cages who were not treated as pets.

Steven Rose of the Open University goes one stage further. Not only can a protein-and stimulation-deprived infancy affect a person's intellectual development, but it may also affect the intellectual development of her children and perhaps even of her grandchildren. Malnutrition in a female rat in infancy, for example, may affect her physical and behavioural development: her womb may not develop properly, and she may not develop normal patterns of rat behaviour. Even if she is well fed in later life, the conditions in her womb and her maternal behaviour may be sub-standard, so that the offspring which she rears will themselves be in a deprived environment. This *transgenerational transmission* – so called because it can affect the animal's development before birth – looks like a genetic effect but is in fact an environmental effect. Rose belives that this same process may occur in humans and can be a contributor to the apparently genetic factor in the development of intelligence.

Conversely, however, it is very difficult to pinpoint specific environmental factors which will improve intelligence, because any one environmental alteration may help the development of some intellectual abilities but hinder the development of others; also the timing of the stimulation is crucial. Any 'good' environment, therefore, may only be good if it occurs at a particular time in development. It seems that the only basic rule which can be applied is therefore something like, 'As varied and stimulating an environment as possible, as early as possible.'

Summary

1 Intelligence is not a 'thing'; it may be a whole number of different abilities, but should best be regarded as a descriptive term, used of behaviour which is appropriate to the environment.

2 Psychologists use the Intelligence Quotient (IQ) as the operational definition of intelligence; this indicates how well an individual compares with others in tests involving logical thinking.

3 It is not possible to find out whether genetics or environment is the major influence on an individual's IQ, but we can try to find out how much they cause differences in IQ between different people.

4 Twin studies are the major research tool for this, but there are severe practical difficulties in carrying them out which make their results rather unreliable.

5 Probably no universal perfect environment exists to help the development of intelligence, because it is not a single ability. Varied stimulation, as early as possible, seems the best recommendation at present.

Further Reading

Cohen, D. and Shelley, D., 'High IQ as high speed thinking', *New Scientist* (1982), vol. 95, p. 773.

Eysenck, H.J., *Race, Intelligence and Education* (1974, Temple Smith).

Flynn, J., 'Race IQ and grandparents', *New Scientist*, 5 April 1984, p. 29.

Kamin, L. J., *The Science and Politics of* IQ (1974, Halsted).

Weinreich-Haste, H., 'A multiplicity of intelligence', *New Scientist*,
7 June 1984, p. 19.

Chapter 13

The Nature/Nurture Debate on Perception

Introduction

We experience the world through our sense organs which send information to the brain in the form of nerve impulses. For most of us this experience is something that we take for granted; the brain produces a model of the world without our thinking about it – it just happens! This disguises the fact that the brain does a very complicated job of organizing and interpreting information from the sense organs, a process known as *perception*.

In the process of perception the brain has to make decisions about shape, size, distance, colour, brightness and many other factors. In this chapter, we are looking at how it is that we come to have perceptual abilities. Before we do, though, try this:

Look at Figure 13.1(a). What is it? It can be perceived in a number of ways but many would say that it is simply a jumble of black blobs. In fact it is a picture of a long-haired man with a beard, but simply being given this information is unlikely to change your perception. Now look at Figure 13.1(b) on page 216, which is a 'cleaned up' version of the picture; it is not exactly the same but when you look back at the original, you will be able to 'see' the long-haired man. (If this doesn't happen immediately, compare the two figures for a little longer.) The message from your eye hasn't changed but now the brain is interpreting it in a different way. It may be that what you first saw in the picture was something like William James's blooming, buzzing confusion (see p.163). But now, experience has enabled you to perceive it differently. Some people argue that babies perceive the world in the sort of way that you first perceived Figure 13.1(a) and that it is only through experience that the brain learns to interpret what it sees.

Figure 13.1(a)

The Nature/Nurture Debate on Perception

Like the debate on intelligence, this discussion is about the relative importance of inherited and environmental influences. (Before reading this section you should consult the general introduction to the nature/nurture problem on pp.162–4.)

The empiricist side of the debate stresses the role of experience in the development of perception; in its extreme form it maintains that only the simplest form of perception, *figure/ground* (the ability to perceive that there is 'something there' standing out from the background), is innate, and that all the rest of our perceptual abilities are learnt or are determined by the environment.

The nativist side of the debate stresses that, under normal circumstances, perceptual processes develop in an orderly manner controlled by the genetic 'blueprint'. If the baby's perception at birth is not the same as that of an adult it is largely because the perceptual system is immature and needs time to develop.

Until the 1960s many psychologists held the empiricist view that infants had very little perceptual ability. The idea was that although the eyes worked, the brain was not able to make much sense of the information it received until it had had the chance to learn from experience. As our methods of studying infants have improved we have found that their capacities are far greater than was previously thought.

Babies use gestures rather than words to communicate, so we can find out what they perceive by studying what they do.

Infants often fall down steps and it had been thought that one of the reasons for this was that they could not perceive depth. The work of E.J. Gibson and R.D. Walk in 1960 demonstrated that they can, in fact, tell that one surface is lower or further away than another. They constructed as apparatus known as the 'visual cliff' (see Figure 13.2). Towards one end of the apparatus, immediately under the glass 'floor', was stuck some black-and-white check material; towards the other, the material was placed about four feet below the glass. The effect was therefore of a visual cliff on the right-hand side of the apparatus in the Figure.

Figure 13.2 The 'Visual Cliff' (Gibson and Walk's Experiment)

Shallow side   Baby   Deep side

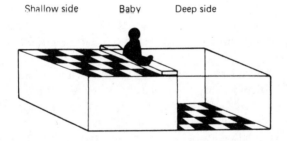

Gibson and Walk studied babies aged between six and fourteen months. They were placed on the central plank and their mothers then called them from the 'deep' or the 'shallow' side. The infants would crawl to their mothers over the 'shallow' side, but would not move over the 'deep' side. Occasionally babies would fall onto the glass over the 'deep' side; they were alright until they looked down, when they showed obvious signs of fear. It seems, then, that if infants of this age fall down steps and off chairs it is not because they do not see the depth but because they have yet to develop adequate control of their movements. This study cannot be performed until the child is old enough to crawl and so it does not tell us whether the child has developed this ability or whether depth perception is possible from birth. Other animals, such as cats, sheep and chickens can be tested a few hours after birth and all show an avoidance of the deep side.

Campos (1978) placed babies onto the visual cliff apparatus and found that infants as young as two months old showed a change of heart-rate when placed on the deep side but not when placed on the shallow side. Infants of this age could obviously perceive the depth but they showed no fear, suggesting that this fear has to be learnt by experiences of falling.

When you move your head or your eyes, objects which are close to you move quickly across your field of vision but objects that are at a distance move more slowly. This can be seen most clearly when moving in a car. A hedge at the side of the road seems to fly past but a tree two hundred yards beyond the hedge seems to drift slowly across the visual field. The brain can use this information, amongst others, to help perceive distance; if an object swings wildly across the visual field when the eyes are moved the brain assumes that it is close, if it moves more slowly it must be further away. This clue to distance is known as *motion parallax*, and Gibson and Walk suggest that this is the main way in which depth is detected by young infants.

The *visual preference method* has been used by a number of researchers to discover the quality of infant perception. Using this method babies are shown two pictures at the same time. If these two pictures are exactly the same, babies should, on average, spend the same amount of time looking at each of them; if, on the other hand, they are very different it is likely that the baby will prefer one to the other and will spend more time looking at that picture. If infant perception is poorer than ours we might find that objects which look different to us appear the same to a baby.

R. L. Fantz (1961) was one of the first people to use this method. He showed that babies between one and fifteen weeks old were able to distinguish many patterns; for example, he found that a bull's-eye pattern was preferred to stripes, checks and geometrical shapes, and that a drawing of a human face was preferred to all these patterns. Fantz suggested that babies may be innately programmed to prefer human faces to other objects, although others have argued that they simply prefer complicated patterns to simple ones and that in this study the faces were the most complicated pictures.

Fantz presented diagrammatic versions of faces like those in Figure 13.3. On average the 1–15-week-olds preferred to look at the 'normal' rather than the scrambled face. This does not definitely mean that there is an innate preference to the human face; the preference may simply develop quickly due to exposure to faces.

Figure 13.3. Face Shapes of the Type Used in Fantz's Experiment

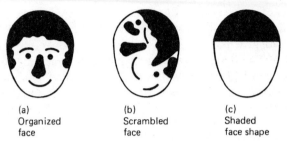

(a)
Organized
face

(b)
Scrambled
face

(c)
Shaded
face shape

More recent research has shown us that newborn babies do seem to take particular notice of human faces and can distinguish between them. Bushnell, Sai and Mullin (1989) have shown that two-day-olds show a preference for their mother's face compared to that of a stranger.

The visual preference method has shown us that before the age of six months infants cannot see fine detail. This ability to see fine detail is known as *acuity*. If you have had difficulty telling the difference between C and G in the small letters of an optician's chart you have experienced the limits of your own visual acuity. Young babies show no preference between a grey card and a card with thin black and white lines on it. The pictures that a baby experiences would seem very fuzzy to us because their acuity is between ten and thirty times poorer than ours.

Size constancy is a perceptual process which allows us to judge correctly the size of objects no matter how close or how far away they are. An elephant on the other side of a field looks big, and a ladybird on your hand looks small, yet the images of them both on the retina of the eye may actually be the same size. With increasing distance an object's image size decreases, but size constancy enables us to overcome this false information from the retina, and to realize that the elephant is not really as small as the ladybird but is just much further away. Without size constancy, objects would appear to grow or shrink as they moved toward or away from us. Some investigations by T.G. Bower in 1967 showed very young babies do in fact have the size constancy mechanism.

In Figure 13.4 the two-month-old baby is placed on the table in a comfortable cot from which he can see an object. He comes to learn that if he turns his head to one side he is rewarded by an adult playing peek-a-boo and tickling him. This is an example of Operant Conditioning (see p.70). Once the baby has been conditioned in this way he will give many head-turns when the original object is placed in front of him, but if the object is changed for something completely different he will give far fewer head-turns. The number of head-turns given to an object will tell us how similar the baby considers the new object to the original one.

Figure 13.4. General Layout of Bower's Experiment

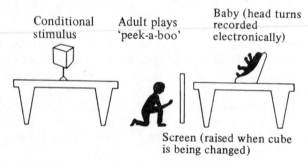

Bower conditioned babies to turn their heads when a 30 cm cube was placed one metre in front of them. He wanted to know whether the infant would recognize this cube when it was shown further away or whether they would confuse it with a 90 cm cube place three metres in front. The reason for using a 90 cm cube at three metres is that it produces an image on the retina of the eye which is exactly the same size as the image produced by the smaller cube at one metre.

If babies cannot use the size constancy mechanism, the 30 cm cube at three metres would seem like a new object and therefore stimulate few head-turns. To a baby without size constancy the 90 cm cube at three metres would look very like the original cube and would be greeted by many head-turns.

Bower showed that his babies (aged two months) did in fact use the size constancy mechanism. They were able to recognize the 30 cm cube even though it had been moved further away. They were not confused by the 90 cm cube and gave far fewer head-turns to this stimulus when it was placed at three metres. They gave a few more to the 90 cm cube at one metre, presumably because they recognized that although it was a new cube it had some similarities to the original and was placed in the same position. By far the most head-turns were given to the 30 cm cube whether it was at one or three metres.

Figure 13.5. Cubes Used in Bower's Experiment

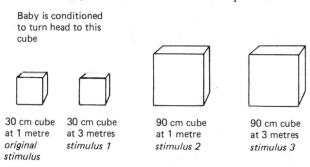

Baby is conditioned
to turn head to this
cube

30 cm cube	30 cm cube	90 cm cube	90 cm cube
at 1 metre	at 3 metres	at 1 metre	at 3 metres
original	*stimulus 1*	*stimulus 2*	*stimulus 3*
stimulus			

Although Bower showed that two-month-old infants have the size constancy mechanism, there has been much disagreement about whether the mechanism is present at birth (the nativist view) or has to develop with experience (the empiricist view).

Slater, Mattock and Brown (1990) have provided evidence for the nativist view by showing that newborn infants are able to recognize objects at different distances. They used a method known as an *habituation procedure* which relies on the fact that if an infant is shown an object for a long period of time it loses interest in it and will prefer to look at a new object. On many occasions they showed cube A to babies at a number of different distances from the child. When cube A was later shown together with a different size cube (B), the babies preferred to look at the new cube even though A and B were placed at different distances so that they both produced the same size image on the retina. If the newborns were not able to use the size constancy mechanism there would be no reason to prefer one cube to the other.

Studies of babies have shown that they have a much more well developed perceptual system than many of the early empiricists believed. William James's description of the perceptual world of an infant as a blooming buzzing confusion seems to be a great exaggeration but nevertheless we should not assume that the infant's perceptual experience of the world is the same as ours. We have the advantage of being able to use our previous experiences to relate what is in front of us now with what we have seen before. Our previous experiences help us to pick out the most relevant parts of a visual image and pay attention to them while ignoring irrelevancies. The view of an infant may therefore be far more confusing. Gordon (1989) suggested that an infant's normal perception may be very like our own during the first few seconds of waking up in a strange room: 'we see everything but nothing makes sense'.

Deprivation Studies

It would be wrong to assume that because the infant has a fairly sophisticated perceptual system, experience does not have a great influence. There is a sensitive period during the first two or three years during which children must have a variety of active visual experiences if they are not to suffer lasting perceptual damage. Most of the studies which show the effect of visual deprivation were done with animal subjects because it is not ethically acceptable to deliberately deprive children in order to see the effect. There is a widely held view, with which we have some sympathy, that it is not right to subject animals to the sort of deprivation that occurs in some of these studies no matter what the value of the findings.

In 1947 A. N. Riesen kept a group of chimpanzees in darkness from birth until they had matured, and compared them with normally reared chimpanzees. The group deprived of light showed markedly inferior perceptual abilities. L. Weiscrantz found that this was due to the fact that the retinas of the chimps reared in darkness had not developed properly and contained fewer retinal cells. Riesen's experiment shows that light is necessary to maintain the visual system or to help it mature.

Riesen then tested chimps which had been raised wearing translucent goggles, which allowed only diffused light to enter the eye. The experience of wearing translucent goggles is like looking through thick bathroom windows: light comes through but there are no clear images. Under these conditions the retina was not damaged but the chimps still had very poor perceptual abilities compared with normally reared animals. At the time of the study it was felt that this result could be used as evidence that perceptual abilities develop as a result of experience rather than being present at birth.

D. H. Hubel and T. N. Wiesel (1962) found that kittens reared in translucent goggles did not develop the normal connections between the retina of the eye and cells in the visual cortex of the brain. In normally reared animals, particular cells in the visual cortex are stimulated when a line of light pointing in a particular direction is shone onto a particular part of the retina. This area of the retina is known as the *receptive field* of the cortical cell. Some cortical cells have receptive fields which stimulate them when a vertical line is shone onto the retina; others are only stimulated by horizontal or diagonal lines. Receptive fields are very important in the perception of shape because differently shaped objects will stimulate different combinations of cells in the cortex.

In 1966 C. Blakemore and G. F. Cooper brought up cats in a 'vertical world', a drum which had only vertical lines drawn on it. The cats were therefore presented with images, but these were very specific, being vertical only. When the cats had matured their perceptual abilities were tested, and it was found that they were unable to perceive horizontal lines. Their receptive fields had developed, but only those which registered vertical lines would operate: horizontal lines had no effect on them. Suggestions were made that this result showed that that line recognition has to be learnt. But it is more likely that receptive fields capable of registering lines at all angles are present at birth but that unused fields deteriorate, or are 'taken over' by fields registering vertical lines.

Thus it seems the type of environment is important in the development of perception: this in turn suggests that learning plays at least some part in perception, and that it is not all innate. However, visual experience alone is not enough. R. Held and A. Hein (1963), for example, showed that for perceptual development to take place fully the tested subject must be allowed to use its eyes and also to manipulate, or at least move around in its environment. In Figure 13.6 both kittens, A and B, are given exactly the same amount and type of visual experience. Kitten A's movements are transmitted via a system of pulleys to kitten B's basket so that any movements made by kitten A are transmitted automatically to kitten B. Both kittens have exactly the same amount of movement in their environment, the only difference being that kitten A's movements are active (it moves itself) and kitten B's are passive (it does not control its movement).

Figure 13.6. The apparatus used by Held and Hein.

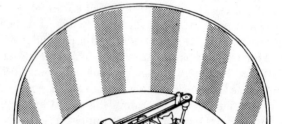

The passive kitten showed much less perceptual development than the active kitten, which suggests that activity in, or interaction with, the environment is necessary for full perceptual development.

Although it is not possible to conduct experiments which deliberately cause deprivation to humans, there are examples of people who have suffered deprivation through illness or accident and the effect of this on later perception can be seen. One of the best known studies of this type is that described by R. L. Gregory in 1963. In this case a 54-year-old man who had been blind since birth was given his sight as a result of the development of a new surgical technique to remove cataracts from the eye. At first the patient could only experience the figure/ground phenomenon: he was aware of objects standing out against a background but was unable to recognize them by sight alone. When allowed to handle objects he found it much easier to see them. This ability to use information from one sense to assist a different sense is known as *cross-modal transfer*. After a fairly short period of time the patient was generally able to overcome the initial problems and to perceive fairly normally.

The results of this type of case study were at one time taken as evidence that perception had to be learnt. But now that we are more aware of the visual abilities of young babies it seems safer to assume that the visual perceptual abilities of these patients had declined due to lack of use.

Children who are born with bad squints are deprived of the normal input to the brain from both eyes working together, and as a result can lose their ability to focus using both eyes and may have impaired depth perception. Studies show that damage is much more likely if the squint is not treated early. In the past it was thought best to delay treatment until the child was older and more ready to withstand the rigours of surgery, but now the operation is performed much earlier.

Distortion or Readjustment Studies

The aim of this type of study is to show that adult perceptual systems are not inflexible and can adjust to a new visual environment. If this can be shown in adults then it is likely that the newborn babies also possess such a flexible perceptual system which is shaped by learning rather than one which is inflexible and innately determined.

Lower animals – lizards, frogs and chickens for example – do not appear able to adjust to a distorted visual world. Chickens wearing goggles that distort their vision by 10 degrees to the right never adapt enough to compensate for the distortion and miss the grain at which they are pecking by 10 degrees each time (E. H. Hess, 1956).

However, studies of adult humans wearing distorting goggles have shown that humans have a much greater ability to adapt to a changed visual world. Ivo Kohler wore goggles in which the left half of each lens was red and the right half green. At first his visual world appeared red when he looked at the left and green when he looked to the right. After only a few hours this apparent division was no longer experienced: he had evidently adjusted to compensate for the change. However, when he removed the goggles, Kohler found that his visual world seemed to be coloured in the opposite direction to that experienced when first wearing goggles, but only for a short time, after which it returned to normal. Once more he had been able to adjust. Kohler also experimented on himself and others using goggles which inverted or displaced objects in their visual world. At first he experienced great disorientation and nausea, but after several days he was able to adjust and live reasonably normally.

G. M. Stratton performed similar experiments on himself using inverting goggles. After a few days' adaptation he was able to move around normally and his visual world appeared to be the right way up except when he really concentrated. On removal of the goggles there was again a reversed after-effect, which lasted only a short time.

Such evidence from readjustment studies shows that human perceptual systems retain a flexibility and an ability to alter in the light of experience even in adulthood. The perceptual system is certainly not inflexible, as some of the early nativists believed.

Cross-Cultural Studies

Cross-cultural studies demonstrate the effects of different life experiences on some aspects of perception. Many studies show that people from different cultures are affected differently by illusions such as the *Muller-Lyer illusion*. To most of us the horizontal line at the bottom of Figure 13.7 looks longer than the one above it, even though in fact the horizontal lines are the same length. Segall, Campbell and Herskovits (1963) found that members of African tribes living in jungle conditions were much less susceptible to this illusion and tended to see the lines as the same length.

Figure 13.7. The Muller-Lyer Illusion

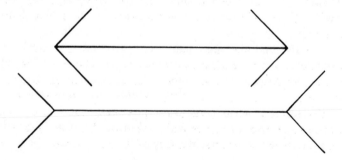

There have been numerous explanations put forward for the differences in the susceptibility to illusions, but it is probably due to the extent to which people are accustomed to interpreting two-dimensional drawings and pictures (a skill which we take for granted in our world which is so full of photographs).

Some studies have shown that size constancy (see page 181) is not used for far objects by people whose normal experience does not include distant views. Turnbull (1961) reported an experience with a pygmy from the rain forests of the African Congo. He took the pygmy to an open plain and pointed out a buffalo in the distance; the pygmy refused to believe that this was a large animal, arguing that it looked like an insect. Only when Turbull drove the pygmy over to the animal did he believe that it actually was large. The pygmy's perceptual system had not applied size constancy to the small image on the retina of his eye to take account of the fact that the animal was far away. This is probably because the pygmy had no experience of seeing great distances and so his perceptual system had not learned to recognize the clues to distance contained in the view; with no recognition of distance the size constancy mechanism will not be used.

Conclusions

The research on the nature/nurture debate on perception has shown us that animals which are low on the evolutionary scale have very inflexible perceptual systems which are preset from birth. For example, certain species of frogs have genetically-determined perceptual systems which, without any need for learning, make them very sensitive to small dark images which move quickly. When the frog detects such a stimulus it automatically extends its tongue and is therefore very efficient at catching flies. If such a frog were surrounded by dead flies it would starve to death because its innate, inflexible perceptual system is not sensitive to still flies, only to moving ones.

As we move up the animal kingdom, perceptual systems become more flexible and able to learn from experience. The human newborn has a perceptual system which, although it cannot detect fine detail, has a fair level of competence in skills such as shape, size and depth perception. These develop as the nervous system matures and becomes capable of more detailed processing. We now believe that infants are able to recognize the face of their mother at a very early age, although, it is likely that this is as a result of much less detailed analysis of facial features than that performed by an adult.

The development of the perceptual system requires a variety of stimulation and active participation of the individual with their environment, and it looks as though there is a period during the first two or three years when the developing perceptual system is most sensitive to those experiences.

The studies that we have discussed show that it is not sensible to take an extreme nativist or empiricist position on the nature/nurture debate. Perception develops as an interaction between innate and environmental factors.

Summary

1 Perception is the process by which the brain organizes and interprets information from the sense organs. In this chapter we have concentrated on visual perception which involves the interpretation of information from the eyes to determine qualities such as shape, size, colour and distance.

2 Nativists stress the importance of genetic factors in the development of perception and tend to regard the perceptual system as fairly fixed and unalterable. Empiricists stress that it is much more flexible and is altered as a result of experience. The debate between people holding these two viewpoints is known as the nature/nurture debate.

3 Studies of babies' perceptual abilities demonstrate that although the 'picture in their head' is fuzzy they are able to make judgements on shape, size and distance amongst other things.

4 Deprivation studies, in which an individual is reared without being allowed to practise normal perception, suggest that the environment does play an important part in the development of perception. Deprivation may lead to a degeneration of existing perceptual systems, especially if it occurs early in life. To develop normally an individual must have an active involvement with a variety of visual stimuli.

5 Distortion studies, which show that an adult can readjust and learn to perceive the world accurately again after his vision has been distorted, demonstrate the flexibility of the perceptual system.

6 Cross-cultural studies reveal that individuals from different cultures have differences in their perceptual abilities.

7 The range of studies considered suggests that innate and environ-

mental factors interact to produce a well-functioning mature perceptual system.

Further reading

Bower, T.G.R., *The Perceptual World of the Child* (1977, Fontana/Open Books).

Gordon, I.E., *Theories of Visual Perception* (1989, New York: Wiley).

Gregory, R.L., *Eye and Brain* (4th edn, 1990, Weidenfeld and Nicolson).

Gregory, R.L., *The Intelligent Eye* (1970, Weidenfeld and Nicolson).

Chapter 14

Psychology Practicals

Psychology is a practical subject. You will have noticed in previous chapters that we do not simply sit in our armchairs and *think* about how children behave; we go out and test our theories either in the laboratory or in the real world.

Psychology practicals can take many forms. In some cases we simply *observe* behaviour in its normal setting. For example you might want to know whether there is any difference between boys and girls in the types of games they play. This could be done simply by watching a variety of different playgrounds and recording which games were being played by each sex. It would probably be better if the children didn't know that you were watching and recording because if they knew this they might 'behave properly' or 'show off' and not behave normally. The way in which people change their behaviour when they know that they are being observed is known as the *Hawthorne Effect*, and many observational studies are done without the subject's knowledge in order to avoid this.

Another way in which we could study sex differences and games would be to *interview* boys and girls and ask them questions about how often they played certain games. We could even write these questions down in the form of a *questionnaire* and let children fill it in themselves. One major problem with these techniques is that we can't be sure that children (or adults) will tell us the truth; they may forget or they might not want to admit that they play some sorts of games. The interview/questionnaire techniques can often, however, be very useful, especially since they tell us about how people feel about things as well as what they actually do.

Lots of people talk about *experiments* and *practicals* as if they were the same things. But it is important to realize that the term 'experiment' has a specific technical meaning and that many practicals such as Observational Studies or Interviews are not experiments.

The Experimental Method

In observational studies all you do is *look* at what is going on. The experimental method, however, involves changing things to see what happens. You start off with an idea about what might happen if the subjects did one thing rather than another. This is known as an *hypothesis*. For example you might put forward the hypothesis that children would drink more orange juice if they were in a hot room than if they were in a cold room. To test this hypothesis experimentally you would simply put some children into a hot room and other (similar) children into the same room when it was cold. Both groups would be supplied with as much orange juice as they desired and you would measure how much was drunk.

The thing that you change in an experiment (the temperature of the room in this one) is known as the *independent variable* and we note the effect of this change by measuring the *dependent variable* (how much orange juice was drunk). Of course, there are lots of other things that might affect the amount of juice that was drunk and we would have to make sure that these did not upset the experiment. It would be silly to allow one group to have crisps if the other group only had the orange juice, or to have some subjects who had just been playing football and another who had been sitting down in a classroom. These other variables are known as *extraneous variables* and we try to *control* them so that they have the same effect in both conditions.

The great advantage of the experiment is that it is the only method that directly studies cause and effect.

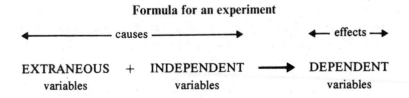

Formula for an experiment

←————— causes —————→   ← effects →

EXTRANEOUS   +   INDEPENDENT   ⟶   DEPENDENT
variables   variables   variables

All experiments can be fitted into this 'formula'. In an experiment to test the hypothesis that there is a difference in the speed that people react to visual and auditory stimuli the independent variable would be whether the stimulus was a sound or a light, the dependent variable would be the time taken to respond to these stimuli. In an experiment to test the effect of a drug on memory the amount of drug received by the child would be the independent variable and the dependent variable would be some measure of memory.

Examples of extraneous variables and their control. In the auditory and visual reaction-time experiment above, you would probably decide to use the same people in both conditions: if you used different people in each condition any difference in the results might simply be due to ability differences between these two groups of people rather than anything to do with the difficulties of the two types of task. Using the same people to react to both visual and auditory stimuli, however, introduces another set of extraneous variables; these are called *order effects*. If all people responded to the auditory stimulus first, then it could be argued that any difference in the results of the two conditions were due to practice (if visual reaction time was best) or fatigue (if auditory reaction time was best). This would be a confounding nuisance when it came to interpreting the results of the experiment; uncontrolled extraneous variables are called *confounding variables*. Order effects can usually be controlled by *counterbalancing*, which involves half the people doing condition A first and the other half doing condition B first. You will notice that this does not get rid of order effects, it simply makes sure that they have the same effect on each condition.

There are some extraneous variables that can be simply *eliminated*. These are such things as noise or distractions, and we simply get rid of them.

We can't get rid of other variables such as sex or time of day, but we can make sure that these don't effect the difference in the results of the two conditions by making sure that they are the same for both. If all the children in one condition are boys then all those in the other condition should also be boys (unless of course you are studying the difference between boys and girls). This method of control is known as *matching* or *constancy*.

When we put some people into one condition and the rest into the other it is important that the two groups are as similar as possible. The most usual way to do this is by *random allocation* which can be done by putting the people's names into a hat and picking them out at random to see who goes into each condition. In this way there should be no bias built in to the groups; other techniques such as asking all the children who sit in the front of the class to be in condition A and the rest in condition B have the disadvantage that the sort of people who choose to sit at the front may be different from those who sit at the back. If the experimenter makes the choice himself all sorts of things might affect the choice and so it is best to rely on random allocation.

In all experiments people should, as far as possible, be treated the same way in each condition and care should be taken to avoid such things as competition between people or letting them know how you expect the experiment to turn out, unless of course this is what you are investigating.

It is impossible to control all extraneous variables but we must design our experiments to avoid any constant difference between the conditions other than the independent variable. Some variables change in a random manner; these are chance factors and cannot be controlled because we can't predict them. Chance variables make life interesting and are the basis of gambling but they are a pain in the neck for experimenters. It is these uncontrollable factors that produce the need for *statistical tests* which are used to make an estimate of how likely it was that any difference between the results of the experimental conditions was due to chance.

A survey of the statistical tests that are available to researchers is beyond the scope of this book. Any reader who would like to know more about statistical tests should read *Starting Statistics* (see the end of the chapter for a full reference).

EXTRANEOUS VARIABLES		INDEPENDENT VARIABLES		DEPENDENT VARIABLES
	+		⟶	
		Condition A		Result A*
		Condition B		Result B*

* The difference here is due to the difference in the variables on the left. If *extraneous* variables were controlled to prevent *confounding* variables, then the difference in the results of the two conditions is due to the *independent variable* or to *chance*.

Experimental Design

Sometimes we use the same people in both conditions of an experiment; at other times this is not possible. Experimental design refers to the way that we use people either in one or both of the experimental conditions.

(a) *Repeated measures design*. In this design, each person performs in both the control and the experimental condition (i.e. in both condition A and condition B).

(b) *Independent subjects design*. In this design, some people perform in condition A and others in condition B. (Note that psychologists often use the term *subject* to refer to a person who is taking part in an experiment.)

(c) *Matched pairs design*. From the results of a pre-test, the subjects are sorted into matched pairs (pairs of equal abilities on the task to be measured). One from each pair performs in condition A and one in condition B.

Table 14.1. *An example of Allocation of Children to Conditions in Repeated Measures and Independent Subjects Designs*

| (a) Repeated Measures | | (b) Independent Subjects | |
Condition A	Condition B	Condition A	Condition B
Tim	Tim	Tim	Ben
Matthew	Matthew	Matthew	Sally
Carol	Carol	Carol	Isabelle
Tom	Tom	Tom	George
Laura	Laura	Laura	Jenny

Advantages and Disadvantages of the Designs

(1) As you can see, you need twice as many people for an independent subjects design.

(2) Since the same people are tested in conditions A and B in the repeated measures design, this method automatically ensures that there are no personality or ability differences between the two groups.

(3) In some experiments, performance in one condition changes the subject in such a way that they could not reasonably be included in the other. This is often the case in learning experiments. For

example, it would not be possible to use repeated measures design to investigate different methods of learning to drive a car.

(4) Matched pairs design controls for personality and ability differences between conditons by the method of constancy (see page 194), and can be used in situations where repeated measures design is not possible.

(5) The choice of characteristics to match in matched pairs design is a subjective decision and pre-testing can take a long time. Independent subjects design is more commonly used in situations where repeated measures is not appropriate.

Populations and Samples

Before you perform an experiment you should decide which *population* you want your results to apply to; you might want them to apply to all humans (good luck!), or just to males or females, to students or to children under the age of seven, etc. It is usually impossible to study the whole of a population, so you must choose a smaller group of subjects from within the population. This is known as a *sample*. If you decided that you wanted to study students at a college it might be tempting to simply ask the people that you know to take part in the experiment. This might not be a good idea because they are a special group within the population of college students and might be different from students in general. You must choose a *representative sample*, i.e. a sample which has the same characteristics as the population. Remember that if you take an unrepresentative sample of the population you might not be able to generalize your results.

There are two main types of methods by which you can achieve a representative sample. These are *random* and *quota sampling*.

Random sampling. For this method a sample is drawn in such a way that every member of the population has an equal chance of being selected, for instance the use of a pin stuck at random into a list of names or drawing names out of a hat. This should produce a representative sample.

Quota sampling. For this method the population is analysed by picking out those chracteristics which are considered important as far as the research is concerned. Individuals are then systematically chosen so that the sample has these same characteristics. The system will produce a representative sample as long as the right characteristics were chosen in the first place.

In practice you may be limited when choosing your subjects to children from a particular school or those that live near to you. Try to avoid personal bias in choosing who you will ask to become involved in your experiment and use a random sampling technique if possible. If you can only study your brothers and sisters don't let this put you off, you might still find something interesting, but do be aware that these subjects are not representative of children in general and point this out in any report of your practical. (You might also find that your brothers and sisters will react differently with you than they would with another experimenter.)

Cross-Sectional, Longitudinal and Cross-Cultural Studies

If you wanted to study a question like: 'does watching TV alter children's behaviour?', how could you do it? Firstly, you'd need to find some way of measuring the amounts and types of TV which children watched, and secondly, you'd have to find some way of measuring children's behaviour. But which children would you study, and over how long a period would you study them?

You might decide to study a group of 5-year-olds, a group of 6-year-olds, 7-year-olds and so on, for as many ages as you wished. If you obtained a *representative sample* of each age-group, the results of your study of each age could be applied to all children of that age; that is, you would be able to say how TV affects the behaviour of all children aged 5, 6, or 7. This is known as the *cross-sectional method*. It is a fairly quick method to use (you could carry out your study in a few days only) – but it does have one main disadvantage. Suppose you found that 7-year-olds' behaviour was much more affected by TV than 5-year-olds. Does this means that TV really does have more effect on 7-year-olds.' Possibly, but it could mean that there was something in the 7-year-olds' upbringing which makes them respond more to TV, and that 'something' was missing from the 5-year-olds' upbringing. Using cross-sectional studies, you cannot be sure that your various age-groups have had the same upbringing; what may be true for your 7-year-olds now, may not be true of today's 5-year-olds when they become 7.

Longitudinal studies are a way of overcoming this problem. Instead of studying groups of children of each age-group, you could test a group of 5-year-olds, and then retest them when they were 6, again at 7, and so on. (A Granada TV series called '7 up' used this method. A group of 7-year-olds were studied, and they were studied again at ages 14, 21 and 28.) This method has the advantage that you can see how children are affected by TV over a period of time, so you can see how changes both in a child's age and in its environment affect its behaviour.

There is a big drawback to longitudinal studies, however – if you were studying children from 5 until they were 20 years old, your study would take 15 years to complete, and you may well lose touch with some of your subjects over that length of time. What started out as a representative sample of subjects aged 5 may be very far from representative when they reach the age of 20.

Whether you use the cross-sectional or the longitudinal method of study, you would probably be studying British children, so your results could only be applied to British children, not to children from different cultures or countries. The cross-cultural method of study allows you to see if children from different countries or cultures behave differently from British children. So, in your TV study, you could find out whether children in Britain are affected as much by TV as children in the USA, or Greece, or wherever, by testing samples of children in each country. Cross-cultural methods tend to be expensive (you have to travel a lot), and they suffer from one other disadvantage: suppose you had studied a group of British children and were comparing them with a group of children from country X. If you found that children from country X became more aggressive after watching TV than the British children did, can you be sure that children from country X respond differently to TV than do British children? Unfortunately not – it may be that country X's TV allows more aggression than does British TV; or it may be that parents in country X are more prepared than British parents to allow their children to be aggressive. Cross-cultural studies are also really just cross-sectional studies of different countries, so they suffer from the deficiencies of cross-sectional studies, too.

Experiments – A General Planning Sequence

(1) Decide what you want your experiment to find out. This means producing a hypothesis which can be tested to see if it is likely to be true; for example: 'A group of subjects asked to recognize words from a list previously learnt will remember more than subjects asked to recall the words.' When you have done the experiment you can either accept this hypothesis (if they did recognize more words than were recalled) or reject it.

(2) Decide which population you want your results to apply to and how you will obtain a representative sample.

(3) Design the experiment. This involves making decisions about whether the subjects will perform in both conditions (repeated measures design) or whether half of them will be in one condition and the other half in the other condition (independent subjects). Also think about possible extraneous variables and design the experiment to control them using methods such as elimination, matching, counterbalancing and randomization.

(4) Write down your instructions to subjects so that you give the instruction in the same way to each subject. Make sure you know exactly how you are to record the subjects' responses. If there is more than one experimenter, check that you all agree everything you are going to do.

(5) Always perform a pilot study. This means doing the practical with a small group of people before going ahead with the full-scale study. The pilot study often shows up weaknesses in things like instructions to subjects or difficulties in measurement. These should be sorted out before continuing with the real thing.

(6) Collect your subjects together. Act in as professional a way as possible. If you take the experiment seriously your subjects will.

(7) Perform the experiment.

(8) Debrief your subjects. Thank them for their involvement in the study and give them a brief explanation of what you were doing. If you are going to get some more subjects later it might be wise to ask this group not to discuss the experiment with anybody else. Assure your subjects that they will not be named in any report that is written.

Some experiments involve deception and can embarrass subjects. Under these conditions the debriefing sessions are most important to reassure the subjects that they are not abnormal and that their embarrassment will not be made public. We suggest that you avoid this type of experiment.

(9) Organize your results into a form which makes them clear (see pages 206–15) and decide what they mean. Do they support the original hypothesis or not? Remember that it is possible that the difference in the results of the two conditions is due to chance; this is especially so if the difference is small. If other people in your group have done the same experiment and got the same answer it makes it less likely that it was a chance result, but the best way of finding out is by performing one of the statistical tests to be found in *Starting Statistics*.

(10) You must now decide how your findings relate to other comparable psychological studies. If you are performing a replication of a previous study, the comparison of findings is relatively straight-forward. Even most non-replication studies are highly likely to have similarities with other studies.

If your results are substantially different from other studies you will need to offer explanations for this; consider the following:

(a) was your subject sample biased/unrepresentative/too small?
(b) were your instructions standardized? were they the same or similar to those used by previous researchers?
(c) did you use different measurements of the dependent variable?
(d) did you use the same type of experimental design?
(e) be honest! were there flaws in the design or in the way the study was carried out?

If none of the above checklist gives you an idea for the discrepancy between your results and other published work, *always consider the possibility that you may be right and they might be wrong!*

(11) Write up your report.

Observational Methods

There are many situations where behaviour is very complicated and cannot be simplified enough to fit into an experiment. In addition, when researchers are starting to look at a type of behaviour not previously studied, observational studies must first be made before any hypothesis about the causes of such behaviour can be tested.

A major problem with observational studies is the lack of time which an observer has in making a record of his/her observations. If the observer also has to record the type of behaviour seen, so much time has to be spent in writing that observations may be missed altogether. To overcome this problem, *behavioural categories* can be developed. Before the study begins the observer decides what types of behaviour are to be recorded and then draws up a table of categories which can simply be ticked when the particular behaviour occurs. Operational definitions of behaviour must be devised so that the observer has clear criteria for what constitutes a particular category of behaviour.

For example, if you were conducting an observational study of the behaviour of boys and girls on zebra crossings, you would need an operational definition of what constitutes 'correct' use of the crossing. If, for example, a child walks across the road one metre to the side of the crossing, have they used the crossing correctly? You would need to define exactly what constitutes 'correct' and 'incorrect' methods of crossing, and agree this in advance so that all observers record the behaviour in the same way.

Figure 14.1 Operational Definitions of Correct and Incorrect Crossings

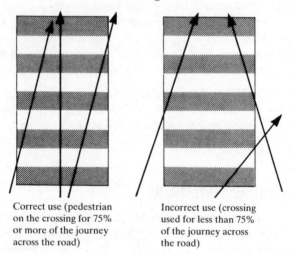

Correct use (pedestrian on the crossing for 75% or more of the journey across the road)

Incorrect use (crossing used for less than 75% of the journey across the road)

Once the definitions are agreed, observers simply use ticks on a tally record to show how many boys and girls used the crossing correctly and how many used it incorrectly. For example:

Boy correct	~~HHH~~ IIII	(9)
Boy incorrect	~~HHH~~ ~~HHH~~ ~~HHH~~ ~~HHH~~ III	(23)
Girl correct	~~HHH~~ ~~HHH~~ ~~HHH~~ ~~HHH~~ ~~HHH~~ ~~HHH~~ I	(31)
Girl incorrect	~~HHH~~ II	(7)

When devising categories make sure that they are meaningful and not so large that they ignore important differences in behaviour or so small and numerous that they are impossible to use.

The Sociogram is another useful way of recording interactions between children (see page 151).

Observational Studies – a General Planning Sequence

(1) Having decided the behaviour(s) to be observed, draw up a checklist for observers in order to make the recording of the behaviour easier and more reliable. The most common type of checklist is one which uses behaviour categories (see above).

(2) Make sure that all your observers are using the checklist in the same way. Get them all to watch the same event and record it on their checklists. If they do not all agree, discuss any differences and get them to agree what should have been recorded. Then watch and record another event. Repeat this until all your observers agree. When they all agree, you have established *inter-observer reliability*.

(3) Estimate the minimum observation time needed for accurate recordings of the behaviour. This will vary according to the complexity and frequency of the behaviour, but as a general guide you should spend a minimum of two hours on your observations.

(4) Time Sampling. You may not have time to observe behaviour for 24 hours each day – or the behaviour you wish to observe may only occur at a particular time each day. Often therefore you can only make observations of samples of behaviour. Two main methods are used to obtain representative samples of behaviour:

(a) The length of time over which the behaviour occurs is divided into 'time units', usually of a few minutes each. You then decide what proportion of the total time units you wish to observe and select the required number at random. For example, if the total time of 240 mintues were made up of 40 time units of 6 minutes each and you decided that you wanted to sample 30 per cent of the total time, you would need to choose 30 per cent of 40 = 12 time units at random, to observe.

(b) As an alternative, you could record observations every (say) three, or five or ten minute throughout an hour, and choose a different hour each day.

(5) As with experimental designs, it is often very useful to conduct a small-scale pilot study first, in order to sort out any 'bugs' in your techniques.

Probably the major advantage of observation studies over experimental methods is that you can observe children performing naturally in their normal environments (when observations are made in the children's normal environment it is often known as *naturalistic observation*). Do remember, however, that experiments can be carried out in the 'normal environment' rather than in the laboratory though it is more difficult to control extraneous variables (experiments performed in this way are often called *field experiments*).

Asking Questions

If you want to ask children questions about their thoughts, feelings or behaviour, rather than observe or experiment, the same guidelines apply regarding the sample you choose and your professional approach.

Make sure any questions are clearly phrased, unambiguous and encourage the children to answer truthfully. Closed-ended questions which simply require a choice of predetermined answers such as Yes or No are easy to record and quantify but may not give as much information as more open-ended questions which allows the child to expand on their answers. The interpretation of answers to open-ended questions may be difficult and can be affected by your own biases. If you decide to use Yes/No or other multiple-choice-type questions, it might be useful to do a preliminary investigation using open-ended questions to help you to decide how to phrase the closed-ended question and which possible responses should be included in the multiple choices.

If you are going to ask lots of questions, try to avoid building in a response bias which might cause incorrect answers from a careless child. Response biases can occur when a series of questions have all been answered in the same way. For example, a series of questions such as 'Have you suffered from smallpox?' and 'Have you ever mugged an old lady?' would all be answered 'No' by most people. If this series is immediately followed by a question such as 'Do you eat sweets' many sweet eaters, especially those in a rush to finish, will answer 'No' to this question as well. Careful preparation of the list of questions can avoid the build-up of these habitual responses.

Is It Right? The Question of Ethics

There are often costs to subjects who take part in our research. Unless we are simply observing them going about their everyday activities the subjects have to give some of their own time in our study, they may have to put effort into learning something, they may risk making a fool of themselves, in some studies they may find out things about themselves that they would rather not know; all these are examples of costs to the people that we study.

On the other hand our studies, hopefully, have benefits such as an addition to existing knowledge about behaviour. This knowledge may at some stage prove useful in the treatment of behaviour disorders or might lead to better advice on how to bring up children.

The question of ethics is a question of balancing the benefits to be gained from a piece of research against the costs to the individuals that we study. In general if the costs are great then we would have to be fairly certain of great benefits before we would go ahead with the research, and even then we would hestitate. Most researchers think that their own work is of great importance. So if there is likely to be be any great cost to the people that we are studying it is important that the work is discussed with impartial experts in the subject area who are more able to make a fair decision because they are not personally involved in the research.

People vary greatly in the extent to which they regard a study as questionable on ethical grounds, and so professional bodies lay down guidelines to help people make decisions about whether or not a study should be carried out in the way that it has been planned by the researcher of whether it should be altered to protect the interests of the individuals under study. The British Psychological Society (BPS) has produced such guidelines for human research, and some of these are summarised below:

Always consider the effects of your research on the individuals that you are studying.

Whenever possible, the people being studied (subjects) should be told why you are doing the research and should later be informed of your results.

Do not deceive your subjects unless it would be impossible to conduct the research in any other way. If deception does occur your should inform your subjects as soon as possible after the study and let them know that they have the option of withholding their own results and preventing you from using them.

If your research involves deception, psychological or physical stress or invades privacy, you must get the opinion of an independent expert before you go ahead with your study.

Make sure that your subjects are aware that they can withdraw from the study if they want to.

Keep information gained about individuals confidential. Do not publish subjects' names.

When studying children get permission from parents or from people *in loco parentis* (e.g. teachers).

Presenting Your Results

When you have done a practical you may end up with masses of numbers; every subject will have at least one score, often more. These results may appear confusing to you, so imagine what they would be like to the person who is simply reading your report. Your job is to summarize the results in a clear and understandable fashion. In this section we will show a number of ways in which this can be done.

Table of Results

Draw up a table showing each subject's score. If individual subjects have only one score this is easy, but if they all have a few scores it is best to put an 'average' score for the subject in each condition.

Make sure that the table is clearly labelled so that a reader can immediately see what it is about. If the numbers refer to seconds or minutes or some other unit of measurement, say what it is rather than leaving the reader to guess. Table 14.2 shows one way of presenting a table of results.

Table 14.2. To Show the Results of an Experiment to Test the Hypothesis that Subjects will take Longer to Climb a Set of Stairs after Drinking Three Pints of Beer than when Completely Sober

Subject	Time taken to climb the stairs when sober (in seconds)	Time taken to climb the stairs after drinking (in seconds)
1	30	35
2	32	34
3	35	37
4	29	29
5	27	30
6	33	38
7	40	49
8	42	43

When presented on its own like this the reader has to inspect the table very closely to see which condition was fastest, and so it is important to give some sort of summary statistic that gives an overall idea of what happened in each condition. An 'average' for each condition would do this.

'AVERAGES'

Work out the average of the following numbers:

2, 2, 3, 5, 8

You probably came up with an answer of 4 by adding up all the numbers and dividing by the number of numbers. This average is the *mean* average, but the average for the above figures could also be 2 or 3. That really does sound like juggling the figures! The problem with the term 'average' is that it includes a number of different sorts of measures; as well as the mean it includes the *mode* (the most common number) and the *median* (the number in the middle when the group of scores are placed in ascending order).

Mean. The arithmetic average. (Add up all scores and divide by the number of scores.)

$$\text{e.g.} \quad 5, 7, 4, 8, 6 \quad \text{MEAN} = 30/5 = 6$$

Median. The middle score of a group of scores. This value has as many scores above as below it. Place the scores in order of size and find the middle number.

$$\text{e.g.} \quad 3, 5, 6, \underline{7}, 9, 11, 13 \quad \text{MEDIAN} = 7$$

$$2, 2, 3, -, 4, 7, 8 \quad \text{MEDIAN lies between 3 and 4} = 3.5$$

Mode. The score which occurs most frequently.

$$\text{e.g.} \quad 2, 3, 3, 4, 6, 7, 2, 3, 3 \quad \text{MODE} = 3$$

$$4, 7, 6, 3, 4, 9, 4, 4, 1 \quad \text{MODE} = 4$$

Sometimes the mean, median and mode of a group of scores are exactly the same, but this is not always the case so you should say which one you are using. The most common one is the mean, but there may be times when you decide you want to use one of the others. It is largely up to you to decide but the following points may affect your decision.

ADVANTAGES (+) AND DISADVANTAGES (−) OF MEAN, MEDIAN AND MODE

Mean
(+) Takes into account the total and the individual values of all scores.
(−) Laborious to calculate for a large number of scores.

(−) Less representative than the median when the group of scores contains a few cases that are markedly higher or lower than the rest.

e.g.   2, 3, 4, 5, 6, 7, 57   MEAN = 12   MEDIAN = 5

(Note: without the 'different' score of 57 the mean would be only 4.5.)

Median
(+) More representative than the mean when there are a few scores which are markedly higher or lower than the rest.
(+) Usually easier to calculate than the mean
(−) It extracts less information than the mean since it does not use the precise numerical values of the scores.

Mode
(+) Easy to find.
(−) Very crude, especially if there is not much difference in the frequencies of the scores.

THE RANGE
A mean, median or mode gives a one-figure summary of a set of scores, making it much easier to make comparisons between the results of different conditions. It can, however, be useful to have information about the *spread* of scores.

These two sets of scores have the same mean:

21, 30, 45, 50, 60, 70, 85, 95   MEAN = 57

54, 55, 56, 57, 57, 58, 59, 60   MEAN = 57

Although these two groups of scores have the same mean, you can see that the first group is more widely spread out (dispersed) than the second. The mean cannot show the difference between these groups of scores. Some measure is needed to describe the variation in the data. There are a number of measures which do this but we shall limit ourselves to the simplest which is known as the *range* (others are discussed in *Starting Statistics* – see full reference at the end of the chapter).

The *range* of a group of scores is the difference between the lowest number and the highest.

21, 30, 45, 50, 60, 70, 85, 95   MEAN = 57   RANGE = 74

54, 55, 56, 57, 57, 58, 59, 60   MEAN = 57   RANGE = 6

When given the range the reader can immediately get an idea of the variation in the scores.

Problem with the range. Since it only takes into account the two extreme scores it cannot give a good description of a group which has an odd score which is markedly higher or lower than the rest. For example the following scores have a range of 71, which is not very representative of the group as a whole.

2, 4, 4, 5, 7, 9, 10, 73

Make sure that you don't use the range when the scores are arranged like this.

Graphs and Charts

As with tables of results the important thing is that these are clear and easily understood. Always label the axes and give an explanatory title.

If we were to draw a graph showing the relationship between the time of day and the temperature, the temperature would go on the vertical axis. The temperature is called a *dependent variable* because its value depends on what time of day it is. If it is possible to identify a dependent variable when drawing a graph, it is customary to put it on the vertical axis.

Don't use line graphs in situations where other visual forms are most appropriate. A common mistake that we have seen students make is to present the scores of individual subjects as a line graph. But as you can see in Figure 14.2, the shape of the graph simply depends on which order you decide for the individuals. If you want to present this data visually, try using a bar chart which shows the individual score without linking it to its neighbour.

Frequency Distribution Curves

It is often useful to plot a graph which shows how frequently particular scores occur in your results.

For example, if you wanted to show how intelligence is distributed in the population at large, you would choose a lot of people at

Figure 14.2

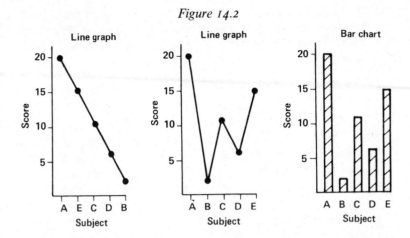

random and ask them to do an IQ test. You would probably present your results in the form of a *frequency distribution* graph. Since the subjects were chosen at random and there are many chance factors which may increase or decrease an individual's IQ, the graph you obtain would probably look like this:

Figure 14.3

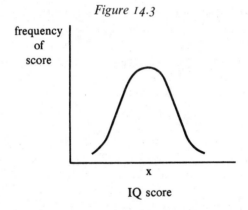

Mean, Median and *Mode* all have the same value (at point *x*).

A graph which looks like this is called a *normal distribution*. It has the following three properties:

(1) Mean, median and mode occur at the same value.
(2) It is bell-shaped and has the same shape either side of the mean.

(3) The curve falls away relatively slowly at first on either side of the mean (i.e. many scores occur a little above or below the mean). Fewer and fewer scores are found with increasing distance from the mean.

A normal distribution is found when the following criteria are met:

(a) The data is continuous (like measures of height and weight which can vary by small amounts all the way along a scale rather than separate or discrete measures like male/female or pass/fail in an exam where a person falls into one category or another).
(b) Each score is the result of a number of randomly distributed effects, some of which tend to increase the score whilst others decrease it (e.g. your height is the result of a combination of many genes passed on from your parents, some of which tend to increase it, some to decrease it, and environmental variables such as the amount and type of food you eat which may also increase or decrease height).
(c) There are a large number of scores drawn randomly from the population.

Normal distributions are not always found when frequency graphs are plotted. The *skewed distribution* takes two forms – the median may have a higher or lower value than the mode: see Figure 14.4.

The characteristic of skewed distribution is that the mean, median and mode have different values.

A skewed distribution is found when:

(a) a small number of scores are taken.
(b) a biased sample is taken of a population that may be normally distributed. For example, plot the frequencies of the heights of males in the room in which you are sitting. Plot the distribution of University students' IQs.
(c) one end of the measuring scale has an attainable cut-off point. For example, with reaction time (the time taken to react to a stimulus), there is no definite cut-off point for slow times since people can take as long as they like, but at the fast end of the scale it is not possible to better O seconds, a reaction time which is quite attainable (usually produced when the subject has anticipated the stimulus).

Figure 14.4

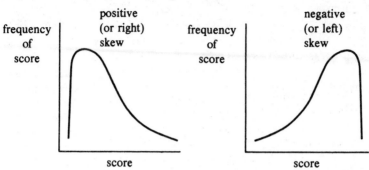

Correlation

We often want to find the relationship between two sets of variables. For example, we might want to know whether there was a relationship between the amount of television that children watch and their intelligence. To do this we could ask parents to record the amount of TV their children watched over a particular period and also give them an IQ test. The results could be shown as in Figures 14.5(a) and (b) in the form of a *scattergram*, where each point represents one child's score on the two variables (IQ and amount of TV watched).

A number of different results might be found from this study. For example, there might be a strong relationship between children's IQ and the amount of TV they watch. Figure 14.5(a) shows this type of relationship between the two variables. Those subjects with the highest IQ watch the most TV. This type of relationship, where those who score highly on one variable tend also to do well on the other, is known as a *positive correlation*.

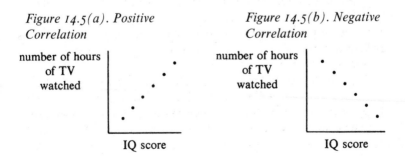

Figure 14.5(a). Positive Correlation

Figure 14.5(b). Negative Correlation

Figure 14.5(b) is another possible result which also shows a strong relationship between the two variables, but this time children with higher IQs tend to watch least TV. This type of relationship, where those who score highly on one variable tend to have a low score on the other, is known as a *negative correlation*.

In practice it is unlikely that we should find a very strong relationship between these two variables. The relationship shown in the scattergram in Figure 14.6 is near zero.

Figure 14.6. Zero Correlation

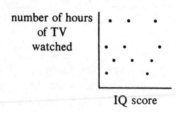

Producing a scattergram from your data will give a quick visual impression of the relationship, but a correlation coefficient can tell you the extent to which two variables correlate. Correlation co-efficients may be anything between +1 and −1. The closer the co-efficient to +1 or −1, the more perfect the relationship; the closer it is to 0, the weaker is the relationship.

For a correlation of +1, every rise in variable A is reflected by a rise in variable B.

For a correlation of 0, there is no relationship between A and B.

For a correlation of −1, every rise in variable A is reflected by a fall in variable B.

Those readers who wish to work out a correlation coefficient from their own data should consult *Starting Statistics*.

A very common mistake is to assume that because two variables correlate, one causes the other. It is vital that you do not make this assumption, because:

CORRELATION DOES NOT IMPLY CAUSATION.

There is a correlation of +0.95 between the length of railway line in a country and the incidence of certain types of cancer. This does not mean that railways cause cancer – there may be some underlying cause which affects both factors, such as industrialization. If two variables correlate, one may cause the other, but the correlational technique cannot confirm this.

Only the experimental method can study cause and effect. This is because it manipulates independent variables whilst controlling other variables in order to discover the effect on dependent variables (see page 193).

Summary

1 Psychologists use many different practical techniques to investigate child behaviour. These include:

The experiment

Naturalistic observation

Survey interviews and questionnaires

Case study (see page 97)

Cross-cultural studies

2 After performing a practical it is important to organize your results in a way which will make them easily understood by someone reading your report. This may involve producing clearly labelled tables of results and graphs. Giving the mean average and the range of a group of scores often makes it easier to see the basic differences between two or more sets of results.

3 The relationship between two variables can be shown by working out a correlation coefficient or drawing a scattergram. It is important to remember that if two variables are highly correlated one *may* be the cause of the other but we should not assume this unless we have other evidence.

Further Reading

Heyes, S., Hardy, M., Humphreys, P. and Rookes, P., *Starting Statistics in Psychology and Education* (1986, Weidenfeld and Nicolson).

Figure 13.1(b)

References

Ainsworth, M.D. (1972) 'Attachment and dependency: A comparison', in J.L. Gewirtz (ed.), *Attachment and Dependency*, Washington: V.H. Winston.

Ainsworth, M.D. (1973) 'The development of infant-mother attachment', in Caldwell, B.M. and Ricciuti, H.N. (eds), *Review of Child Development Research*, vol. 3, University of Chicago Press.

Ainsworth, Bell & Stayton (1974) 'Infant-mother attachment and social development', in M.P.M. Richards (ed.), *The Integration of a Child into a Social World*, Cambridge University Press.

Argyle, M. (1967), *The Psychology of Interpersonal Behaviour*, Harmondsworth: Penguin.

Argyle, M. (ed.) (1973) *Social Encounters*, Harmondsworth: Penguin.

Ausubel, D., Joseph, D. and Hanesian, H. (1978) *Educational Psychology: Cognitive View*, New York: Holt, Rinehart and Winston.

Axline, V. (1947) *Play Therapy, Boston, Mass: Houghton Mifflin.*

Axline, V. (1971) *Dibs: In Search of Self*, Harmondsworth: Penguin.

Bandura, A. (1965) 'Influences of a model's reinforcement contingencies on the acquisition of imitative responses', *Journal of Personal and Social Psychology*, 1, pp.589–95.

Bandura, A. (1977) *Social Learning Theory*, Englewood Cliffs, NJ: Prentice-Hall.

Bandura, A., Ross, D. and Ross, S.A. (1961) 'Transmission of aggression through imitation of aggressive models', *Journal of Abnormal and Social Psychology*, 63, pp.575–82.

Bandura, A., Ross, D. and Ross, S.A. (1963) Imitation of film-mediated aggressive models, *Journal of Abnormal and Social Psychology*, 66, pp.3–11.

Bandura, A. and Walters, R.H. (1963), *Social Learning and Personality Development*, New York: Holt, Rinehart and Winston.

Bee, H. (1985) *The Developing Child*, New York: Harper and Row.

Bellman, M. and Cash, J. (1987) *The Schedule of Growing Skills* (Developmental Screening Procedure), Windsor: NFER-Nelson.

Berkowitz, L. (1974) 'Some determinants of impulsive aggression: the role of mediated associations with reinforcements of aggression, *Psychological Review*, 81, pp.165–76.

Biller, H.B. (1971) *Father, Child and Sex Role: Paternal Determinants of*

Personality Development, Lexington: D.C. Heath.

Blakemore, C. and Cooper, J.F. (1970) 'Development of the brain depends on the visual environment', *Nature*, 241, pp.467–8.

Bouchard, T.J. and McGue, M. (1981) 'Familial studies of intelligence: A review', *Science*, 212, pp.1055–9.

Bower, T.G.R. (1967) 'The visual world of infants', *Sci. Amer.* offprint no. 502, pp.80–91.

Bower, T.G.R. (1977) *The Perceptual World of the Child*, London: Fontana/Open Books; Cambridge, Mass.: Harvard University Press.

Bowlby, J. (1951) *Maternal Care and Mental Health*, Geneva: World Health Organisation.

Braine, M.D.S. (1963) 'The ontogeny of English phrase structure: The first phase', *Language*, 39, pp.1–13.

Brand, C., cited in Cohen, D. and Shelley, D. (1982) 'High IQ as high-speed thinking,' *New Scientist*, 95, pp.773–5.

Brown, R. (1973) *A First Language: the Early Stages*, Cambridge, Mass: Harvard University Press.

Bruner, J.S. and Kenney, H. (1966) 'The development of the concepts of order and proportion in children,' *Studies in Cognitive Growth*, New York: Wiley.

Bryant, B., Harris, M. and Newton, D. (1980) *Children and Minders*, London: Grant McIntyre.

Buck, R. (1975) 'Nonverbal communication of effect in children', *Journal of Personality and Social Psychology*, 31, pp.664–753.

Burt, C., quoted in Jensen, A.R. (1969) 'How much can we boost IQ and scholastic achievement?', *Harvard Educational Review*, 39, pp.1–123.

Bushnell, I.W.R., Sai, F. and Mullin, T. (1989) 'Neonatal recognition of the mother's face', *British Journal of Developmental Psychology*, 7, pp.3–15.

Clark, M.M. (1976) *Young Fluent Readers*, London: Heinemann.

Condon, W.S. and Sander, L. (1974) 'Neonate movement is synchronised with adult speech: interactional participation and language acquisition', *Science*, 183, pp.99–101.

Cravioto, J. and De Licardie, E.R. (1968) in Scrimshaw, N.S. and Gordon, J.E. (eds), *Malnutrition, Learning and Behaviour*, MIT Press.

Curtiss, S. (1977) *A Psycholinguistic Study of a Modern-day Wild Child*, New York: Academic Press.

De Casper, A. and Fifer, W. (1980) 'Of human bonding: Newborns prefer their mothers' voices', *Science*, 208, pp.1174–6.

Delgado, J.M.R. (1956) 'Study of some cerebral structures related to transmission and elaboration of noxious stimulation', *Journal of Neurophysiology*, 18, pp.261–75.

Dennis, W. (1960) 'Causes of retardation among institutional children: Iran,' *Journal of Genet, Psychol.* 96, pp.47–59.

Diener, E., and DuFour, D., (1978) 'Does television violence enhance programme popularity?', quoted in Zimbardo, P.G., *Psychology and Life* (10th edn, 1971), Scott, Foresman and Company.

Dollard, J., Doob, L.W., Miller, N.E., Mowrer, O.H. and Sears, R.R. (1939) *Frustration and Aggression*, New Haven: Yale University Press.

Douglas, J.E. and Sutton, A. (1978) 'The development of speech and mental processes in a pair of twins: a case study', *J. Child Psychology and Psychiatry*, 19, pp.49–56.

Douglas, J.W.B. (1970). 'Broken families and child behaviour', *Journal of Royal College of Physicians*, vol. 4, pp.203–10.

Douglas, J.W.B. and Turner, R.K. (1970) 'The association of anxiety-provoking events in early childhood with enuresis', *Proc. Fifth International Scientific Meeting of International Epidemiological Associations* Belgrade: Savremena Adinstracija.

Dunn, J. and Kendrick, C. (1982) *Siblings: Love, Envy and Understanding*, Oxford: Basil Blackwell.

Eibl-Eibesfeldt, I. (1975) *Ethology: The Biology of Behaviour* (2nd edn), New York: Holt, Rinehart and Winston.

Eimas, P.D., Signeland, E.R., Jusczyk, P. and Vigorito, J. (1971) 'Speech perception in infants', *Science*, 171, pp.302–26.

Elliott, C.D., Murray, D.J. and Pearson, L.S. (1979) *British Ability Scales*, Slough: NFER.

Elliott, C.D., Murray, D.C. and Pearson, L.S. (1979) *British Abilities Scale – Revised*, Windsor: NFER-Nelson.

Erikson, E.H. (1972) *Play and Development*, New York: W.W. Norton.

Eron, L.D., Huesmann, L.R., Lefkowitz, H.M. and Walder, L.O. (1972) 'Does television violence cause aggression?' *American Psychologist*, 27, pp.253–63.

Eron, L.D., 'Parent-child interaction, television violence and aggression of children', *American 1980*, 25, pp.244–52.

Eysenck, H.J. (1975) 'What is wrong with psychology', *New Behaviour*, May 1st, pp.62–6.

Eysenck, H.J. (1977) *Psychology is About People*, Harmondsworth: Penguin.

Fantz, R. (1961) 'The origins of form perception', *Scientific American*, 204(5), pp.66–72.

Ferguson, C.A. and Slobin, D.I. (eds), *Studies in Child Development*, New York: Holt, Rinehart and Winston.

Flynn, J. (1984) 'Race, IQ and Grandparents,' *New Scientist*, April 5th, pp.29–31.

Francis, H. (1982) *Learning to Read: Literate Behaviour and Orthographic Knowledge*, London: George Allen and Unwin.

Freedman, J.L. (1984) 'Effects of television violence on aggressiveness,' *Psychological Bulletin*, 96, pp.227–46.

Freeman, N., Lloyd, S. and Sinha, C. (1980) 'Learning tests on babies', *New Scientist*, 88, pp.304–7.

Freud, A. and Dann, S. (1951) 'And experiment in group upbringing', *Psychoanalytic Study of the Child*, 6, pp.127–68.

Friedman et al. (1982) 'Perceptions of cries of full-term and pre-term infants', *Infant Behaviour and Development*, 5, pp.161–73.

Galton, F. (1869) *Hereditary Genius*, London: Fontana, 1962.

Gardener, R.A. and Gardener, B. (1969) 'Teaching sign-language to a chimpanzee', *Science*, 165, pp.664–72.

Garland, C. and White, S. (1980) *Children and Day Nurseries*, London: Grant McIntyre.

Garvey, C. (1977) *Play*, London: Fontana/Open Books.

Garvin, J.B. and Sacks, L.S. (1963) 'Growth potential of pre-school-aged children in institutional care: a positive approach to a negative condition', *American Journal of Orthopsychiatry*, 33, pp.399–408.

Geschwind, N. (1979) 'Specializations of the human brain', *Scientific American*, 241, pp.180–99.

Gibson, E.J. and Walk, R.D. (1960) 'The Visual Cliff', in W.T. Greenough (ed.), *The Nature and Nurture of Behaviour: Developmental Psychology*, Freeman and Co.

Goldberg, P. (1968) 'Are women prejudiced against women?', *Transaction*, vol. 5, pp.28–30.

Gordon, I.E. (1989) *Theories of Visual Perception*, New York: Wiley.

Gregory, R.L. (1990) *Eye and Brain* (4th edn), London: Weidenfeld and Nicolson.

Grossman, K. and Grossman, K. (1982) 'Parent and infant attachments', in Barlow, G.W., et al. (eds), *Behavioural Ontogeny*, Cambridge University Press.

Guildford, J.P. (1967) *The Nature of Human Intelligence*, New York: McGraw-Hill.

Halliday, M.A.K. (1975) *Learning How to Mean – Explorations in the Development of Language*, London: E. Arnold.

Harlow, H.F. (1949) 'The formation of learning sets', *Psychol. Rev.*, 56, pp.51–65. Also in *Sci. Amer.*, 181(2), pp.36–9.

Harlow, H.F. (1958) 'The nature of love', *Am. Psychol.*, 13, pp.673–85.

Harlow, H. (1959) 'Love in infant monkeys', *Scientific American*, 200(6), pp.68–74.

Hartshorne, H. and May, M.A. (1928) *Studies in the Nature of Character, 1: Studies in Deceit*, New York: Macmillan.

Hayes, K.J. and Hayes, C. (1952) 'Imitation in a home-raised chimpanzee, *J. Comp. Physiol. Psychol.*, vol. 45, No. 450, pp.450–59.

Hebb, D. (1949) *The Organisation of Behaviour*, New York: Wiley.

Heim, A.W. (1954) *The Appraisal of Intelligence* London: Methuen.

Held, R. (1965) 'Plasticity in sensory-motor systems', *Scientific American*, 213(5).

Held, R. and Hein, A. (1963) 'Movement-produced stimulation in the development of visually guided behaviour', *Journal of Comparative Physiological Psychology*, 56, pp.607–13.

Hendrickson, A. and E. (1980) 'IQ and Brainwaves', *New Scientist*, 85, pp.308–11.

Hess, E.H. (1956) 'Space perception in the chick', *Scientific American*, 195, pp.71–80.

Heyes, S., Hardy, M., Humphreys, P. and Rookes, P. (1986) *Starting Statistics*, Weidenfeld and Nicolson.

Hill, W. (1980) *Learning* (3rd edn), London: Methuen.

Hinde, R.A. (1970) *Animal Behaviour* (2nd edn), New York: McGraw-Hill.

Horton, R.W. and Santogross, D.A. (1978) 'The effect of adult commentary on reducing the influence of televised violence', *Personality and Social Psychology Bulletin 1978*, 4, pp.337–40.

Hubel, D.H. and Wiesel, T.N. (1962) 'Perceptive fields, binocular interactive and functional architecture in the cat's visual cortex', *J. Physiol. Psychol*, 160, pp.106–54.

Hug-Hellmuth, Heartha von (1921) 'On the techniques of child analysis', *Int. J. Psychoanal.*, vol. 2.

Hutt, C. (1966) 'Exploration and play in children', *Symp. Zool. Soc.*, London, 18, pp.61–81.

James, W. (1980) *The Principles of Psychology*, New York: Holt, Rinehart and Winston.

Jensen, A.R. (1969) 'How much can we boost IQ and scholastic achievement?', *Harvard Educational Review*, 39, pp.1–123.

Jolly, H. (1969) 'Play is work: The role of play for sick and healthy children', *Lancet*, 2, pp.487–8.

Kagan, J. (1979) 'Overview: Perspectives on human infancy', in Osofsky, J.D. (ed.), *Handbook of Infant Development*, New York: Wiley-Interscience.

Kamin, L.J. (1974) *The Science of Politics of IQ*, New York: Halstead Press. Press.

Kellogg, W.N., and Kellogg, L.A. (1967) *The Ape and the Child*, New York: Hofner.

Kellogg, W.N. (1968) 'Communication and language in home-raised chimpanzees', *Science* vol. 162, pp.423–7.

Kohler, I. (1962) 'Experiments with goggles', *Scientific American*, offprint no. 465.

Koluchova, J. (1972) 'Severe deprivation in twins: a case study,' *Journal of Child Psychology and Psychiatry*, 13(2), pp.181–8.

Langois, J.H. and Downs, A.C. (1980), Mothers, fathers and peers as socialization agents of sex-typed play behaviour in young children,' *Child Development*, 51, pp.1237–47.

Latané, B. and Darley, J.M. (1969) 'Bystander apathy', *American Scientist*, 57, pp.268–74.

Leyens, J-P, Camino, L., Parke, R.D. and Berkowitz, L. (1985) 'Effects of movie violence on aggression in a field-setting as a function of group dominance and cohesion', *Journal of Personality and Social Psychology*, pp.346–601.

Lewin, K., Lippit, R. and White, R.K. (1939) 'Patterns of aggressive behaviour in experimentally created 'social climates', *Journal of Social Psychology*, 10, pp.271–99.

Lewis, M., Young, G., Brooks, J. and Michalson, L. (1975) 'The beginning of friendship', in M. Lewis and L. Rosenblum (eds), *Friendship and Peer Relations*, New York: Wiley.

Locurto, C. (1988) 'On the malleability of I.Q.', *The Psychologist*, November.

Lorenz, K. (1952) *King Solomon's Ring*, London: Methuen.

Lorenz, K. (1966) *On Aggression*, London: Methuen.

Maccoby, E.E. and Jacklin, C.N. (1974) *The Psychology of Sex Differences*, Stanford, Calif: Stanford University Press.

Macfarlane, A. (1977) *The Psychology of Childbirth*, Cambridge, Mass.: Harvard University Press.

MacKinnon, D.W. (1938) 'Volition and prohibitions', in Murray, H.A. (ed.), *Explorations in Personality*, New York: Oxford University

McGarrigle, J. and Donaldson, M. (1974) 'Conservation accidents', *Cognition*, 3, pp.341–50.

Malina, R.M. (1987) 'Motor development in the early years', in S.G. Moore and C.R. Cooper (eds), *The Young Child: Reviews of Research* (vol. 3), Washington, DC: National Association for the Education of Young Children.

Maratsos, M. (1983) 'Some current issues in the study of the acquisition of grammar', in J.H. Flavell and E.M. Markman (eds), vol. 3 of the *Handbook of Child Psychology*, New York: Wiley.

Mason, M.K. (1942) 'Learning to speak after six and one-half years of silence,' *J. Speech Hear. Disord.*, 7, pp. 295–304.

Mead, M. in Benedict, R. (ed.) (1968) *Patterns of Culture*, London: Routledge and Kegan Paul.

Meltzoff, A.N. and Moore, M.K. (1977) 'Imitation of facial gestures', *Science*, 198, pp.75–80.

Millar, S. (1968) *The Psychology of Play*, Harmondsworth: Pelican.

Mischel, W. (1976) *Introduction to Personality* (2nd edn), New York: Holt, Rinehart and Winston.

Moon, C. and Wells, C.G. (1979) 'The influence of home on learning to read', *Journal of Research in Reading*, 2, pp.52–62.

Money, J. (1975) 'Ablatiopenis: Normal male infant sex-reassigned as a girl', *Archives of Sexual Behaviour*, 4, pp.56–72.

Money, J. and Ehrhardt, A.A. (1972) *Man and Woman, Boy and Girl* Baltimore: John Hopkins University Press.

Murray, J.P. (1980) *Television and Youth – 25 Years of Research and Controversy*, Stanford, California: The Boys Town Centre for the Study of Youth Development.

Newson, J. and E. (1965) *Patterns of Infant Care in an Urban Community*, Harmondsworth: Pelican.

Opie, I. and Opie, P. (1961) *The Lore and Language of School Children*, Oxford: Clarendon Press.

Parke, R.D., Berkowitz, L., Leyens, J.P., West, S.G. and Sebastian, R.J. (1977) 'Some effects of violent and non-violent movies on the behaviour of juvenile deliquents', in L. Berkowitz (ed.), *Advances in Experimental Social Psychology*, Vol. 10, New York: Academic Press.

Parsons, J.E., Adler, T.F. and Kaczala, C.M. (1982) 'Socialization of achievement attitudes and beliefs: Parental influences', *Child Development*, 53, pp.310–21.

Patterson, G.R., Littman, R.A. and Bricker, W.A. (1967) 'Assertive behaviour in children: A step towards a theory of aggression', *Monographs of the Society for Research in Child Development*, Serial No. 113.

Patton, R.G. and Gardner, L.I. (1963) *Growth, Failure and Maternal Deprivation*, Illinois: C.C. Thomas.

Paulsen, K. and Johnson, M. (1983) 'Sex-role attitudes and mathematical ability in 4th, 8th and 11th grade students from a high socioeconomic area', *Developmental Psychology*, 19, pp.210–14.

Pavlov, I.P. (1927) *Conditioned Reflexes*, Oxford University Press.

Piaget, J. (1948) *The Language and Thought of the Child*, London: Routledge and Kegan Paul.

Piaget, J. (1951) *Play, Dreams and Imitation in Childhood*, London: Heinemann.

Piaget, J. (1954) *The Origins of Intelligence*, London: Routledge and Kegan Paul.

Piaget, J. and Inhelder, B. (1956) *The Child's Conception of Space*, London: Routledge and Kegan Paul.

Piaget, J. and Inhelder, B. (1972) *Memory and Intelligence*, New York: Basic Books.

Power, M.J., Alderson, M.R. and Others (1967) 'Delinquent Schools?' *New Society*, 10, pp.542–3.

Power, M.J., Ash, P.M., Schoenberg, E. and Sorey, E. (1974) 'Delinquency and the family', *Journal of Social Work*, vol. 4, pp.13–38.

Quinton, D. and Rutter, M. (1985) 'Parenting behaviour of mothers raised "in care"' in Nichol, A.E. (ed.), *Longitudinal Studies in Child Care and Child Psychiatry*, New York: John Wiley.

Raven, J.C. (1958) *Standard Progressive Matrices*, London: H.K. Lewis.

Rheingold, H.L., and Cook, K.V. (1975) 'The contents of boys' and girls' rooms as an index of parents' behaviour', *Child Development*, 46, pp.459–63.

Riesen, A.N. (1950) 'Arrested vision', *Sci. Amer.* offprint no. 408.

Robertson, J. and Robertson, J. (1967) *Young Children in Brief Separation: I, Kate Aged Two Years Five Months in Fostercare for 27 Days*, Tavistock Child Development Research Unit

Robertson, J. and Robertson, J. (1967) *Young Children in Brief Separation: II, Jane Aged Seventeen Months in Fostercare for 10 Days*, Tavistock Child Development Research Unit.

Rose, S. (1976) *The Conscious Brain*, Harmondsworth: Pelican.

Rosenthal, R. (1966) *Experimenter Effects in Behavioural Research*, New York: Appleton.

Rosenthal, R. and Jacobson, L. (1968) *Pygmalion in the Classroom: Teacher Expectations and Pupil's Intellectual Development*, New York: Holt, Rinehart and Winston.

Rosenzweig, M.R., Love, W. and Bennett, E.L. (1965) *Physiology and Behaviour*, vol. 3, pp.819–25.

Rothbart, M.K. and Maccoby, E.E. (1966) 'Parents' differential reactions to sons and daughters', *Journal of Personality and Social Psychology*, 3, pp.237–43.

Rutter, M. (1972) *Maternal Deprivation Reassessed*, Harmondsworth: Penguin.

Saario, T.N., Jacklin, C.N. and Tittle, C.K. (1973) 'Sex role stereotyping in the public schools', *Harvard Educational Review*, vol. 43, pp. 386–516.

Sander, L.W. (1969) 'Regulation and organisation in the early infant-caretaker system', in Robinson, R. (ed.), *Brain and Early Behaviour*, New York: Academic Press.

Scarr, S. and Weinberg, R.A. (1976) 'IQ test performance of black children adopted by white families,' *American Psychologist*, 31, pp.726–39.

Schaffer, H.R. and Emerson, P.E. (1964) *The Development of Social Attachments in Infancy*, Monograph of the Society for Research in Child Development, no.29.

Schaffer, H.R. (1977) *Mothering*, London: Fontana/Open Books.

Sears, R.R., Maccoby, E.E. and Levin, H. (1957) *Patterns of Child Rearing*, Evanston: Row, Peterson.

Segall, M.H., Campbell, D.T. and Herskovits, M.J. (1963) 'Cultural differences in the perception of geometric illusions', *Science*, 139, pp.769–71.

Selman, R.L. (1980) *The Growth of Interpersonal Understanding*, New York: Academic Press.

Selman, R.L. and Jaquette, D. (1977) 'Stability and oscillation in interpersonal awareness: a clinical-development analysis', in Keasey, C.B. (ed.) *The Nebraska Symposium on Motivation*, vol. 25, Lincoln: University of Nebraska Press.

Sheridan, M. (1973) *From Birth to Five Years: Children's Developmental Progress*, Windsor: NFER-Nelson.

Sheridan, M. (1977) *Spontaneous Play in Early Childhood 0–6 Years*, Windsor: NFER-Nelson.

Sinclair-de-Zwart, H. (1969) 'Developmental psycholinguistics' in Elkind, D. and Flavell, J.H. (eds), *Studies in Cognitive Development*, Oxford University Press.

Skeels, H.M. (1966) *Adult Status of Children with Constrasting Early Life Experiences*, Monograph of the Society for Research in Child Development, no.46.

Skinner, B.F. (1938) *Science of Human Behaviour*, London: Macmillan.

Skuse, D. (1984) 'Extreme deprivation in early childhood – II: Theoretical issues and a comparative review', *Journal of Child Psychology and Psychiatry*, 25, pp. 543–72.

Slater, A., Mattock, A. and Brown, E. (1990) 'Size constancy at birth: Newborn infant's responses to retinal and real size', *Journal of Experimental Child Psychology*.

Slobin, D. (1973) 'Cognitive prerequisites for the development of grammar', in Ferguson, C.A. and Slobin, D.I. (eds), *Studies in Child Development*, New York: Holt, Rinehart and Winston, pp.175–208.

Sluckin, W. (1972) *Imprinting and Early Learning*, London: Methuen.

Smith, C. and Lloyd, B.B. (1978) 'Maternal behaviour and perceived sex of infant: Revisited', *Child Development*, 49, pp.1263–5.

Smith, P.K. and Connolly, K.J. (1980) *The Ecology of Pre-School Behaviour*, Cambridge: Cambridge University Press.

Snow, C. and Ferguson, C.A. (eds) (1977) *Talking to Children*, Cambridge: Cambridge University Press.

Snow, M.E., Jacklin, C.N. and Maccoby, E.E. (1983) 'Sex-of-child differences in father-child interaction at one year of age', *Child Development*, 54, pp.227-32.

Spearman, C. (1904) 'General intelligence objectively determined and measured', *Am. J. Psychol.*, 15, pp.201-93.

Stern, D.N. (1977) *The First Relationship: Infant and Mother*, London: Fontana/Open Books.

Stratton, G. M. (1897), described in Gregory, R.L. (1990) *Eye and Brain* (4th edn), London: Weidenfeld and Nicolson.

Sylva, K.D., Roy, C. and Painter M. (1980) *Childwatching at Playgroup and Nursery School*, London: Grant McIntyre.

Thomas, A. and Chess, S. (1977) *Temperament and Development*, New York: Brunner/Mazel.

Thompson, S.K. (1975) 'Gender labels and early sex role development', *Child Development*, 46, pp.339-47.

Thorndike, E.L. (1911) *The Fundamentals of Learning*, College Bureau of Publications, 1932.

Thurstone, L.L. (1938) *Primary Mental Abilities*, Psychometric Monographs No. 1, University of Chicago Press.

Tizard, B. (1986) *The Care of Young Children – Implications of Recent Research*, London: Thomas Coram Research Foundation.

Vernon, M.D. (1962) *The Psychology of Perception*, Harmondsworth: Penguin.

Vernon, P.E. (1972) *Intelligence and Cultural Environment*, London: Methuen.

De Villiers, P.A., and de Villiers, J.G. (1979) *Early Language*, London: Fontana Press.

Waters, E., Wippman, J., and Sroufe L.A. (1979) 'Attachment, positive affect and competence in the peer group', *Child Development*, 50, pp.821-9.

Watson, J.B. (1925) *Behaviourism*, New York: Norton.

Watson, J.B., and Rayner, R. (1920) 'Conditioned emotional reaction', *Journal of Experimental Psychology*, vol. 3, pp.1-14.

Wechsler, D. (1974) *Wechsler Intelligence Scale for Children: Revised*, New York: Psychological Corporation.

Wells, C.G. (1985) *Language Development in the Pre-School Years*, Cambridge: Cambridge University Press.

Wells, G. (1985) *Language, Learning and Education*, Windsor: NFER-Nelson.

Weir, R.H. (1963) *Language in the Crib*, The Hague: Mouton.

Whiting, J.W.M. and Child, I.L. (1957) *Child Training and Personality*, New Haven: Yale University Press.

Witkin, H.A., Moore, C.A., Goodenough, D.R. and Cox, P.W. (1977) 'Field-dependent and field-independent cognitive styles and their educational implications', *Review of Educational Research*, 47, pp.1-64(9).

Useful Organisations

British Association for Early Childhood Education (BAECE)
Studio 3:2, 140 Tabernacle Street, London EC2A 4SD
(Tel: 071–582 8744)
Commission for Racial Equality
Elliot House, 10/12 Allington Street, London SW1E 5EH
(Tel: 071–828 7022)
Pre-School Playgroup Association
Alford House, Aveline Street, London SE11 5DH
(Tel: 071–582 8871)
National Playbus Association
St Thomas's Church, St Thomas Street, Bristol BS1 6JJ
(Tel: 0272 25951)
The Voluntary Organisations Liaison Council for the Under Fives (VOLCUF)
c/o The Thomas Coram Foundation for Children, 49 Brunswick Square,
London WC1N 1AZ
(Tel: 071–278 3459/8365)
Voluntary Council for Handicapped Children
8 Wakley Street, London EC1V 7QE
(Tel: 071–278 9441)
Workplace Nurseries Campaign
Room 205, South Bank House, Black Prince Road, London SE1 7SJ
(Tel: 071–582 7199/587 1546)
National Children's Bureau
8 Wakley Street, London EC1V 7QE
(Tel: 071–278 9441)
National Child Care Campaign
Wesley House, 70 Great Queen Street, London WC2B 5AX
(Tel: 071–405 5617/8)
Gingerbread
35 Wellington Street, London WC2E 7BN
(Tel: 071–240 0953)
Mudiad Ysgolion Meithrin
(Welsh Medium Nursery Schools and Playgroups)
10 Park Grove, Cardiff CF1 3BN
(Tel: 0222 36205)

Welsh Playgroups Association
2a Chester Street, Wrexham, Clwyd LL13 8BD
(Tel: 0978 358195)
Scottish Child and Family Alliance (SCAFA)
56 Albany Street, Edinburgh EH1 3QR
(Tel: 031–557 2780)
Scope (Scottish Pre-School Playgroups Association and Stepping Stones)
16 Sandyford Place, Glasgow G3 7NB
(Tel: 041–221 4148/9)
Northern Ireland Pre-School Playgroup Association
11 Wellington Park, Belfast BT9 6DJ
(Tel: 0232 662825)
Save the Children Fund
41 Wellington Park, Belfast BT9 6DN
(Tel: 0232 681171/2)

Index